Luminos is the Open Access monograph publishing program from UC Press. Luminos provides a framework for preserving and reinvigorating monograph publishing for the future and increases the reach and visibility of important scholarly work. Titles published in the UC Press Luminos model are published with the same high standards for selection, peer review, production, and marketing as those in our traditional program. www.luminosoa.org

T0329899

In recent years, the issue of how regions are connected and what kinds of cultural exchanges take place on a global scale has become of increasing importance. The term *transpacific* has come to signify the nexus of these flows of culture, capital, ideas, and labor across the Pacific. Drawing from Asian Studies, American Studies, and Asian American Studies, a new generation of scholars is developing new models for considering the geopolitical struggle over the Pacific and its attendant possibilities for inequality and exploitation. The word and concept of the transpacific can be harnessed for purposes of both domination and resistance.

The Transpacific Studies series seeks to publish monographs that look at cultural and political movements and artistic works that have arisen to contest state, corporate, and military ambitions and attempt to place them in a context that should be more dynamic than older ideas of the "Asia Pacific" or the "Pacific Rim" of global trade.

1. *Becoming Global Asia: Contemporary Genres of Postcolonial Capitalism in Singapore*, by Cheryl Narumi Naruse

Becoming Global Asia

Becoming Global Asia

*Contemporary Genres of Postcolonial Capitalism
in Singapore*

Cheryl Narumi Naruse

UNIVERSITY OF CALIFORNIA PRESS

University of California Press
Oakland, California

Suggested citation: Naruse, C. N. *Becoming Global Asia: Contemporary Genres of Postcolonial Capitalism in Singapore*. Oakland: University of California Press, 2023. DOI: https://doi.org/10.1525/luminos.169

Library of Congress Cataloging-in-Publication Data

Names: Naruse, Cheryl Narumi, 1984– author.
Title: Becoming global Asia : contemporary genres of postcolonial
    capitalism in Singapore / Cheryl Narumi Naruse.
Description: Oakland : University of California Press, 2023. |
    Includes bibliographical references and index.
Identifiers: LCCN 2023017132 (print) | LCCN 2023017133 (ebook) |
    ISBN 9780520396661 (paperback) | ISBN 9780520396678 (ebook)
Subjects: LCSH: Postcolonialism in literature. | Postcolonialism—
    Singapore—20th century. | Capitalism—Singapore—20th century. |
    Globalization—Singapore—20th century. | Social change—Singapore—
    20th century. | Singapore—Economic conditions—20th century.
Classification: LCC PN56.P555 N37 2023 (print) | LCC PN56.P555 (ebook) |
    DDC 809/.933585957—dc23/eng/20230621

LC record available at https://lccn.loc.gov/2023017132
LC ebook record available at https://lccn.loc.gov/2023017133

32   31   30   29   28   27   26   25   24   23
10   9   8   7   6   5   4   3   2   1

To Steven, Naomi, and Ushi

CONTENTS

ILLUSTRATIONS

ACKNOWLEDGMENTS

I have been looking forward to the moment when I would be in the position to write my acknowledgments since that would signal the end of a very long journey. Now that it is here, I am realizing what a difficult task this is because I will never have the right language to convey the level of gratitude I have for the friends, colleagues, teachers, and mentors who supported me throughout the writing of this book. I hope these acknowledgments show how immensely fortunate I have been.

This book began as a dissertation at the University of Hawai'i at Mānoa under the guidance and dedication of Laura Lyons. My too many emails, sloppy drafts, and unannounced office visits demanded unreasonable amounts of time from Laura, but she always offered me intellectual, professional, and personal guidance. Laura let me stay true to my ideas, and I continue to be grateful for the education she gave me. Thank you, Laura.

My dissertation committee—Cristina Bacchilega, Monisha Das Gupta, Cynthia Franklin, John Rieder, and S. Shankar—gave me important feedback that shaped the trajectory of what this book has now become. Whether it was in courses, hallway interactions, teaching assistantships, department colloquia, reading groups, committee work, job advising, chats over coffee, or an offer to read a chapter draft, I also had the good fortune of learning from Katharine Beutner, Stephen Canham, S. Charusheela, Anna Feuerstein, Candace Fujikane, Vernadette Gonzalez, Craig Howes, Lisa King, Sankaran Krishna, Michael Shapiro, Jack Taylor, Mari Yoshihara, and John Zuern. Greta LaFleur was and continues to be a generous mentor. Coffees with Jeffrey Carroll were a grounding source of support throughout my graduate study. Paul Lyons and Bob McHenry left us too soon. Through fun times, good food, shared coursework, and late-night conversations, my smart friends—Ranjan

Adiga, Kim Compoc, Phillip Drake, Joy Enomoto, Keala Francis, Sahoa Fukushima, Kai Gaspar, Monica Ghosh, Diana Leong, Yin Peng Leong, Rajiv Mohabir, Madoka Nagado, Deanna Ramsay, Noʻu Revilla, Nikki Rosenblatt, Anjoli Roy, Jennifer Sano-Franchini, Chad Shomura, Rawi Sophonpanich, Lyz Soto—offered important camaraderie, making the challenging pursuit of a PhD more bearable. Kristine Kotecki was a bestie at first sight and continues to be a life inspiration.

It was in the calming green of Pālolo Valley where I learned how to focus and write. Bryan Kuwada and Aiko Yamashiro taught me so much about community and living a full and meaningful life. Tula always brought good humor to the household. The good memories of laughter, cooking, cookie fits, overgrown dill and sweet potato plants, and shared fashion choices at Millipede Mansion bring me joy to this day.

The transition to my first job at the University of Dayton was challenging after my life in Honolulu, but friendships with Rachel Bloom-Pojar, Fatima Esseili, David Fine, Lynn Itagaki, Denise James, John McCombe, Tom Morgan, and Shannon Toll sustained me. Ari Friedlander has become one of my most important friends. Whether for a game of Golden Tee or talking me through my latest existential crisis, Ari is a rare and reliable friend.

I cannot imagine being where I am today if it were not for the 2015 summer seminar, "Migratory Aesthetics and Asian/American Studies," organized by Tina Chen at Penn State. Tina's visionary work at *Verge* and the Global Asias Institute has gifted me new colleagues and receptive audiences for my work. Tina has also given me generous amounts of her time and mentorship over the years. At the seminar, I met Crystal Baik, Akash Belsare, Chris Eng, Christopher Fan, Michelle Huang, Andrew Leong, Vinh Nguyen, Leland Tabares, Sunny Xiang, and Hentyle Yapp. Initial giggles over pho led to summer writing groups, conference panels, and special issues. I have learned so much from this incredibly smart bunch, and I am proud to call them friends. I especially appreciate Vinh, who has been a generous Toronto host and someone who understands me like no other. Chris Eng became a friend before we even met in person and has been a constant source of support that I am lucky to have. Spending time with Sunny is one of my favorite pastimes—Sonny and Cher forever!—and I have learned so much from her incredible mind. Michelle always has the right things to say. The "aesthetic migrants" seminar also spawned another writing group, one that has been important throughout the more isolated periods of the pandemic. Thank you to Chris, Michelle, Douglas Ishii, for their reliable company and on-demand feedback on my writing. Justin Mann and Maia Gil'Adí added to the virtual fun.

In 2016, I had the opportunity to return to Singapore for a year for a post-doctoral research fellowship at Nanyang Technological University with the Global Asia research cluster. Thank you to K. K. Luke and Erin Lee for their support: it was a wonderful, generative year. During that time, I had the chance to connect with old friends and family and make new colleagues. Nadine Chan was a wonderful collaborator and has been an especially important influence for my thinking.

Times spent with Janessa Choong, Philip Holden, Claire Hua, Jee Leong Koh, Lydia Kwa, Fiona Lee, Debbie Lin, Shaoling Ma, Yun Sian Ng, Suan Ong, Angelia Poon, Sheo Rai, Kevin Riordan, Dan Feng Tan, Jeremy Tiang, Cyril Wong, and Mayee Wong were nourishing. Special thanks to Seow Leng Ang at the National Library for always being ready to answer my idiosyncratic questions and to Shawn Hoo for his research assistance, particularly for chapter 1.

The work of organizing the Southeast Asia Forum for the Modern Language Association brought together a special group of people committed to bringing more critical attention to the region. Weihsin Gui, Joanne Leow, Sheela Jane Menon, and E. K. Tan were the original coconspirators. Shortly after, Brian Bernards, Philip Holden, Fiona Lee, Shaoling Ma, Nazry Bahrawi, Ben Tran, Alden Sajor Marte-Wood, Mayee Wong helped get it all together. They have provided a convivial intellectual community that has made the convention feel like a highlight of the year.

At Tulane University, I have had the privilege of having many wonderful colleagues. Whether it has been through hallway conversations, yard drinks, coffees, pies, tarot salons, text messages, or co-teaching, Mohan Ambikaipaker, Patricia Burns, Hongwei Thorn Chen, Rosie Click, Mariana Craciun, Guadalupe García, Z'étoile Imma, Elizabeth Kalos-Kaplan, Erin Kappeler, Michelle Kohler, Camilo Leslie, Scott Oldenburg, Selamawit Terrefe, Ed White, and Anne-Marie Womack have made pretenure life a little less grueling. I am also incredibly thankful to Scott and his leadership as department chair. Times spent with the Mohan family were life giving, as were the late-night drinks with Z'étoile and Zazi Dlamini. My life in New Orleans has also been enriched by many family friends. Britton Stewart has been a dear friend, and she and her family have made settling down in New Orleans much easier. Special thanks to Max Dulaney and Leslie Raymond for all their help as we were transitioning to our new home. I have also treasured the times we have spent with the Drexler-Drakes and the Pitres.

Books are very hard to write, and I am grateful to have had institutional support to have done so. Thank you to the Tulane University Office of Academic Affairs and Provost for the Faculty Book Manuscript Workshop support. The Tulane University School of Liberal Arts also provided generous research support through the Andrew W. Mellon assistant professorship and the Book Subvention Award as well as the means to participate in the National Center for Faculty Development and Diversity. Elizabeth Kleinfeld, Kimberly McKee, and Jay Sibara helped me get my brain working again after coming off of parental leave.

Portions of this book were published in other venues. An earlier version of chapter 2 first appeared in "Singapore, State Nationalism, and the Production of Diaspora," *CLCWeb: Comparative Literature and Culture*, vol. 15, no. 2, 2013. An earlier version of chapter 3 first appeared in "Hwee Hwee Tan's Mammon Inc. as Bildungsroman; Or, the Coming-of-Career Narrative," *Genre: Forms of Discourse and Culture*, vol. 49, no. 1, pp. 95–115, by the University of Oklahoma. All rights reserved. An earlier version of chapter 3 also first appeared in "Overseas

Singaporeans, Coming-of-Career Narratives, and the Corporate Nation," *Biography: Hawaiian glottal stop Interdisciplinary Quarterly*, vol. 37, no. 1, 2014, pp. 145–67, University of Hawai'i Press. All have been republished by permission of the publisher.

There are a number of friends and colleagues who are not easily categorized by academic life itineraries. Thank you to Susy Wu and Semion Raynes, who have been solid and lifelong friends. I am thankful for the Canada times spent with the Gin and Yan families, Garrett and Amy Peck, Thy Phu, Michael Tang, Janis Tong, Adrian Tse, and Victor Wong. The Elskies, Kate Okamoto, Sunny Xiang, and Jan Vuong have been incredible New York City hosts. Whether over conference dinners or texts, exchanges with Nasia Anam, Frank Cha, Stephanie Elsky, Colleen Lye, Ragini Tharoor Srinivasan, and Shashi Thandra were always meaningful sources of friendship, inspiration, and collaboration. I am grateful to the very extended Lim family and my cousins, who are always up for another food adventure and important sources of support. I have no doubt confused my parents, Fuminori Paul and Boon Keow Judy, with many of my life decisions, and I am thankful for their support. At the University of California Press, Enrique Ochoa-Kaup has been a wonderful editor, finding me astute readers and efficiently ushering the project through each stage. I am very grateful to my copy editor, Sheila Berg, for her careful eye, and to Emily Park, production editor, for her speedy problem-solving skills. Thank you to Janet Hoskins, Viet Thanh Nguyen, and the Transpacific Studies Editorial Board for believing in this project.

Writing has never come easily to me, and I have toiled over the years to strengthen it. Any improvements in my writing have been because my friends and colleagues have given me their precious time and incredible care. Jini Kim Watson, Philip Holden, and Kate Adams gave me amazing feedback on early drafts of the manuscript. I have admired Jini's and Philip's work throughout my career, so it was a real privilege to have their guidance. Lydia Woolley was an incredible note taker during my book manuscript workshop and a student I was lucky to learn from. Special thanks to Nadine Chan, Chris Eng, Ari Friedlander, Steven Gin, Weihsin Gui, Michelle Huang, Laura Lyons, Kristine Kotecki, and Sunny Xiang, who helped me untangle convoluted ideas and sentences and connect the dots, particularly in the final stages of revision. These friends, themselves incredible thinkers that I immensely respect, have taken good care of me and my ideas, and I am indebted to them.

My family has taught me what really matters. Naomi has brought unexpected joys into my life and is now my inspiration for how to be. Ushi, the hungriest and sweetest dog ever, has spent as much time at my desk as I have. The most important person I have to acknowledge is Steven Gin. Whether saving me from an exploded tube of salsa or taking on extra childcare to give me more time to write, Steven has always been there for me. Thank you for helping me make this possible, Steven. Everything is better with and because of you.

Introduction

Global Asia, a Wayward Postcolonialism

In 2007, a *Smithsonian Magazine* article declared, "Singapore Swing: Peaceful and Prosperous, Southeast Asia's Famously Uptight Nation Has Let Its Hair Down." Remarking on his return trip to Singapore, David Lamb, former Southeast Asia bureau chief of the *Los Angeles Times*, marveled, "This tiny nation—whose ascendancy from malaria-infested colonial backwater to gleaming global hub of trade, finance and transportation is one of Asia's great success stories—is reinventing itself, this time as a party town and regional center for culture and the arts."[1] Implicit in Lamb's fawning language is recognition of Singapore's wealth: in 2021, Singapore boasted a gross domestic product (GDP) higher than that of 80 percent of the world's nations, a feat the former British colony accomplished within roughly fifty years of independence.[2] After its ejection from the Federation of Malaya, Singapore gained independence in 1965 and became one of the wealthiest countries in Southeast Asia under the leadership of former prime minister Lee Kuan Yew and the People's Action Party (PAP), the governing party that still manages Singapore today. Even more impressively, Singapore in "the early 1990s . . . reached rough parity, in terms of per capita Gross Domestic Product, with the United Kingdom, its former colonial power."[3] Though many may not know these exact details of Singapore's economic ascendency, most are by now familiar with its "Third World to First World" arc.[4] It is at this point well worn, almost a cliché.

Although other Asian nations, such as India, South Korea, and China, similarly position themselves as vibrant sites of capitalist flourishing, Singapore stands out for its constant citation as an economic model for political leaders to reproduce elsewhere. "Africa's Singapore Dream," announced one recent *Foreign Policy* headline in an article detailing Rwandan president Paul Kagame's admiration for Singapore's first prime minister, Lee Kuan Yew.[5] In contrast to Rwanda, where Singapore is held up as an aspiration, Singapore is used as evidence for Jamaica's

1

economic failures. "When you consider that in 1967, Jamaica and Singapore had about the same per capita GDP," Jamaican Parliament member, Dr. Peter Philips, declared, "and that today, Singapore is in the order of 10–12 times higher than ours, it is an indictment, collective indictment on Jamaica and its political leadership on all sides over the four decades."[6] Ironically, the former British colony has become so compelling that "Singapore-upon-Thames" was floated as a possible post-Brexit model by a British member of Parliament.[7] In an even more unlikely wielding of the nation-state as exemplar, in 2019, Jared Kushner of the Trump administration cited Singapore in his "Peace to Prosperity" plan as the economic model for Palestine to follow.[8] The geographic and geopolitical diversity of these brief examples demonstrates the strength of Singapore's appeal, rooted in the implausibility of its rags-to-riches narrative. More importantly, it demonstrates how crucial Singapore is to global fantasies of economic success and effective governance.

But more than just another instance of praise for Singapore's economic story, the *Smithsonian* feature article marks a different transformation: the nation is now regarded as a globally significant bearer of *cultural* capital. Considering that Singapore's reinvention of itself as a site of art and pleasure comes in the shadows of the 1997 Asian financial crisis, a time of economic pain and uncertainty, Singapore's flourishing may seem the stuff of melodrama. The magnitude of Singapore's cultural transformation, as Lamb writes, is even starker when considering what Singapore used to be:

> This, after all, was Singapore, long ridiculed as a prissy, soulless place, with no DNA for fun, culture or the arts. Singapore? Isn't that where chewing gum is illegal and *Cosmopolitan* magazine is banned as too racy? Where bars closed before anyone starts having a good time, and everyone is so obsessed with work that the government launched a smile campaign to get people to lighten up?[9]

Lamb's assumptions about Singapore repeat the science fiction writer William Gibson's perceptions of Singaporean governance as technocratic and overly focused on economic profit. Infamously dubbing the country "Disneyland with the Death Penalty," Gibson lampooned the island nation's "white-shirted constraint," "absolute humorlessness," and "conformity" in a 1993 essay for *Wired* (proving Gibson's point, the magazine would go on to be banned in Singapore).[10] For many years, the speed and thus exceptionality of Singapore's trajectory as a so-called Asian Miracle nation was attributed to the authoritarian state's punitive and repressive governance.[11] The no-spitting and no-littering laws, drug offenses punishable by death, restrictions on free speech and assembly, and vandalism offenses punishable by caning (as made famous by the American Michael Fay) came to signal a strong state government that bordered on a dictatorship.[12] Such representations depict Singapore as overly engineered, mechanical, and profiting off of its robotic, compliant citizenry—its economic success more of a point of denigration than

FIGURE 1. A typical sign at a subway station in Singapore, "Singapore MRT Fines." Photo by Steve Bennett, Wikipedia.EN [cropped]. Free to use under a CC BY-SA 3.0 license, https://creativecommons.org/licenses/by-sa/3.0/deed.en.

celebration.[13] But as Lamb notes, "Suddenly people are describing the city with a word that, until recently, wasn't even in the local vocabulary: trendy."[14] Not only does Singapore appear at the top of various ranking lists for "Ease of Doing Business" and "economic freedom,"[15] it also now appears on US cable television and social media as a desired travel destination with abundant shopping, exotic food, architectural wonders, and cultural diversity. In other words, Singapore is lauded for its economic capital *and* regarded as a site with cultural capital. From HBO to Bollywood, Singapore alternately serves as a futuristic cityscape and romantic destination getaway. Its cultural appeal has been further confirmed by the movement of the global elite into the city-state: billionaires such as the Facebook cofounder Eduardo Saverin, for example, have settled in Singapore.[16] As indicated by its recent role in the global cultural imaginary, Singapore is gaining a new kind of power to accompany its authoritarian governance and accumulated wealth.

SINGAPORE AS "GLOBAL ASIA"

Collectively, the various admiring depictions of Singapore index its transformed reputation as "Global Asia," the perception of Singapore as an alluring Asian setting for capitalist flourishing. Such a setting, in this instance, is hospitable to finance, corporations, and the global elite while also productive of a diasporic, cosmopolitan workforce for the global economy. The labels "Global Asia" and "Global Asias" may be more familiar to readers of this book as interdisciplinary academic subfields, with the former seeking to free knowledge production about Asia from the limitations of the East/West binaries that reproduce parochial notions of Asia and the latter aimed at the intersecting subdisciplines of Asian, Asian diasporic, and Asian American studies.[17] My usage here is a historical gesture toward the name of the broad strategy adopted by Singapore's Economic Development Board (EDB) in 2010. The EDB formally named "Global-Asia" as their strategy to establish Singapore as a "home" for multinational corporations and their activities.[18] The naming of this strategy was somewhat belated, considering that many economic programs were already being implemented during the preceding decade with the goal of reinventing Singapore to accrue global capital. But as with other postcolonial Asian contexts (e.g., Malaysia, Hong Kong, the Philippines), the 1997 Asian financial crisis became an occasion to catalyze the island nation into a "knowledge economy."[19] In declaring a transition into this new economy, the then prime minister Goh Chok Tong called for a "reorient[ing of] society to meet the intellectual, emotional, spiritual, cultural and social needs of our people."[20] Knowledge economies, with their emphasis on services, from "health care, education, and finance, to transportation, entertainment, and advertising[,] [are] characterized in general by the central role played by knowledge, information, communication, and affect."[21] But as various policy reports and recommendations from this period show, the post-1997 economic transition was not simply about training a population

FIGURE 2. The Singapore skyline, including a view of Marina Bay Sands. Photo by Hu Chen on Unsplash.

for new forms of labor. The *Renaissance City Report*, for example, proposed "establish[ing] Singapore as a global arts city . . . and a cultural centre in the globalised world. The idea is to be one of the top cities in the world to live, work and play in, where there is an environment conducive to creative and knowledge-based industries and talent."[22] More than renovating Singapore's image, the economic transition to a knowledge economy would mean making Singapore productive of a "creative class."[23] Achieving such an aspiration, the *Renaissance City Report* further noted, would mean a reduced role for the state: "Cultural development is a domain in which [the government] is less likely to succeed purely by its control and dominance."[24] Taken together, what we see is that the knowledge economy of Global Asia would require new kinds of economic ideologies and modes of governance.

But as the *Smithsonian* article illustrates, understanding the possibility, functioning, and success of Singapore as Global Asia entails more than a study of Singapore's state rule and social engineering. The many celebratory depictions of Singapore above, in other words, not only index Global Asia but are also constitutive of it. Global Asia is an aestheticized, transnationalized narrative that exceeds the Southeast Asian nation itself. Critically comprehending Global Asia's allure and "soft power," as Joseph Nye terms it, is an aesthetic matter.[25] As I will further show, Singapore's soft power and increased cultural capital is made possible by Singapore's anglophonic legibility, or its cultural readability as Westernized.[26] English is crucial for understanding the globalized dynamics of power in the Singaporean context, and, indeed, this is the key mode through which Singapore differentiates itself from other Global Asia sites; Shanghai, for example, could be understood more as a sinophonic Global Asia. In Singapore, English is the language of governance, the most prevalent literary language, and a language fraught with class privilege because of its uneven distribution among Singapore's multiracial constituents. It is also, of course, a language with colonial baggage and a language that continues to bring legibility to the island-nation. Through English, imperialisms, both past and current, play out. It is thus a linguistic medium that presents multiple scales of power, mirroring how the state and Singaporeans navigate global, national, and historical terrains.[27]

To study the aestheticized significance of Singapore as Global Asia, this book examines the anglophone forms and genres that materialized concomitantly with Singapore's post-1997 transformation: demographic compilations, coming-of-career narratives, and the princess fantasy. Each chapter defines the formal characteristics of these contemporary genres in order to give readers a sense of my objects of study rather than to stake a claim to their originality. More at stake in my analysis is *why* they make an appearance after 1997 and how the materials offer insights into new narrative logics, aesthetics, and the political unconscious that underpins Global Asia and Singapore's transition to a knowledge economy.[28] I identify these emergent genres as they appear in a diverse range of materials, including government policy documents, political ephemera, state newspapers, literary magazines, tourism industry promotional materials, short stories, film, and novels. While Singapore has long been a special locus of capital accumulation as the result of its history as a global port city, these materials elucidate the ideological shifts that have accompanied Singapore's reputation as Global Asia. Yet, as I discuss later, such newness does not mean Singapore as Global Asia is without history. Rather, Global Asia is a cultural and political veneer requiring deeper historicization and cultural analysis.

THEORIZING POSTCOLONIAL CAPITALISM

Many of the literary works this book studies emphasize Singapore's anglophonic legibility as a problem of interpretation; they also critique understandings that oversimplify Singapore's readability as evidence of US or British hegemony. Take, for example, Jeremy Tiang's depiction of a Swiss McDonald's as an emotional refuge for his protagonist, who is in distress about her marriage, in the short story "Sophia's Honeymoon." One interpretation might assume that Tiang is critiquing Overseas Singaporeans like Sophia, who find meaning and comfort in the factory-produced food from a Western corporate franchise like McDonald's.

Sophia, in other words, evidences the deleterious, culturally homogenizing effects of Westernization. And yet, in Singapore, McDonald's can also serve as a nostalgic cultural setting. For many, the fast-food restaurant's air-conditioning offered a place to comfortably study with friends for national exams. In this frame, a different kind of interpretation emerges, one that might otherwise get lost when assuming that McDonald's only signifies Western capitalism: McDonald's is a childhood site of friendship, a site of learning, and a respite from the experience of scholastic stress shared by many Singaporeans. Certainly, that McDonald's means something different across local contexts is not necessarily a unique insight in itself. But Tiang and the many other Singaporean writers under study in this book invite us to consider the limitations of Eurocentric interpretations of global signifiers. Undoubtedly, signifiers of Global Asia in Singapore—whether they are corporate franchises or the English language—*can* be attributed to the West. Singapore might appear *as if* it is Western, the texts tell us, but that is not the whole story, for that attribution to the West can operate as a cover for the real maneuvers of power.

At the same time, the state curation of Singapore as Global Asia means that the island nation Singapore presents itself as quintessentially "Asian." The cultural representation of Singapore's multiracial, multilingual, and multireligious constituents—Chinese, Malay, Indian, Eurasian, and Peranakan—is at once touted as a point of multicultural distinction from other Asian countries, evidence of Singapore's racial difference from the West, and as pan-Asian exotic cultural appeal to the West. Eng-Beng Lim cogently writes, "It is precisely because Asia and Asian do not exist in any stable terms that Singapore needs and wants to be a part of it and identified as such."[29] In this spirit, many of the writers in this book subtly and humorously play with the codes of Asian legibility, critique the state's Asian essentialism (particularly as it manifested during the Asian Values era), and call attention to the ways *readers* desire and maintain Asia and Asians as coherent. In this way, we see how the critiques of Singapore as Global Asia—whether through global signifiers or essentialized notions of Asia—rest not simply on the fact of its construction, but on how its very representation is interpreted.

Academic critics must contend with such problems of interpretation: the machinations of Global Asia compound the existing difficulties of reading Singapore, obstacles shaped by the limitations of critical paradigms offered by neoliberalism, postcolonialism, and empire to apprehend the unprecedented nature of Singapore's economic trajectory. While analyses of Singapore and other Asian Tiger sites commonly apply the descriptor "neoliberal" to Singapore, doing so can reproduce what Naoki Sakai describes as an emanation model,[30] whereby capitalist formations originating in Euro-America in the late 1970s spread to the non-Western world. Such is the charge that Aihwa Ong makes of David Harvey, who she argues presents neoliberalism's instantiations in East and Southeast Asian contexts as exceptional and against the norm.[31] Understanding Singapore as an exceptional economic success (as the state would like it) can carry troubling implications, for it suggests that Singapore is untheorizable or outside the trajectory of history.

Notably, in work preceding the critique she makes of Harvey, Ong rejects the postcolonial explanatory frameworks for Singapore's economic trajectory, arguing that Singapore and other Asian Tigers "would not consider their own engagements with global capitalism or metropolitan powers as postcolonial but seek rather to emphasize and claim emergent power, equality, and mutual respect on the global stage."[32] For Ong, "postcolonial" problematically marks "an analysis based on colonial nostalgia or colonial legacies,"[33] which is an inadequate framework for capturing the dynamics of countries like Singapore and for studying "how economic and ideological modes of domination have been transformed in excolonial countries."[34] Ong's rejection of postcolonial frameworks resonates with general perceptions of Singapore. Indeed, when I have taught any of the Singaporean literary texts discussed in this book in courses on postcolonial literature, undergraduate students expect the literature to depict "a rationalization of and pragmatic adjustment to, if not quite a celebration of, the downturn in the fortunes and influence of insurgent national liberation movements and revolutionary socialist ideologies [of] the early 1970s."[35] Encountering images of Singapore's gleaming, modern skyline and wealth, my students wonder: How can this be postcolonial?

Not only does Singapore present theoretical and conceptual difficulties for understandings of neoliberalism and postcolonialism; it is also an unlikely site of consideration in Americanist fields that engage with Asian nations and postcoloniality, most notably, Asian American studies and US empire studies. Though Singapore was aligned with the United States during the Cold War, it has not experienced the brutal violence of US empire through war or militarization like other East and Southeast Asian nations like Japan or Vietnam. Neither has Singapore produced a particularly large immigrant population in the United States. And while Singapore is economically successful, it does not pose a threat to the United States in the way that China does.[36] Yet US empire is the context from which Singapore's independence, economic policies, and ensuing trajectory has formed. Singapore, in other words, is a post-British/Japanese imperial formation *and* a nation continually re-forming in the milieu of US empire. As Jini Kim Watson writes, the decolonization struggles in Singapore, Malaysia, Indonesia, the Philippines, and Korea are formations "*simultaneously* postcolonial and the result of bipolar complications [of the Cold War]."[37] As Wen-Qing Ngoei further shows, Singapore played a significant but underexamined role in American attempts to contain communism in the region.[38] Moreover, when considering how Singapore is a regional power,[39] as Viet Thanh Nguyen and Janet Alison Hoskins write, one whose desirability, I would add, works in tandem with the perceived threat of China to produce a sense of "Rising Asia" or the "Asian Century," it emerges as a necessary site for comprehending the broader cultural and political dynamics of the transpacific, of which the United States is a part.

Singapore's economic and political trajectory thus challenges the normative assumptions and typical methodologies of the very fields usually engaged to understand Singapore as Global Asia. Even as Ong advocates for a pluralized understanding of neoliberalism to counter its Eurocentric discourse, she rejects postcolonialism as the appropriate critical approach for comprehending a site like Singapore. To be fair, the field of postcolonial studies itself rarely engages Singapore (and other Asian Tiger sites); after all, how often do the literary or political works from these sites feature in introductory courses to or readers on postcolonial literary and theory?[40] Nonetheless, as the archive I examine continually returns us to themes of nationalism, nation formation, cultural difference, and developmental lag, I show throughout this book that Global Asia *is* postcolonial, though not the kind that is occupied with established questions of political or cultural resistance, subalternity, or cultural hybridity.

Rather than affirm Singapore as an exemplar of Westernized neoliberalism or as an economic exception, I argue Singapore serves as but the latest instantiation of *postcolonial capitalism*. This is the term I use to describe how capitalist cultures are motivated, rationalized, and strategized through a consciousness of colonial subordination and racial capitalism, both past and present. Whereas Ong suggests that "the postcolonial" is antithetical to or irrelevant in a state's drive to global capitalism, I analyze the strategic ways in which states leverage their postcolonial status to "claim power, equality, and mutual respect."[41] In the case of Singapore, Global Asia builds on earlier phases of postcolonial capitalism, namely, state developmentalism (1965–85) and Asian Values (1985–2000), which I discuss in more depth in chapter 1. One might describe Global Asia as the economic phase of neoliberalism in Singapore—and to be sure, neoliberalism is conceptually interrelated with knowledge economies—but doing so would periodize it with respect to Euro-American developments. Postcolonial capitalism offers Global Asia a different kind of historical gloss than neoliberalism by situating it within the trajectory of decolonizing nationalisms following the post-1945 restructuring of the world into a three-world order.

My thinking about the culture of postcolonial capitalism finds its way between theorists who emphasize the multiplicity of capitalism (e.g., Sandro Mezzadra, Kalyan Sanyal) and those who call for a stronger grappling with the history of race and colonialism (e.g., Couze Venn, Cedric J. Robinson).[42] While both schools of thought share a critical perspective of Eurocentrism, they diverge in their handling of how to read colonialism in the present: Does it figure as the empire in new clothes, or does it figure as the violence whose legacies have not yet been fully grappled with? To my mind, it is not an either/or proposition: the thesis of multiplicity is not eroded by the fact of colonialism so long as we acknowledge that colonialism is one among many influences at work. While the expressions and techniques of postcolonial capitalism are context dependent and change over time, a consciousness of colonialism helps represent capitalism as a politicized, moralized, and curative response to historical injustices, even as capitalism reproduces the very economic systems that facilitate the spread of extractive, colonial violence. "Helps" is the key word here because it situates the question of colonialism as not one where we are evaluating the significance or totality of its power. Rather, we are looking to the ways that postcolonial cultural and political formations are interpreting and retooling colonial history for its *own* expressions of power.

The emergent genres I study are not only crucial for tracking new logics of Global Asia, but for historicizing Global Asia with respect to postcolonial capitalism since genres are themselves a "process of textual change."[43] To track the continuity across different iterations of capitalism in Singapore, my readings of Global Asia texts take a historical and formal approach to the representations of the nation. I trace the structural pattern between the nation as a consolidating and identity-making form for Singapore's export-oriented, industrial manufacturing economy to a branding technique that sells Singapore as distinct for its knowledge economy. Tracking such shifts of the nation enables my palimpsestic analysis of "the postcolonial" as a shorter, heterogeneous historical period of distinct economic ideologies. Because of its importance as a political form for independence from empire, the nation and nationalism have long been central concepts in postcolonial studies for comprehending governance, solidarity, kinship, and culture. While many critical works discuss the significance—and insignificance—of the nation in a globalized world, it is not my intention to enter those discussions. Rather, I see the nation as the form through which postcolonial capitalism in Singapore makes itself historically legible and nationalism as the ideology through which postcolonial capitalism expresses and normalizes itself. The nation thus forms the basis of my reading methodology. Approaching the nation as a mutable form that performs different kinds of capitalist functions is what makes it possible for me to bring together, as I do in the next section, two very different kinds of nationalist texts—one more conventionally nationalist and the other less so—to track the ways the trauma of colonial occupation can be mobilized toward postcolonial capitalist ends. In other words, my point here is not to be either for or against the nation or to make claims about its strength or weakness. Rather, I recognize the nation as a variable form that changes over time according to the imperatives of postcolonial capitalism, in much the same way that Marxist formalists view literary genre as a register of political and historical change. In this way, genre operates throughout this book as a selection principle for the archive I study, an organizing principle for the chapters that unfold, and a critical orientation through which I read my archive.

At the core of postcolonial capitalism is the seeming tension between the terms of the appellation. Because many former colonies are now major players in the global economy, "postcolonial" cannot be assumed to imply an "anticapitalist" stance, as Aimé Césaire once intimated.[44] In Singapore, postcoloniality is regarded as an obstacle to national aspirations, whose Third World/class connotations must be overcome for the nation to succeed rather than a state of political and economic freedom. Such rags-to-riches narrative structures in "Asian Century," "Rising Asia," and "New India" discourses similarly frame postcoloniality as a condition to get over. Globally, postcoloniality is becoming the basis for forming economic blocs like BRICS, which only further amplify some of the most oppressive and exploitative effects of unregulated capitalism.[45] Consequently, postcolonial capitalism is what I call a "wayward postcolonialism," or a postcolonialism that has come unmoored from the traditional political, economic, and cultural significations of its original and still-dominant usages, reminding us of the need to more precisely disaggregate concepts of the "postcolonial," "anticolonial," and "decolonial."[46]

This centering of "the postcolonial" rather than "the colonial" as the active agent of capitalism and thus a locus of power is the key theoretical provocation of the term "postcolonial capitalism." But I do not celebrate the exertion of reclaimed power inherent in postcolonial capitalism, since it wields Singapore as an economic wedge against the Global South. Nevertheless, treating the postcolonial as the agent of postcolonial capitalism moves us beyond a theoretical impasse noted by many scholars. When Ong argues that "we must move beyond an analysis based on colonial nostalgia or colonial legacies,"[47] she is registering a certain frustration with imperial-centrism. And indeed, "placing colonialism/imperialism securely in the past [or] suggesting a continuous line from that past to our present," Gayatri Chakravorty Spivak warns, "sometimes serve[s] the production of neocolonial knowledge."[48] Those economic transformations to which Ong refers cannot be adequately explained by theories of colonial mimicry, which might posit that these states are unwittingly parroting colonial powers in their drive to capitalism, nor is it simply the result of a draconian state and a conservative or deluded populace. In fact, in an apparent sign of protest against Global Asia, in 2011, the PAP, the party responsible for the policies advancing this economic image, lost the largest number of parliamentary seats since it took power in 1965. Certainly, as I argue, imperial legacies persist in Global Asia, but empire is no longer the center of this story of power.

Singapore as Global Asia insists that it is *not that kind* of postcolonial, with vague strawman references to bedraggled Third World countries ubiquitous in local political rhetoric. In a 2002 National Day Rally speech, for example, Goh rationalized the need to bring in "foreign talent" to build Singapore up as Global Asia: "But if we now shut our doors to talent, we will soon become like any other Third World city of 3 million people. Then we will find life quite different. We will become a small fish—a guppy—in a small pond."[49] Here we see the characteristic flattening of postcoloniality as a condition of underdevelopment in service of the promotion of postcolonial capitalism and as a slight to the Global South. Official state histories attribute the beginning of Singapore's history to its "founding" by Sir Stamford Raffles as a British trading post in 1819, a historical narrative roundly criticized by Singaporean writers, academics, and political commentators and yet one that continues to be upheld, as demonstrated by the state-sponsored bicentennial celebration of Raffles in 2019. Faris Joraimi, Siew Sai Min, and Alfian Sa'at, moreover, point out how Singapore's postcolonial independence is "regarded as a dangerous predicament" and how Singapore is "constantly spooked . . . by multiple threats of failed nationhood—of which colonialism is not one."[50] Such an observation resonates with C. J. W.-L. Wee's remarks: "[For Singapore,] the *imperial past* is not necessarily a debasing one, for it laid the foundation for present sociopolitical developments. . . . Singapore is probably distinct among postcolonial societies in its *valorization* of the imperial."[51] Besides having the effect of making Singapore appear forgiving of colonialism, such historical narratives attempt to obscure both the actual role that the anticolonial platform played for the PAP in the 1950s and 1960s and the exact ways in which postcolonial governance shapes capitalism. By valorizing the imperial, the Singapore state implies that it is simply following a tutelage model and, consequently, abdicates its influence. Of course, there is hardly anyone with illusions about the state's role in constructing Singapore into a haven for capitalism. That the state is representing Singapore as the paragon of *colonial* capitalism should invite us to consider why it so readily deploys the narrative of colonial complicity.

Besides performing its continuity with colonialism, Singapore's use of "the global" often acts as another way of erasing postcoloniality. Take, for example, the state's presentation of diasporic Singaporeans as the protagonists of Global Asia. The emergence of a cosmopolitan, diasporic workforce seemingly aligns Singapore more with the ideological priorities of a deregulated, globalized free market economy and has the further effect of dissociating Singapore from traditional markers of postcoloniality that insist on a nationalist sense of sovereignty. And there is the rub: tracing postcolonial capitalism through representations of Global Asia is the conceptual challenge precisely because Global Asia does not intuitively register as "postcolonial." This book takes that challenge head-on in its focus on what are ostensibly genres of Global Asia—that is, post-1997 texts that easily lend themselves to neoliberal or global approaches. Certainly, that is what they are and this book elucidates how biopolitical governance, neoliberal individualism, and neo-orientalism function for Global Asia. But *Becoming Global Asia* also demonstrates how genres of Global Asia put pressure on our conceptions of "new," as these contemporary texts consistently reference earlier moments of Singapore's independence and nation formation: they must *also* be read as contemporary genres of postcolonial capitalism. Centering postcolonial capitalism counters the colonial alibi. My book therefore retheorizes postcoloniality to clarify its crucial role in the material and ideological movement of global capitalism. I argue that it is precisely the obfuscation of postcoloniality's entanglements with global capital that has enabled Singapore to be reduced to an imitative colonial state rather than a postcolonial state. Ironically, this obfuscation has been promoted both by the

Singaporean state and by its critics, each having their own reasons for tying post-coloniality to a particular time, locale, and politics.[52]

Postcolonial capitalism understands postcoloniality as an ongoing, globally uneven condition. For its more contemporary instantiations, postcolonial capitalism thinks through the ways that Singapore's economic trajectory develops in the aftermath of British and Japanese imperialisms alongside the assertion of US empire in Southeast Asia. In pursuit of a methodology that grapples with US empire while not inadvertently recentering it, I follow the "transpacificism" developed in Nguyen and Hoskins's work. In their formulation, Nguyen and Hoskins offer the transpacific as a way of breaking free of an Asian American or American studies that insists "on the United States as the primary object of inquiry."[53] *Becoming Global Asia* contributes to this project of transpacificism by thinking through the more attenuated role of US empire. At times, this means reckoning with the *context* of US imperialism as it interacts with the global economy rather than examining a relation of power that is connoted by understandings of the transpacific as a contact zone. At other times, reckoning with such a context appears in brief historical details or notes, as in chapter 1, when I discuss how initial perceptions of diasporic Singaporeans as national traitors were in part shaped by the ways US immigration policies were unsettling Singapore's worker pool. Still at other moments, understanding the attenuated role of US empire simply means not assuming that all things Western should be read as a symptom of Singapore pandering to or glorifying the United States. For example, in forming language policies so that Singapore could offer the world a workforce fluent in English, the state was able to attract transnational corporations to set up headquarters in Singapore in the 1980s and 1990s—American ones among them. Obviously, English as a language has an audience beyond the United States. Still, of course, the United States is a significant and desired audience. The point is that through the English language, we can see how Singapore's governance was negotiating and constantly aware of its positionality within a US-led global configuration. Rather than directly responding to US power, it was devising ways to benefit from that world order.[54] The book demonstrates that the goal of transpacificism does not simply mean leaving the fact of US empire to Americanists.

Although *Becoming Global Asia* is routed into Asian American studies as the result of Singapore's transpacific geography, it is more directly indebted to Asian Americanist theories and methodologies that situate the significance of Asian racialization—of both people and place—within systemic frames of oppression and inequality.[55] When perceived as a nation that has successfully transcended its postcolonial condition of underdevelopment and therefore one worthy of emulation, Singapore, in its prescribed role as a model nation, is vital in symbolically reinforcing global inequality and rationalizing postcolonial capitalism on a global scale. Distinguishing Singapore as "model" nation operates as an economic wedge between the Global North and the Global South, much in the way that model minority Asian Americans serve as a racial wedge and anti-Black buffer in the United States. This wedge function obscures the subaltern forms of migrant labor that build the cityscape and maintain homes to keep Singapore functional at all. When Jared Kushner cited Singapore as an economic model for the Peace to Prosperity plan, he minimized—if he did not completely erase—the role that Israeli occupation plays in Palestine's ability to "meet the daunting challenges" of determining a "better future," thereby positioning Palestine as incompetent (and we know that is exactly the point).[56] Like Kushner, Lamb's unctuous admiration for Singapore appears to be based in part in his disdain for other postcolonial nations: "At independence, instead of tearing down the overt symbols of colonialism in a burst of ultranationalism, Singapore accepted the reality of the past."[57] Studying Global Asia and postcolonial capitalism is never simply what *Singapore* or its wealth is about; it is about the many scales of power that Singapore makes possible.

HISTORICIZING GLOBAL ASIA; OR, READING FOR THE CONTINUING LOGIC OF POSTCOLONIAL CAPITALISM

What does postcolonial capitalism look like in literary narratives? Let us first turn to "The Japanese Invaders," a chapter from the famed 1998 memoir, *The Singapore Story*, by Prime Minister Lee Kuan Yew, who shares his harrowing experience of living under Japanese occupation during World War II. The memoir itself tells the story of Singapore's postcolonial nation formation and helps us establish a historical perspective on postcolonial capitalism. Alongside Lee's memories of terrifying encounters with Japanese soldiers are his reflections on running a chewing gum business, construction firm, and trade company. In describing the challenges of the time, Lee muses, "But one needed capital to get richer. I was able to raise some money and quickly accumulated more. I knew that the moment I had cash, the important thing was to change it into something of more permanent value."[58] In the same way that a CEO's memoir might surreptitiously pass off interior dialogue as advice for its readers, the subtext of Lee's ruminations is that his thinking under such duress—what some would describe as Lee's "pragmatism"—is what enabled the eventual economic success of Singapore. Lee writes that the "three and a half years of Japanese occupation were the most important of my life" because of the way they provided "vivid insights into the behavior of human beings and human societies, their motivations and impulses."[59] This suggests that occupation was a lesson in the workings of and responses to brutal power. In what may come as a surprise, Lee goes on to praise the "smart and the opportunistic" individuals who worked with the Japanese, and he singles out the Shaw brothers as "the luckiest and most prosperous of all" for the gambling farms they were licensed to run.[60] Rather than condemn these individuals for war profiteering or detailing the difficult choices they may have faced in aligning themselves with the Japanese, Lee's language takes on a congratulatory if not wondrous tone. In this way, Lee attributes the "survival" of Japanese occupation to business acumen.[61]

For Lee, Japanese occupation was, moreover, the catalyst for his anticolonial thinking. As the historians Hong Lysa and Huang Jianli put it, the dominant account of Singapore's postcolonial history "begins with the harsh years of the Japanese occupation, when the people of Singapore realized that as long as they were ruled by foreigners their interests would be secondary to those of their colonial rulers."[62] Indeed, Lee's account of Japanese occupation tells not only of the Imperial Army's brutality but also of the British Empire's fallibility; the latter proved profoundly disappointing to him. Japanese occupation destroyed the myth of "the superior status of the British . . . [as] the greatest people in the world,"[63] inspiring Lee to later advocate for independence from them. Japanese occupation thus represented the beginnings of Lee's decolonizing political consciousness, one that is intertwined with his valorization of the survivors who had the necessary "improvisational" abilities to thrive during this dark period of history.[64] In other words, capitalist accumulation is rationalized as fundamental to a decolonizing political consciousness and process.

Two decades later, echoes of Lee's thinking resound in an unlikely literary work that thematizes Singaporean survival under Japanese occupation: Kevin Kwan's 2017 *Rich People Problems*. In this final installment of Kwan's popular *Crazy Rich Asians* trilogy—paradigmatic texts of Global Asia and Singapore's cultural capital—the protagonist, Nicholas Young, is given the old diaries and private correspondence of his recently deceased grandmother, Su Yi. After reading a letter from King George VI, Nicholas realizes that Su Yi and her family were World War II heroes who used their wealth as a ruse to forward anticolonial causes. Their family business justified travel and allowed them to help others escape Singapore during Japanese occupation and "hide some of Singapore's most crucial anti-Japanese activists."[65] Tyersall Park, the gigantic family estate, was used as an "Underground Railroad" and "a place for secret high-level meetings and a safe house for some of the key people who were being hunted down by the Japanese."[66] Historically, Tyersall Palace, or the Istana Woodneuk, was the headquarters for British and Australian armies fighting the Japanese Imperial Army. In Kwan's trilogy, Tyersall Park is notably hidden away; Singaporeans have never heard of it, and it is impossible to view on Google Maps. Tyersall Park thus emerges as an invisible symbol of the immense accumulated capital through which anticolonial endeavors are made possible. That Tyersall Park is invisible even though it is located in the middle of the island further comments on the unconscious centrality of such logic in Singapore: to be properly post- and anticolonial requires immense capital.

While one of the novel's plotlines gives wealth an anticolonial motivation, Japanese occupation explains and justifies unfettered consumption as a symptom of colonial trauma in a different subplot, taking Lee's notion of anticolonial capitalist survival to its logical conclusion. Charlie, the former boyfriend of the other pro-tagonist, Astrid, notes his mother's childhood experience at a wartime concentra-tion camp in Malaysia, musing, "I'm sure that's why my mother is the way she is now. She makes her cook save money by buying the discounted, three-day-old bread from the supermarket, but she'll spend $30,000 on plastic surgery for her pet fish. It's completely irrational."[67] Notably, the Endau settlement Charlie refers to was famed for the success of the "Grow More Food" campaign. In order to prepare for the possibility of food shortage, the Japanese had the prisoners grow food crops. The settlement's eventual self-sufficiency earned it the name, New Syonan Model Farm.[68] The history of the Endau settlement thus reads as an alle-gory for Singapore itself insofar as state narratives often present the city-state's movement toward political autonomy as enforced by circumstance. While this juxtaposition of wartime-inspired frugality alongside lavish extravagance seems to illustrate some kind of contradiction, Charlie draws a causal relation between the colonial trauma of Japanese occupation and his mother's consumptive behaviors. The excessive wealth expressed by Charlie's mother's consumption—and any new oppressions or exploitations caused by it—is vindicated by trauma.

In this unlikely pairing of a revered statesman's memoir and a bestselling novel, a distinct rationality of postcolonial capitalism emerges. Wealth and business strategy signify autonomy from colonial power and are attached to a decolonial imaginary. Consumption is posed as a means of working through and overcom-ing colonial trauma. Taken together, these texts point to the ways that capital-ism is a logical redress for colonialism. Since the Japanese occupation, the state has expanded on the kernel of this logic in varying ways. Sometimes it wields national precarity and the potential return of colonial inferiority to facilitate its economic agenda, moments that invoke what Geraldine Heng and Janadas Devan describe as state "narratives of crisis" to justify its hard rule.[69] At other times, the state exploits the colonial-era East/West binary to justify paternalistic governance. At yet other times, it uses the history of colonial dispossession to sell Singapore's "Third World to First World" narrative to emphasize its status as a model post-colonial nation. What these different state expressions of postcolonial capitalism illustrate is how Singapore's colonial experience and its postcolonial desires for autonomy and respect are instrumentalized to galvanize the nation's citizenry for the purpose of capital accumulation.

Literary narratives offer a way of tracking postcolonial capitalism's different his-torical manifestations. Indeed, it is our objects of study that result in the divergence between my literary/cultural theorization and Ong's ethnographic theorization of Singapore—as examples of postcolonial capitalism and "small *n*" neoliberal-ism, respectively. Although I primarily focus on how postcolonial history moves through to our present, literary texts like Lee's and Kwan's can also help histori-cize Singapore's soft power as Global Asia. Through Lee's status as the mastermind of Singapore's success and Kwan's as a bestselling, Hollywood-adapted author, we see different kinds of cultural capital propelling Singapore's exalted status. Study-ing postcolonial capitalism and Global Asia together through literary and cultural materials offers insights into the cultural imaginary and historicity of capitalism, insights that can only be accessed by means of literary methodologies that study language and narrative.[70]

GLOBAL ASIA PRODUCTIONS OF DIASPORA

Key for Singapore under Global Asia is the reimagined form of diaspora. Such a reimagination is partly a way of recruiting diasporic citizens into the national fold, but more significantly for this book is their role in building Singapore's cultural capital by styling the nation as global and cosmopolitan. In this way, diasporic Singaporeans—often highly professionalized, anglophone subjects—are cast as Global Asia's main protagonists. Indeed, many of the Global Asia texts under study in this book are also diasporic ones. The significance of diasporic Singaporeans for the transition into the Global Asia knowledge economy became apparent after a controversial 2002 Singapore National Day Rally speech, when former Singaporean prime minister, Goh Chok Tong, questioned the loyalty of Singaporeans living abroad:

> Fair-weather Singaporeans will run away whenever the country runs into stormy weather. I call them "quitters." . . . I take issue with those fair-weather Singaporeans who, having benefited from Singapore, will pack their bags and take flight when our country runs into a little storm. . . . Look yourself in the mirror and ask, am I a "stayer" or a "quitter?" Am I a fair-weather Singaporean or an all-weather Singaporean?[71]

Responding to the nation's economic uncertainty after the 1997 Asian financial cri-sis, Goh's speech invoked typical nationalist rhetoric. In contrasting "stayers" and "quitters," he asserted that Singaporeans at home were somehow truer than their overseas compatriots, traitors who had deserted the nation in a time of need. Cap-turing the ever-present consciousness of Singapore's status as a relatively young and small island city-state, Goh's remarks revealed a long-standing anxiety of the Singaporean state: the loss of human capital, purported to be Singapore's primary natural resource.

Given Goh's firm admonition, it might seem shocking that the government reversed course only a few years later, launching in 2006 the Overseas Singaporean Unit (OSU) as a "directorate under the National Population and Talent Division of the Prime Minister's Office . . . [and a] part of the Singapore government's overall efforts to engage its citizens."[72] Distancing itself from the alienating sentiments expressed in Goh's speech, the government, in establishing the OSU, demonstrates the state's clear attempt to foster more positive relations with Singaporeans living abroad. Instead of traitors and quitters, the diaspora was heralded as necessary for Singapore's future as Global Asia.

The state's positive attitude toward, treatment of, and instrumentalization of diasporic Singaporeans signify a pivotal change accompanying Singapore's increased orientation to a knowledge economy following the 1997 Asian financial crisis.[73] This instrumentalist function of the diaspora is especially evident in the language Deputy Prime Minister and Minister for Home Affairs Wong Kan Seng used at the launch of the OSU: "I believe in and share the unit's mission—to create an interconnected Overseas Singaporean diaspora with Singapore at its core."[74] The diaspora would come to represent the "Singaporean of the 21st century" as someone "who is familiar with global trends and lifestyles and feels comfortable working and living in Singapore as well as overseas," as put by the *Singapore 21* report.[75] Put a little differently, the twenty-first-century Singaporean, who was also described as the "Renaissance Singaporean,"[76] is a cosmopolitan subject. Cosmopolitanism, as figured by the Overseas Singaporean, is a key part of presenting Global Asia as new, unprecedented, and no longer postcolonial; moreover, it allows Singapore to be represented as an economic model with global reach and influence.

In the Global Asia context, cosmopolitanism and diaspora operate not as descriptors of its values or characteristics but as ideological tools. This is apparent in Wong's use of the word *create* when describing the "Overseas Singaporean diaspora." That is, this diaspora is one that must be claimed by the state, toward particular benefits and advantages. This vision for the "diaspora" is akin to Ong's observation, whereby it is "increasingly invoked by elite migrants in transnational contexts to articulate an inclusive ethnicity that includes disparate populations across the world who may be able to claim a common racial or cultural ancestry."[77] But as Ong points out, "diaspora" "is loose on the information highway and political byways, and elite diasporic subjects have picked up the term in order to mass customize global ethnic identities."[78] While Wong's language underscores the profitability of diaspora, his thinking is not idiosyncratic to him or the Singaporean state; such mass customization is also evident in "diaspora marketing" and "diaspora strategy," terms used in business and public policy, respectively. Even while the instrumentalist logics might appear politically distasteful, they are a constitutive part of diasporic representation. For better or worse, the Singaporean state's diaspora strategy has catalyzed the legibility of its diaspora. That the category "Overseas Singaporeans" is now even legible as constituting a diaspora speaks to the effectiveness of the state's strategies.

Recognizing the ideological significance of diasporic Singaporeans for Global Asia both in state materials and in literary and cultural materials, this book approaches the people making up this "diaspora" less in terms of their changing attachments to the national homeland and more in terms of how they function in the national project as valued representatives on a global stage. My readings therefore focus on how the concept of diaspora is being used, what it does for the nation, and what it gives voice to rather than on how diasporans feel.

To be clear, however, these questions of instrumentality are not limited to the state. Literary productions likewise leverage diasporic Singaporean characters to critique the state.

READING GOVERNANCE IN CONTEMPORARY GENRES OF POSTCOLONIAL CAPITALISM

In this book, genre and form act as selection principles for each chapter but also as an aesthetic mode of synthesizing disparate political positions. That literary forms like demographic collections and the coming-of-career narratives (themselves outgrowths of anthologies and bildungsroman) also appear in state texts demonstrate how governance traffics in culture. Because my archive includes a number of policy recommendation reports and state-authored texts from an authoritarian government, it might appear that I am setting up a power dynamic that centers the state and that positions literary texts as simply reactive to its rule. However, my interest in soft power assumes a tempered role for the state in the Global Asia context. When we consider that Global Asia is a cultural formation that operates within a symbolic order or, as the *Renaissance City Report* puts it, a site "imbued with a keen sense of aesthetics,"[79] the state is situated as but another cultural producer among many and not one that typically holds that much sway. These often well-designed, glossy, English-language texts replete with graphics and photographs look more like corporate brochures inviting a public readership; indeed, they are very accessible materials and can generally be found in public libraries or circulating around the internet.[80] Some of the policy recommendations are more directly aimed at the general population, as indicated by their translation into Singapore's other official languages. Even while some of these reports are not necessarily aimed at the everyday Singaporean, since they offer granular detail on how various governmental bodies or civil servants should implement policy, they are meant to be read, by virtue of their circulation, accessibility, and design.

Some may simply dismiss these state texts as propaganda, undeserving of critical attention because their agenda is straightforward or because there is little evidence that they have explicit effects on the Singaporean populace. In other words, their significance cannot be measured by circulation or reception. But my reading methodology treats state texts as important repositories of governing logics: they are less an expression of dominating power than a grasping for power. They do not articulate the rule of law. Policy papers, speeches, and political ephemera are often meant to be persuasive, which is to say, aspirational. Indeed, many of the reports read like manifestos. Such government materials are cultural texts that contribute to capitalism as a cultural formation.

Notably, many of the literary texts I examine also represent the state in a more tenuous position of power. They are often obliquely critical of the state and do not overtly represent Singaporean governance, as is the case in *Mammon Inc.* and

Crazy Rich Asians, which use subtle passing historical references to socioeconomic policies. While I suspect that many writers want to resist portraying Singaporean life as completely overdetermined by state power (as so often perceived in the West), these texts also remind us that the Singaporean state is but one institution working within a matrix of power.[81] To be clear, I am not suggesting that disciplinary or oppressive power is no longer operating in Singapore as Global Asia. Whether suppression of political dissent, capital punishment, or restrictive immigration laws for migrant workers, there are clear and current examples of authoritarian governance. Yet I contend that state power *does* operate differently under Global Asia and that the top-down models of power, even in this authoritarian context, cannot capture important nuances.

The organization of the book can be described in a few different ways. The first half of the book focuses on compiled literary forms; the latter half examines adapted novelistic genres. Roughly speaking, the chapters proceed chronologically, with the first chapter focused on the period before 1997 to establish historical precedent; the subsequent chapters look at post-1997 Global Asia texts. Each chapter also has a thematic focus that has been central to understandings of the postcolonial nation: global order, territory, work, and cultural difference. Regardless of organizational logic, when taken together, the chapters track the ideological workings and historical operations of Global Asia with respect to postcolonial capitalism.

Tracking earlier permutations of postcolonial capitalism, the first chapter turns to the anthology, an especially prevalent literary form and genre in Singapore. The anthology is, as I argue, an underexamined form of postcolonial nationalism, one that is outward-facing and conscious of the colonial-turned-global gaze. The chapter examines how this compiled form and pedagogical genre changes according to the prevailing economic ideologies of two periods: state developmentalism (1965–85) and Asian Values (1985–2000). The production history of Singapore anthologies exposes the global and local scales of postcolonial capitalism through the ideological and economic influences of UNESCO, local writing competitions, oil and petroleum corporations, and the manufacturing economy. Yet, I argue, it also reveals some of the more utopian national visions of Singapore. For this reason, I suggest that even while the anthology might seem a compromised genre because it seeks to make Singapore legible to the world for capitalist development, it inadvertently established the anthology as an important generative and generous genre that creates the conditions for local writing.

The chapters that follow focus on contemporary genres of postcolonial capitalism to track the emergence of Global Asia. Chapter 2 studies the transformed role accorded to diasporic Singaporeans and how they expand territorial understandings of the nation in service of Global Asia. As with the previous chapter, I examine compiled forms, in this instance what I describe as demographic compilations: the state-controlled newspaper series "Singaporean Abroad" (2008–12) and the literary nonfiction magazine *be movement* (2015). Demographics are not based in a sense of belonging, kinship, or political commitments but instead portray recurring characteristics of a population, recalling the administrative logics of colonialism that continue into postcolonial, biopolitical governance. I show how the "population aesthetic," or the noncontinuous, serialized representation of flat characters, is used in demographic compilations as part of the Singaporean state's efforts to cultivate a cosmopolitan ethic. I also show how this statist genre is retooled by Overseas Singaporeans themselves to critique postcolonial capitalism. The chapter closes with Jeremy Tiang's *It Never Rains on National Day* (2016), a short story collection that thematizes the denouement of diasporic Singaporean fictional narratives as a way of critiquing the formal conventions of demographic compilations.

Chapter 3 centers the analysis on the changing notions of work ethic by showing how the postcolonial nation allies with neoliberalized corporations to compel labor from its subjects. It focuses on the "coming-of-career" genre in Hwee Hwee Tan's *Mammon Inc.* (2001), a satirical novel critical of the state's valorization of Overseas Singaporeans, and *Conversations on Coming Home* (2012), a state promotional booklet encouraging Overseas Singaporeans to return. I examine how postcolonial work is an aestheticized and pleasurable mode of asserting self-sovereignty and protesting empire and how it is also the mode through which Global Asia obscures its postcolonial associations. In *Mammon Inc.* and *Conversations*, this erasure happens when the pleasures of contemporary, corporate work are read as the ideological power of transnational corporations rather than as the rejection of the postcolonial state. As a reminder that the implications of transnationalized, neoliberal work is not limited to the professional classes, I then turn to *Ilo Ilo* (2013), an award-winning feature film about a middle-class Singaporean Chinese family and their Filipina domestic worker. The erasure of the nonelite classes, I argue, is the consequence of posing Singapore as economically exceptional and thus disassociated from the Southeast Asian region and the Global South.

At the center of chapter 4 is the legacy of Singapore's Asian Values discourse and the way in which the perception of Asiatic difference plays out in our current juncture. I argue that a shorter rather than longer view of history is necessary for understanding the workings of postcolonial capitalism. As I show in my readings of Kevin Kwan's novel *Crazy Rich Asians* (2014) and its Hollywood feature film adaptation (2018), portrayals of Singapore's economic success as originating with British colonialism obscures the historical specificity of capitalism and conflates capitalism with colonialism. The chapter demonstrates how postcolonial capitalism exploits colonial fantasies of Asia and in doing so works with histories of orientalist difference to enshrine Singapore's cosmopolitan veneer. Kwan's presentation of Singapore in what I describe as a "princess fantasy," or a fantasy of being the center of attention, having all desires met, and being revered by all, enables us to see the multifaceted appeal of Kwan's work while also diagnosing the changing dynamics of the West's reading of the East.

In the brief conclusion, I examine the controversial closure of Yale-NUS (National University of Singapore) College to discuss the implications of Singapore's soft power as it meets the state's repressive state apparatus. Even in the face of authoritarian, disciplinary rule, I contend, we must think through the entire assemblage of power at the disposal of the modern state.

1

The Cultural History of Singapore Literary Anthologies

The history of Singapore anthologies begins roughly a decade before the city-state's independence with the publication of *L'essai* (1953), a collection of poetry and prose written by Raffles Institution students. On the face of it, the anthology is well suited for Singapore's multilingual and multiracial context as an aesthetic form that coheres multiple, heterogeneous pieces in a single text. Since *L'essai*, the anthology has seen significant growth.[1] One recent headline in a local newspaper, for example, observes "The Rise of the Anthology."[2] Singaporean academic and literary events now feature dedicated panels on the genre and, indeed, Singapore Writers Festival programs from the past decade reveal large numbers of panels promoting and discussing newly published anthologies.[3] Speakers' biographies show that many Singaporean writers are also anthology editors themselves. Anthologies are everywhere in Singapore and a staple of the literary scene.

While noting the prominence of the anthology in contemporary Singapore literature, Weihsin Gui also observes its importance throughout Singapore's literary history as a form in which "concepts of a national literature and national identity are expressed and negotiated."[4] In addition to the anthology's role in producing national literature, editors often perform the invisible labor of building national literary infrastructure. Take, for example, Chandran Nair, an influential figure who shaped Singapore's literary landscape.[5] His press, Woodrose Publications, issued ten titles, including a multilingual anthology, *Singapore Writing* (1977) and an anthology of short stories by women edited by Geraldine Heng, *The Sun in Her Eyes* (1976).[6] On top of establishing an outlet for local writers, Nair's efforts would eventually lead Heinemann and Federal Publications to begin publishing Singaporean works. His editorial labor, in other words, brought both local and international audiences to Singapore literature.[7]

The anthology has played a crucial and influential role in Singapore's literary history, and as I argue in this chapter, it is a form that was at once instrumental for state-led efforts in postcolonial capitalist development and used by Singaporean writers and editors to contest those imperatives. It is a literary and cultural site of contestation. I moreover show that because the changes in aesthetic and political priorities of the Singapore anthology track with shifts in Singapore's economic ideologies—namely, the developmentalism of early independence and Asian Values—the anthology yields understandings of the different cultural and political permutations of postcolonial capitalism. In this way, this chapter is methodologically distinct. Instead of working backward from the present through historicized close readings of post-1997 emergent genres to comprehend the workings of Global Asia, it offers a genealogical account that lays out key historical moments for the rest of the book.[8] Across these two periods, and as I demonstrate in later chapters on Global Asia itself, what constitutes "the global" also transforms. While "global" might typically refer to how neoliberalism of the late 1970s increased the economic and cultural interconnected coherence of the world (i.e., globalization), I use the term more broadly to refer to the external structuring force of the nation-state, a force that has its own internal logic shaped by imperial histories, as illustrated by the very notion of the post-1945 three-world order. The power dynamics of postcolonial capitalism, the anthology reminds us, do not operate in a vacuum between state and subject. Perceptions of the global also frame the nation.

Following a discussion of the theoretical significance of the anthology for postcolonial literary studies, the first section examines what I describe as the "major anthology." These were the most prevalent type of anthology in the first phase of postcolonial capitalism, when "the global" was focalized through institutions. These major anthologies published by state agencies and international publishers were wrought with institutional interests, including those of the Singaporean state as it cultivated a nationalized manufacturing economy, UNESCO in its promotion of book development, and the oil and petroleum industry as it sought to promote a socially conscious image. During this period, the anthology emerges as a key literary form for building Singapore's cultural capital for a global audience and as a compromise that performs book development without requiring the cultivation of full-time, professional writers. Postcolonial capitalism, in this instance, operates with an assimilative logic in its attempt to prove Singapore's capacity for modernity and development. As I show, major anthologies of the 1970s and 1980s rely on already existing ordering logics (colonial-era demographic categories of race), established literary values (great authors), and emergent global values (multiculturalism) to make legible the national literary project. Yet, as I illustrate in a discussion of *The Poetry of Singapore* (1985), editors like Edwin Thumboo subtly push back against the imperatives of legibility with an aesthetic of translation.

The next section considers the Asian Values era of the 1990s, a time of increased wealth and improved global reputation, during which the "popular anthology" proliferates. In this phase of postcolonial capitalism, the "West" (the name used to connote the United States) becomes the face of the global and is understood to be in a culturally binary relation to "Asia." The relatively inexpensive paperbound popular anthologies that emerged had little publishing support from the state and were mostly funded by private benefactors and independent presses. With a focus on the VJ Times horror anthologies, I show how popular anthologies sought to challenge the respectability politics of Singapore's attempts to make itself globally legible. Although popular anthologies rarely feature as literarily significant because of their imbrication with genre fiction, I argue that they perform the important nationalist function of cultivating the recognition that one's fellow Singaporeans can occupy the status of producers of literature. Consequently, I suggest that we understand the Singapore anthology as a generative form. By using the term "generative," I want to capture not only its denotation of production but also its etymological relation to "generosity." If we are then to think about the anthology as Singapore's national form, we see how collaboration, assistance, and goodwill emerge amid a sociopolitical context of intense development.

THE NATIONAL LONGING
FOR ANTHOLOGICAL FORM

The anthology has deep historical roots and can be found in classical Greek and Chinese literatures. The word *anthology* comes from the Greek for "bouquet," referring to a collection of poems. Anthologies have since expanded to include any number of genres, but, as Jeffrey R. Di Leo puts it, "the basic notion of an anthology as a *collection* of writings remains the same."[9] As a genre, the anthology holds an unusual degree of authority because of its historical association with canon formation and preservation. Indeed, the anthology's relationship to the (English) literary canon is a key factor in distinguishing types of anthologies. According to formal literary definitions, anthologies aim to produce a canon and are thus deemed historical texts, whereas miscellanies and collections emphasize contemporary pieces for entertainment.[10] The "anthology" is generally accepted as the broad umbrella term, and I deploy it here as such. However, that the technical differentiation among anthological subgenres falls along the lines of the text's ability to preserve the canon reveals the anthology's conservative politics.[11]

As evidenced by scholarship on racialized or marginalized anglophone literatures, not all anthologies have canonizing aspirations, however, and many in fact seek to unsettle Eurocentric literary values associated with the anthology's role in preserving the canon. Asian North American, Black, and Indigenous thinkers such as Larissa Lai, Brent Hayes Edwards, and Alice Te Punga Somerville frame the anthology as a crucial site of historical contestation and potential subversion.[12] They also note that the anthology's formal capacity for diverse representation can potentially unsettle its complicity in reproducing Eurocentric literary values that are so often associated with the construction of the canon. Critics optimistic about the anthology's political potential see the form as offering community representation. As Te Punga Somerville describes it, anthologies can "create a sense of 'us,'" particularly for writers who have been historically disenfranchised.[13] Considering how anglophone literary values cohere around the production of the liberal, individualized subject, the work of conceptualizing this sense of "us" is no small decolonizing gesture. Anthologies moreover entail "cooperative means of production and multiple authorship," as Barbara Benedict points out, making them "material expressions of a kind of community."[14] As certainly evidenced in the history of Singapore anthologies, we might further add that anthologies often emerge out of and reproduce communal gatherings such as classrooms, readings, and book launches. These theorizations of the anthology from cognate fields to postcolonial studies show how the anthology is a form suited for representing what Benedict Anderson describes as the "imagined community" and thus postcolonial nationalism.

But as some critics such as Colleen Lye and Gayatri Chakravorty Spivak have countered, the anthology's plural form can also reaffirm a problematic racial politics that relies too heavily on the performance of diverse representation and ultimately flattens difference.[15] These critiques are important reminders that while the anthology's plural form can appear as opposed to Eurocentric literary values, its progressive promise can actually reinscribe some of the dominant ideologies that it seems to oppose.[16] Even though historical contexts of disenfranchisement or dispossession may produce counter-anthologies that challenge Eurocentric literary values and empower marginalized groups, counter-anthologies are not necessarily anti-canon formation. Indeed, as I discuss below, anthologies were crucial for performing a literary canon as a way of asserting national sovereignty and modernity in postcolonial Singapore and Southeast Asia. Counter-anthologies are not inevitably anti-canon, just as anticolonial politics are not indubitably decolonial.

Besides its potential to disturb Eurocentric literary values and its capacity to literarily forge communal relations, the anthology's formal capacity for consolidation also resonates with questions of nation formation, a key mode of inquiry in postcolonial literary studies. Like the novel, the typical object of study for postcolonial literary treatments of the nation, the anthology too offers coherence to difference by bringing together, as Timothy Brennan writes, "an unsettled mixtures of ideas and styles."[17] But what is distinct is how that difference is brought together; rather than through narrative, as with the novel, the anthology binds through editorial decisions and the material form (i.e., printing and binding technology that makes possible the portability of long-form writing). Given how, as Philip Holden points out, Singapore cannot draw on established narrative forms to assert its sovereignty, the anthology's reliance on material infrastructure and editors to engineer a non-narrative-based sense of coherence makes it a strikingly apt form for Singapore when considering its independence was gained through its split from present-day Malaysia.[18] Such problems of forming national narrative have only been historically complicated by Singapore's transient, multiracial, and multilingual constituency. From the Singaporean context, we begin to see that the nation as novel premise that is so prevalent in postcolonial literary studies relies on an ideal type, in the sociological sense, of the nation.[19]

While I am building a case for why the anthology should be an important form for diversifying understandings of postcoloniality, the anthology also faces the problem of not being considered an aesthetic object in and of itself. Perhaps the anthology evades literary and aesthetic appreciation because editors are rarely held up as creative beings. Although editor status can confer cultural capital and authoritative status on individuals, seldom are anthology editors recognized, celebrated, or studied for the fact that they *are* anthology editors; if anything, the editor's reputation as an author or academic is what lends the editor role any kind of prestige.[20] In highlighting the ways that Albert Wendt is "making things possible" through his editorial labor, Te Punga Somerville implicitly comments on editorial labor as a kind of care work that is undervalued, as often happens with work traditionally associated with the "feminine." The denigration of editorial work as feminized labor is manifested in the literary criticism and its institutions. Endless journalistic and biographical writings offer insight into the creative minds of authors: their habits, their writing practices, their inspirations, and their politics. Degree programs credentialize authors as such. Literary societies exist for the study of authors. While writing, as the act of crafting language into narrative, is indeed an important source of literature, myriad institutions work in concert to reaffirm the patriarchal, capitalist values of individuality at the expense of other kinds of literary labor.

When we recognize editing as "invisible artistry," as the experimental filmmaker Su Friedrich puts it, rather than as correction, other forms and histories of literary practice emerge.[21] Although film and anthology editing differ in significant ways, they both involve the work of careful juxtaposition in order to create effects, whether those juxtapositions involve images, sounds, words, stories, or authors. Engaging the craft of such invisible artistry means both valuing the curatorial work of the editors and looking at the actual text in its new context, as Kristine Kotecki argues: "The process of being excerpted, translated, and arranged into anthologies . . . emphasizes in other ways the political stakes of the poems."[22] The political implications of the anthology, in other words, can also emerge phenomenologically from the effects produced by the texts in their new arrangement, not just the representational politics of contributors' identities or other elements of the paratextual framing.

The curation practice of anthology editors, moreover, is especially resonant with the engineer, an important postcolonial figure that emerged during the decolonization era and one that continues to be celebrated today as the exalted figure of technocratic governance. In postcolonial literary criticism, where the nation has been treated as a potential liberatory structure, celebrated authors are often valued as revolutionary for their critical role in anticolonial knowledge production. With their abilities to craft language, to inspire, and to imagine new futures, we might say that postcolonial authors are regarded as a kind of literary equivalent of the postcolonial political leader because they share a propensity for narrative and appeal to desires for aesthetic unity. A less romanticized but still significant postcolonial figure is the engineer, as the figure that could solve the *problem* of postcoloniality: substandard material conditions as created by the history of extractive capitalism and when compared to those of the former colonial world. Writing of the Bandung period, Dipesh Chakrabarty points out that the "accent on modernization made the figure of the engineer one of the most eroticized figures of the postcolonial developmental imagination."[23] Although Lee Kuan Yew was regarded as a charismatic and inspirational leader during the independence era, he is arguably more appreciated as a highly successful social engineer. Even though the terms have changed, the problem-solving engineer still remains an exalted figure, as indicated by local rhetoric and global praise regarding Singapore's technocratic governance and its ability to shape national outcomes through design and infrastructure.[24] Might we then say that the engineer is one of the most eroticized figures of the postcolonial capitalist imagination and that its corresponding literary figure is the anthology editor? While the editor certainly shares qualities with Claude Lévi-Strauss's bricoleur, as a figure that recombines preexisting pieces to create something new,[25] the language that celebrates Chandran Nair as an editor of *Singapore Writing* (1977), for example, is the language of engineering insofar as it highlights his role in materializing the anthology, as the person who "worked to get publishers, media and governmental support and acceptance for writers and writing."[26] The editor, in other words, is a crossover figure, one that navigates both aesthetic and political worlds, instrumental for producing the anthology and, in the Singaporean context, instrumentalized by the state to produce national culture.

In short, the anthology is a significant yet understudied literary form for comprehending postcoloniality, whether because it is a form befitting a postcolonial ethos or because it is a form that is resonant with the questions of postcolonial studies around nationalism or nation formation. As a curated and engineered text, the anthology moreover invites non-narrative perspectives on nation formation. Certainly, anthologies can include narrative forms and prose, but narrative is not necessarily the anthology's central aesthetic feature; it is but one possible option. While anglophone literary studies already predisposes its critics to narrative forms, in the context of literary theorizations of the nation, the tendency toward narrative and the novel is the consequence of emphasizing the nation as a cultural and epistemological form. Put a little differently, we have seen narrative study as central for understanding how nation and nationalism have become ideologically meaningful. My discussion of Singapore anthologies below thinks through the nation as a sociopolitical form, offering insights into the ways that nationalism can also be a project of legibility, one seeking to situate itself in a global context. In other words, rather than framing national consolidation as primarily an internal political struggle, my discussion of Singapore anthologies thinks through questions of national consolidation with respect to its changing economic and political dynamic with the world. As I show, these national contexts are both subjected to and responding to the dynamics of the global economy and thus the imperial logics of racial capitalism.

MAJOR SINGAPORE ANTHOLOGIES: ISSUES OF BOOK DEVELOPMENT

Like the rest of the newly independent nations of the so-called Third World, developmentalism (or modernization) was the prevailing socioeconomic ideology of postcolonial capitalism in the 1970s and 1980s. As reflected in the rhetoric of the Bandung Conference of 1955, development and modernization were largely regarded as an issue of rights across the Third World, but in terms of policy, different kinds of economic strategies were taken up by postcolonial states. Singapore opted to focus on export-oriented industrialization (i.e., international trade through export of raw materials or manufactured goods). This was a common developmental strategy among the postcolonial Asian nations that would come to be known as the Asian Tigers (Singapore, South Korea, Taiwan, and Hong Kong) and one distinct from Latin American economies, which favored import substitution industrialization. Without the available raw materials, such as the rubber or timber found in Malaysia and Indonesia, Singapore's exports were all manufactured commodities such as matches, mosquito coils, fishhooks, and books. As I also discuss in chapter 3, the state's developmental discourse of the manufacturing economy drew on Japanese management techniques that emphasized efficiency, productivity, and teamwork among Singaporeans. During this period, as Jini Kim Watson's work teaches us, Singapore sought to signify the island nation's development through urban modernity and built space.[27]

It is against this background of great socioeconomic change, industrialization, and modernization that Singapore's national literary and aesthetic production began. During this period, the production of anthologies is dominated by state-sponsored publishers and institutions (e.g., Educational Publications Bureau, Federal Publications for the Ministry of Culture, ASEAN Committee on Culture and Information) and international publishers based in Europe (e.g., Heinemann Asia and Times International). According to Nair, this was also a time when presses "were adamantly not interested in publishing local literary output and published only school textbooks and supplementary educational materials."[28] The publishing industry in Singapore was also export oriented as it was attempting to position itself as a publishing hub in the region, which meant publishers from the United Kingdom, the United States, and Australia sent materials to Singapore for printing and distribution.[29] The local literature these presses were willing to publish were pieces from the many writing competitions held at the time, as titles such as *Prize-Winning Plays I* (1980) and *Prize Poems: Winning Entries of the First Ministry of Culture Poetry Writing Competition* (1979) make clear. Of course, these writing competitions were not specifically eliciting material for anthologies. Rather, they were used to generate the short-form writing that would later become the composite parts of many early Singapore anthologies. Governmental bodies were the main publishers of anthologies in the 1970s and 1980s because they were also the most financially resourced literary institutions of the time in the context of recent independence. But anthologies need not simply be read as a vacuum of state power. The anthology was very much shaped by the broader developmental imperatives of early postcolonial capitalism in Singapore and the global cultural policies of UNESCO that emphasized so-called book development.

The emergence of the anthology cannot be understood separately from the history of short stories and poetry; that is, the long, anthological form must be understood through the history of its composite parts. As Holden argues, short stories were regarded as a mode of social development and "a form of training for modern national life and citizenship."[30] Though education is one approach to espousing short stories as a mode of development and a number of early anthologies were indeed published out of creative writing classes, writing competitions helped generate actual material en masse. According to Holden, writing competitions that started with Radio Malaya in 1947 and continued with the Ministry of Culture, Radio Singapore, the National Book Development Council, and others played a significant role in bringing the short-story form into the national consciousness.[31] This mode of generating literary material is well suited to both Singapore's industrial manufacturing economy and the cultural developmental logics derived from UNESCO.[32] As Sarah Brouillette writes, UNESCO's 1972 International Book Year was especially influential in promoting ideas of "the book not as an object of portable elite cultural knowledge but instead as an agent of social and economic change in the developing world," or what is known as "book development."[33] UNESCO's influence on Singapore literary production is especially evident in which governmental agencies organized writing competitions: the Ministry of Culture and the National Book Development Council. Such agencies are direct outgrowths of the cultural policy espoused by UNESCO, of which Singapore was a member state from 1965 to 1985.

The abiding belief in the role of literature as a developmental force was not only taken up by state agencies, however; UNESCO's influence was evident in literary circles as well. As indicated by the proceedings for the 1976 seminar "Developing Creative Writing in Singapore," for example, participants were given "Literary Colonialism: Books in the Third World," an essay by Philip G. Altbach, a scholar whose research on publishing in the Third World was supported and taken up by

UNESCO.[34] Nair, who would later go on to work for UNESCO, would frequently offer public comments about the need for Singaporeans to "nurture in our society a national consciousness . . . through the media of our literature."[35] Still, Singapore's creative writers saw themselves as at odds with the state for, as Holden puts it, "overly rationalized attempts to produce national culture," and Nair was certainly critical about the industrialized production of Singapore literature at the expense of quality.[36] There was nonetheless ideological consensus between the state and subject, insofar as literature was mutually regarded as an important developmental force. A clear split emerged between the two in terms of the role of national consciousness, however: for the state it is a mode of performing economic development, whereas for writers like Nair it is a mode of developing critical, decolonial faculties. This tension between function and aesthetic taste would be borne out in the decades to follow.

While the push for literary production through writing competitions in Singapore was certainly a response to notions of book development, that such promotion occurred through short-form writing also speaks to the economic context of industrial manufacturing. In his prize-giving speech for the 1986 National Short Story Competition, Ch'ng Jit Koon speculated that the short story was appealing "to Singaporeans who are always in a hurry and often claim they have not much time for reading."[37] Although Ch'ng was quick to correct the perception that the efficient consumption of short stories did not mean that they were efficiently produced, he closed his speech with a quote from Stephen Vincent Benet, who said the short story is "something that can be read in an hour and remembered for a lifetime." Though Ch'ng's remarks on the short story are oversimplified in a way that seems characteristic of a governmental figure, his explanation for the short story's appeal resonates with earlier assessments made within literary circles. In her paper "The Current State of Creative Writing in Singapore," Nalla Tan lamented the perception that "poems are not as time consuming as prose to write," hence the prevalence of poetry over prose.[38] It is striking that both the reader's and the writer's time are portrayed as impediments to literary production. Tan also points out that Singaporeans face the perennial problem that "a livelihood from writing is not guaranteed."[39] When we consider that the 1970s and 1980s were an era with a strong national emphasis on Taylorist forms of production and thus time management, task completion, and efficiency, there's a way that—rightly or wrongly— short-form writing appeals to those sensibilities. As Ch'ng's use of the Benet quote emphasizes, short stories are a form of literature that is *manageable* because it is an experience that can be completed within the parameters of a schedule. Moreover, that the writing was generated in competition employs the logic of mass production, which is another way we can see the influence of industrial manufacturing on literary production at the time.

Despite all the writing competitions organized by the state and creative writing programs put on by independent creative writing organizations, such efforts were not necessarily producing *books* in service of book development. As Brouillette points out, UNESCO forwarded the notion of books, the physical objects of literature, "as agents of cultural and economic development" and, consequently, "UNESCO made the book industries themselves the subject of intense scrutiny and debate."[40] Book production, then, became a measure of development. A speech by then parliamentary secretary of education Ho Kah Leong at a writer's workshop in 1983 makes UNESCO's influence in Singapore's burgeoning literary scene very clear. Besides the fact that a UNESCO consultant, S. A. Klitgaard, was leading the workshop, the very developmental problem that Ho bemoans is steeped in UNESCO policy thinking: "In 1980, only 44 titles per million persons were published in developing countries as against 500 titles per million persons in developed countries. It is very obvious, then, that in a developing country like ours, there is a real and urgent need to expand and even intensify our book development programmes."[41] While Ho's speech shows that his understanding of literature is not solely about its commodity form—he discusses the need to create a local reading culture for children and the need for good writing and editing—his ultimate concern is to be able to make national development legible according to UNESCO metrics.

As indicated by the publication history of major anthologies, oil and petroleum corporations were also major ideological and financial influences on Singapore's national literary scene.[42] Volumes 1 through 4 of *Prize-Winning Plays*, for example, are listed as part of the "NUS-Shell Short Plays Series."[43] The oil corporation also sponsored the Shell Literary Series in the mid- to late 1980s, which included texts by prominent Singaporean authors such as Ee Tiang Hong, Simon Tay, Shirley Lim, and Angeline Yap.[44] Shell's competitor, Esso, was a powerful financial influence, as illustrated by its partnership with the Ministry of Culture for a 1979 short-story competition and its sponsorship of the aforementioned creative writing seminar. Historically, the oil and petroleum industries have played a significant role in Singapore's economy as a result of its large oil refineries. Undoubtedly, corporate sponsorship of Singapore's literary efforts was meant to earn these environmentally violent corporations goodwill by portraying some notion of social responsibility and humanitarianism. Although anthologies generated by writing competitions and creative writing seminars appear as especially localized phenomena insofar as they seem shaped by the particularities of local debates and culture, the developmental logics that undergird Singapore's literary production reveal the influence of the global economy.

As illustrated by *The Poetry of Singapore* (1985), edited by Edwin Thumboo, evincing national culture was about both empowering Singaporeans with a sense of their recently gained identities and demonstrating Singapore's capacity to keep up with global culture. *The Poetry of Singapore* is distinct as the first locally produced, canon-establishing national anthology published for a readership beyond Singapore. It was commissioned by the ASEAN Committee on Culture and

Information for a series on ASEAN's literary traditions aimed at "enhanc[ing the] consciousness of and sensitivity to each other's literature" and disseminating ASEAN literature "among the ASEAN people and the rest of the world."[45] The hardcover binding and nearly 600-page length of this anthology (five years later, ASEAN published the anthology, *The Fiction of Singapore*, which would total over 1,200 pages) performs the gravitas of the nation in its very material form. Perhaps unsurprisingly, given its length, *The Poetry of Singapore* was initially only locally available at the "National Library and its branches, schools, junior colleges and institutions of higher learning."[46] Thus the volume was treated as a pedagogical text, one that required institutional access.[47] The anthology includes original poems in Malay, Chinese, and Tamil and their translations into English. It is organized according to language group and has both the original and translated preface for the non-English sections. Within each language group, authors are listed in chronological order according to the poet's birth year. The language identity categories organizing *The Poetry of Singapore* replicate the colonial-era logic of demography combined with an emphasis on authorship to perform a sense of "great writers." *The Poetry of Singapore* is not quite the national culture of Fanon's thinking, nor is it an example of the counter-anthologies that imagine new liberatory futures for the postcolonial nation that Lai writes of. In fact, because the anthology appears to reflect Singapore's status quo, it might seem rather unremarkable. But as I show, it in fact reflects a national culture anxious to establish itself in a global order, one that signifies an assimilatory logic to the expectation that everyone "in the modern world . . . can, should, will 'have' a nationality," as Benedict Anderson puts it.[48]

As the title alone suggests, *The Poetry of Singapore* is meant to be understood as an authoritative topology of Singapore's national literary tradition. It teaches readers about the many literary and cultural traditions that comprise Singapore's multiracial population, and it also performs the nation's historical stability, modernity, and development. As Thumboo himself remarked, the anthology's presentation of Singapore's racial diversity through linguistic difference is noteworthy, especially when compared to the other anthologies produced in this ASEAN-commissioned series. Also noteworthy is the presentation of English as one of Singapore's national languages.

> Each nation had literary elements attracting strong politics. Malaysia would only have Malay writing; work in Chinese, Tamil, and English would be excluded. No Wong Phu Nam, sadly. Both Thailand and the Philippines had Malay writers in their southern parts. Unlike in Malaysia, they were included. For political reasons I asked that the Singapore volumes treat each language separately. Otherwise Malay would have a large beginning and then tail off, small.[49]

Thumboo's comments illustrate his awareness that the volume was asserting a national imagination: that is, asserting a politics of how Singapore should be read by the world. Malaysia's decision to include only Malay traditional texts and folklore, despite its similar multicultural and multilingual context, is the literary expression of its *bumiputera* (lit. "son of earth" or "son of soil") policies. Other volumes in the series opted to present oral literature (Indonesia), epics (Philippines), and classical religious texts (Thailand), and they separated English translations into separate volumes. Even while the series was aimed at facilitating cultural exchange within the diverse region, the outward, extraregional glance of the Singapore anthology sets itself apart from its Southeast Asian counterparts.

Unlike the other anthologies in the ASEAN series, *The Poetry of Singapore* forwards a thesis asserting Singapore as modern, bucking the trend of asserting what Étienne Balibar describes as the "myth of national origins" or, as David Lloyd puts it, the "resurgence of atavistic or premodern feelings and practices."[50] Finding a common source of nationalist origin for Singapore, one that is inclusive of its diverse constituents and distinct enough from neighboring nations, has long been a headache for the state and not a controversy that *The Poetry of Singapore* looks to resolve. In fact, as Thumboo's post-publication commentary about Malay literary traditions indicates, he was concerned about evenly presenting Singapore's different literary traditions. This concern, it seems, manifested in selecting poems that were written within the past hundred years, even as the critical introductions to each non-English-language section makes clear that Singaporean poetry emerges from longer historical literary traditions. What are we to make of this major anthological presentation of Singapore through the genre of poetry as multilingual, in translation, recently independent, and driven by the imperative of socioeconomic developmentalism?

We can see the influence of governance in the arrangement and multicultural presentation of Singapore in this edited volume. For one, by organizing the anthology according to racialized language group, *The Poetry of Singapore* draws on the colonial logics of racial taxonomy, which persists in postcolonial Singapore through the CMIO (Chinese-Malay-Indian-Other) scheme that racially types every Singaporean at birth. This official racial typing expands to understandings of language, for each group has a corresponding national language: Mandarin, Malay, and Tamil. In other words, race and language are formally connected by government policy. The use of the CMIO organizing principle reflects Singapore's administrative practices while also performing multiculturalism through linguistic difference. As Chua Beng Huat points out, multiculturalism is an instrument of Singaporean state control and one that, we should add, emerges out of Singapore's colonial history as a port city of trade.[51] Besides acting as an ideological, disciplinary tool of the Singaporean state, multiculturalism follows what Slavoj Žižek has argued is the cultural logic of multinational capitalism. For Žižek, multiculturalism is the celebratory, tolerant view of difference from the perspective of capitalism, a view that "treats *each* local culture the way the colonizer treats colonized people."[52] Moreover, as Jodi Melamed points out, liberal multiculturalism emerged as the official antiracism of the United States in the same period,[53] a value that would expand along with US empire during the Cold War. In short, multiculturalism is in vogue and has increasing global appeal during this period of state developmentalism. The aesthetics of multiculturalism in *The Poetry of Singapore* therefore articulates with the globalized context in which Singapore's nation formation is materializing. Singapore's export-led industrial economy at this time required the disciplining of citizens into efficient workers as well as the assurance of hospitality to foreign investment and multinational corporations. In other words, Singapore's national culture was shaped by the state with an eye toward building investor confidence. Clearly, Singapore did well in this regard; in 1959, 83 multinational corporations operated in Singapore, a figure that increased to 383 by 1973.[54] As illustrated by a 1980 UNESCO report, "The Cultural Impact of Multinational Corporations in Singapore," Singapore's economic approach was unprecedented:

> There appears to be an absence of acrimony and bitterness which characterize the relationship between Latin American countries and the multinational corporations. To put it rather crudely, while the multinational corporation is an ugly word in Latin America, it evokes a different response in South-East Asia. . . . Singapore appears to stand out in South-East Asia as a shining example of how domestic policy may be formulated to accommodate the demands of the multinationals in their search for profits and market shares on a global scale.[55]

Given all this, one could make a claim that the CMIO colonial logic that organizes the anthology and its multicultural appeal demonstrates how Singapore's national imagination in the mid-1980s was still colonized and complicit with the terms of colonial and neocolonial discourse.

But I want to also suggest that we understand anthologies like *The Poetry of Singapore* as operating within the politics of anglophonic legibility, a politics that undergirds Singapore's nationalist project of postcolonial capitalism. As an anthology commissioned and published by ASEAN, an economic and political union between Southeast Asian nation-states, it might not be expected to present what Lloyd describes as nationalism against the state but rather a nationalism acceptable by the state. Put differently, this is a nationalism articulating a respectability politics for the global economy, a politics that is especially evident in the anthology's inclusion of English-language poetry. Certainly, creating an English-speaking population for the global economy is a cornerstone of Singapore's postcolonial capitalist project. In fact, the aforementioned UNESCO report highlights how the state successfully molded Singaporeans to fit corporate needs through English-language education. In other words, English not only marks modern futures for Singapore's inhabitants, but it also has a distinct function of attracting capital. Indeed, Thumboo's introduction to *The Poetry of Singapore* is very clear-eyed about the economic uses of English:

> Two cogent reasons lie behind this unique necessity for multilingual representation and translation into English. The first reflects our multi-racial origins; the second,

the imperative to develop the skills and capacities—best realized through English—essential to the viability of a small modern republic. . . . English performs a number of interlocking roles as the primary language of formal education. In addition to being increasingly the chief linguistic bridge between Singaporeans, English, already the language of international and regional contact, is crucial to training manpower for the financial, industrial, technological, and information and service sectors which make up the economy of Singapore.[56]

In this answer to what must surely have been a question about the inclusion of English in an authoritative nationalist text, one can detect something of a defensive tone in Thumboo's writing that anticipates the critique of English as a foreign, colonial, and politically compromised language.[57] Despite this defensiveness, Thumboo's crucial point that English serves "a number of interlocking roles" is precisely why this book relies on an anglophone archive to investigate Global Asia. One could critique Thumboo for his economic rationale regarding the status of English in Singapore for how it echoes some of the state discourse of the time. However, as illustrated by its address to a non-Singaporean reader, Thumboo's introduction, I would argue, is grappling with how to present the Singaporean nation as a sociopolitical form in a medium assumed to present the nation as a cultural or epistemological form, suggesting that the anthology's function of educating citizens is subordinated to its extranational consciousness.

In other words, *The Poetry of Singapore* is less a working through of what consolidation, homogeneous time, or imagined communities look like in the context of newly won sovereignty and more a presentation of national culture that is legible to power outside of the nation-state. That desire to make Singapore legible to the West operates with a historical consciousness of racial capitalism. This is where we read for the logics of postcolonial capitalism. When we treat *The Poetry of Singapore* as a representation of the nation for an audience outside of Singapore and Southeast Asia, the anthology's CMIO arrangement and multicultural aesthetic offer the myth of origins of multiculturalism rather than the prehistory of the nation. As I have pointed out, multiculturalism already has a capitalist appeal. On top of assuring readers of Singapore's ability to consolidate racial difference and a performance of a respectability politics for the global order, *The Poetry of Singapore* effectively presents the image of Singapore as *already* multicultural and thus *already* developed and modern by featuring poets born before the time that multiculturalism appears as a favored political philosophy or official policy in the West. This is not to suggest that the anthology paints a simplistic picture of Singaporeans happily coexisting. Indeed, poems like "My Lion City" by Masuri S. N., "The Beginning" by S. Markasan, "Who Are We" by Tie Ge, and "An Old Church in Malacca" by Zhong Qi grapple with the hardships of Singapore's independence and its national, modernizing project. Nor is an originary claim about multiculturalism in the former colonies a complete myth. Colonial trade routes helped establish port cities like Singapore, Hong Kong, and Manila, sites that were regarded as polyglot centers of cosmopolitan, urban modernity. Archaeological digs reveal that Singapore was already a port city as early as the fourteenth century.[58] While the anthology does not seek to present Singapore as multicultural since antiquity, we still see that it sets up the conditions to make a claim for emergent power in a global context through its multicultural aesthetic.

Even while the anthology draws on the disciplinary logics of colonial and postcolonial governance to make Singapore legible for the purposes of the global economy, it also has an aesthetic of mediation, one that interrupts a smooth or total concession to economic hegemonies. Thumboo's decision to present Singapore's multicultural modernity through linguistic difference may appear to follow the status quo, but the anthology's calling attention to the role of translation suggests something much more aesthetically and politically deliberate. A Spivakian reading might interpret the anthology's translation of Malay, Tamil, and Chinese poems into English as accommodationist, a political concession to what Minae Mizumura coins the "Age of English."[59] By including the original alongside the translation, itself an aesthetic choice, the anthology nonetheless reminds us that the language we receive as readers is mediated. Such an effect is further amplified by the fact that Thumboo is but one of many people who make the anthology's meaning possible. Masuri S. N., V. T. Arasu, Wong Yoon Wah, and Lee Tzu Pheng, listed as section editors, all authored substantial critical introductions to each section and also presumably contributed their linguistic competency and literary expertise to major editorial decisions. Readers also see the names of translators listed at the end of each poem, serving as another reminder that the text has undergone a process of change. The anthology's paratextual apparatus constantly calls attention to the mediation of meaning, supplementing the use of poetry to depict the nation, which averts the possibility of bringing full legibility to Singapore. As Jahan Ramazani points out, "Poetry, especially in its lyric mode, cannot be adequately studied in translation in the same way that drama, epic, and the novel can be studied within their generic frameworks even when translated into another language."[60] Indeed, Arasu's introduction to Tamil poetry notes the impossibility of translation:

> A major limiting factor . . . was the need to choose poems that will lend themselves to translation—poems that would still retain a strong flavor of the original when rendered into English. It is admitted that translation is a compromise, an approximation of the original. . . . Many of the beautiful Tamil poems with their singing metres, chiming rhymes and their play on words are too alien to be transmitted through English.[61]

Even as it cedes to the postcolonial capitalist politics of legibility, *The Poetry of Singapore* never quite offers full or direct insight into the inner life of Singapore.

In other words, the volume at once performs legibility *and* illegibility: it offers an aesthetic experience that is also about what cannot be understood.

Even though the English-language poetry in the volume is not mediated by as many linguistic modes, *The Poetry of Singapore* reminds its readers that English will never offer full legibility of Singapore's national culture but only offers partial insights as permitted by its multilingual presentation. The consciousness of partiality acknowledges both the borders of various language communities and the fact that English is part of the larger whole. In its consistent emphasis on how meaning is conveyed and on the limits of that meaning, *The Poetry of Singapore* in fact calls attention to the distance between languages—precisely what translation seeks to overcome. The act of translation is a negotiation of what Spivak describes as the "spacy emptiness between two named historical languages."[62] In its aesthetic of mediation, *The Poetry of Singapore* offers a literary and historical consciousness of those spaces between languages that can be incorporated into our reading practices. Here Spivak's notion of the reader-as-translator—or the RAT, as she likes to put it—is useful.[63] The RAT in multilingual Singapore is not someone necessarily thinking about how meaning moves between languages but someone who brings to her reading practice a consciousness of the spacy dynamics among languages and an awareness of partiality. The reader as translator, in other words, is someone who is intensely aware of how language is situated, how it is couched, and how it has developed among others. To read as a translator means that we do not simply think through the anglophone as an autonomous, separate world but that we also think through how we feel the textures of the sinophone, Malay, or Tamil in the anglophone.

As a literary form responsive to the economic conditions of the time, established as they were by colonial histories of racial capitalism, anthologies are produced by miming the cultural logics of postcolonial capitalism. The formation of national culture was both an assertion of cultural autonomy and a performance of Singapore's readiness to integrate into the global economy. The emergence of the Singapore anthology builds on the combined effects of the global and local economic contexts of book development and time management for Singapore's burgeoning manufacturing industries. Just as we see the early Singapore anthologies responding to economic ideologies, we also see the kinds of nationalist work they do for UNESCO, ASEAN, and other institutional permutations of the global. Singapore anthologies do different kinds of nationalist work for local and global audiences. Major anthologies did offer readers a sense of a national culture and local identity—the sense of "us" that Te Punga Somerville writes of—while also offering evidence of the nation-state's success in the cultural sphere through its book development. Although *The Poetry of Singapore* demonstrates how anthologies use the terms of colonial and postcolonial governing logics to appeal to the reigning capitalist sensibilities of the time, multilingual and translated anthologies also trouble the possibility of representing Singapore as fully legible.

ASIAN VALUES, THE ASSERTION OF DIFFERENCE,
AND THE RISE OF POPULAR ANTHOLOGIES

While canon-performing and prize-winning major anthologies edited by well-known Singaporean writers and academics were still proliferating during the Asian Values period, the popular anthology also began to emerge. In contrast to the major anthologies that were published by established institutions, popular anthologies, which were relatively inexpensive, informal, and paperbound, operated by the selection principle of pleasure rather than literary greatness and were published by institutions outside of the state-sanctioned literary system. Within anthology studies, critics typically distinguish between anthologies and miscellanies along the lines of their relationship to history and literary canons. "Miscellanies," Michael F. Suarez explains,

> are usually compilations of relatively recent texts designed to suit contemporary tastes; anthologies, in contrast, are generally selections of canonical texts which have a more established history and a greater claim to cultural importance. The miscellany, then, typically celebrates—and indeed constructs—taste, novelty and contemporaneity in assembling a synchronous body of material. It should be distinguished from the anthology, which honours—and perpetuates—the value of historicity and the perdurance of established canons of artistic discrimination in gathering texts recognized for their aesthetic legitimacy.[64]

In its emphasis on pleasure, the popular anthology as I have defined it has much in common with the eighteenth-century anglophone miscellanies that Suarez writes of, but I depart from him in my desire to foreground the institutional conditions of production in a fashion similar to the distinctions made between independent aesthetic productions and the culture industry. In doing so, I mean to also situate understandings of popular anthologies within local and global systems of power, specifically, the economic contexts and power dynamics shaped by the history of imperialism. If we are to take canonicity as the defining feature of anthologies, as it so often is, then compiled literary texts from recently independent nations or disenfranchised groups would be excluded. Primarily defining anthologies in terms of establishment, in other words, does not entirely make sense for contexts in ongoing formation and has the further effect of reproducing notions of historical lag.

While the developmentalism of the decades before cultivated a taste for easily produced and consumed short literary forms by virtue of its producibility and manageability, anthological production during the Asian Values period grew alongside the increasing local appetite for short genre fiction—namely, horror. Anthologies flourished during this period, with 110 published between 1985 and 2000, in contrast to the 40 that were published in the twenty-year span that preceded it. Of these 110 books, roughly 40 were major anthologies and 70 were popular anthologies.[65] Certainly, the proliferation of anthologies and Singaporean literature more generally can and should be understood as a phenomenon reflecting the wealth and thus new spending power that Singaporeans had accrued. "Singaporeans with more spending power and leisure time," a 1989 *Straits Times* article declares, "are famished for books set in Singapore, about Singapore and penned by Singaporeans. Singaporean books have come of age. They have at last captured the public imagination."[66] Moreover, the article claims, the desire for local literature was a result of an education system that saw a generation of Singaporeans who were "brought up on stories written by Singaporeans."[67] Although increased wealth and national education undoubtedly produced a reading public amenable to local literature in the ways that the article suggests, these factors cannot fully explain the appeal of genre fiction or anthologies at this time. With a particular focus on the popular anthologies put out by Pugalenthi Sr's VJ Times, I suggest that we see pleasure in national culture emerging during this period. This localized pleasure tracks with the inward-facing, nativist posture of Asian Values but rejects the state developmental imperatives of early postcolonial capitalism (i.e., book development and institutionalized values of what constitutes "the literary"). It is precisely because the anthology as a genre is historically mired in institutional politics that ideological challenges to institutional values emerge from it. Like Lai's counter-anthologies, popular anthologies "emerge from outside the academy," but they are not themselves conceptualized as a direct challenge to the major anthologies, nor are they attempting to make legible socially marginalized communities.[68] Rather than try to reclaim the historical time of the nation, these popular anthologies emphasize pleasure in the present and encourage less-established or amateur writers to be received as aesthetic producers. In this way, popular anthologies begin to take a stronger inward orientation compared to the major anthologies. Whatever counterhegemonic politics they enact are oblique.

In contrast to the early years of independence, an era characterized by the desire to demonstrate how Singapore's industrial modernity was on par with the so-called First World, the later decades of the twentieth century were guided by the assertion of Singapore's cultural difference and the rise of what is variously referred to as "Confucian capitalism," "Asian Values," or "communitarianism." This assertion, as we will see in chapter 4, is foundational to the neo-orientalist formations of Global Asia. Following the global shift toward neoliberalism, or free-market capitalism, the unprecedented rate of development of the "newly industrialized economies," "Asian Tiger nations," or "Asian Miracle nations" of Singapore, Taiwan, South Korea, Hong Kong, and Malaysia was viewed as anomalous because of their strong, interventionist states. These "single-party-dominant states, with or without military backing," Chua writes, "were as glaringly successful economically as they were ruthless in suppressing political dissent on the road to successful national capitalist growth."[69] While critics point out that states are, in fact, very involved in implementing deregulatory policies, the general narrative put out by Western proponents of the "free market" is that neoliberalism means a receding of the state and hence freedom. Thus, Asian Miracle nations defied the prevailing economic theories of the time, ones that were rooted in US and Cold War notions of freedom. Rather than revise neoliberal free-market theories, Western intellectuals argued that "high work ethics, education attainment, family and group orientation [that came from] major 'Asian' civilization and traditions" explained the economic successes of these exceptional postcolonial Asian nations.[70] The orientalist appeal of explanatory frameworks like Confucian capitalism and Asian Values, Chua argues, coincides historically with the collapse of socialism in the former USSR and Eastern Europe; thus, the Asian Miracle nations would come to replace the socialist world as the new Other to what he describes as globalizing liberal capitalism.[71] Similar theories about Asian American model minorities would also intensify around the same time. In Chua's account, this Western, culturalist explanation for Asian economic success was quickly appropriated and promoted by a number of Asian politicians and "discursively transformed into a political value and an attitude towards 'collective' orientation, which in turn finessed an explanation for the supposed absence of 'popular demands' for liberal democracy."[72] Lee Kuan Yew and other politicians essentialized tenets of Confucianism as "Asian" and deployed Asian Values discourse to fend off human rights critiques of authoritarian Asian states and to maintain the status of economic exceptionalism. In other words, what we see during this period is a turn back to presenting the nation as a cultural and epistemological form using the terms of self-defined orientalism and occidentalism rather than presenting the nation as a sociopolitical form as in the earlier years of independence.

While Asian Values had a representative function on the global stage, it had more of a disciplinary function in the national context of Singapore. The discursive shift to pronounced difference from the West accompanied Singapore's increasing wealth, economic stability, and improved global reputation. Even though the manufacturing sector was still driving Singapore's economy at this time, the commodities it was producing—electronics and petrochemicals—had greater global importance in the 1980s. Moreover, as Chua writes, the improved standards of living and increased affluence in 1985 were evident in the "possession of consumer durables . . . at the level of the developed nations," increased fashion consciousness, more cars, and modern buildings.[73] Although such material improvements and increased consumerism served as evidence of Singapore's economic success, Singapore and many of the other Asian Miracle nations viewed such excesses as ideologically dangerous. Indeed, Goh Chok Tong delivered a 1988 speech, "Our National Ethic," that warned against the perils of individualism:

> Our society is changing. . . . Singaporeans have become more affluent. We have become more English-educated. We travel widely, read foreign newspapers and journals, listen to BBC and watch American TV programmes. . . . There is a clear shift toward emphasis on self, or individualism. If individualism results in creativity, that is good, but if it translates into a "me first" attitude that is bad for social cohesion and the country. . . . We are concerned because it will determine our national competitiveness, and hence our prosperity and survival as a nation.[74]

As Goh's language reveals, the West is the cultural threat. For the way that such discourse positions itself as a defense against Euro-American neoimperialism, we see a subtle shift in postcolonial capitalism from a motivational, liberatory rhetoric supporting development and industrial modernity to a protective position justifying and maintaining postcolonial capitalism's continuation. Yet even as state figures repudiate the Western cultural influence outright, Singapore's postcolonial capitalism accepts the imperial terms of the global economy. At all times, Singapore's relation to the former imperial powers are still operative in the nation's capitalist formation.

The turn to Asian Values not only articulated with the state's defensive posturing, but it also built on an ongoing national controversy over questions of what constitutes Singaporean identity. State anxieties over a shared national ethos began to heighten in the 1980s when there was a sense that state developmental imperatives were no longer motivating or meaningful among Singaporeans. As asserted by Stephan Ortmann, it was during this time that "the government increasingly became aware that economic growth alone cannot be the only basis for Singapore's national identity."[75] The drive to invent a shared national identity was eventually codified in a 1991 parliamentary White Paper known as the Shared Values. According to the paper, the Shared Values were drawn from Confucian ideals and encapsulated by five statements: "Nation before community and society above self; Family as the basic unit of society; Regard and community support for the individual; Consensus instead of contention; Racial and religious harmony."[76] The implementation of the Shared Values came in the form of public education as schools administered civics and moral education lessons. It also involved building on Singapore's bilingual language policies that required that all students learn English, as Singapore's official language, alongside one of their "Mother Tongue" languages (Mandarin, Malay, or Tamil), in order to maintain a sense of cultural heritage. Parents were also asked to help develop a sense of national identity. "All parents," the White Paper declares, "have a responsibility to bring up their children, not just to meet their physical needs, but to prepare them to be good parents and citizens in their turn."[77] Although the Shared Values were seen as something of a corrective to the developmentalism of the years before, the formalization of national identity and ideology was still given an economic justification, as underscored by Goh's point in the aforementioned speech about the need for Singapore to both "prosper" and "survive"—economic success is postcolonial survival in a world shaped by imperialism.

In this context of increased wealth and heightened anxiety over national identity, VJ Times's publications began to take hold and the anthological landscape too began to shift. In many ways, Pugalenthi Sr's VJ Times has much in common with Nair's Woodrose Publications. Both were small presses that sought to bring visibility to Singaporean writers and cultivate a local reading public. Although the two share a common literary ambition, they also have very different relations to established, national institutions. For one, Nair is himself a celebrated poet in Singapore's literary canon and held a number of positions that would confer literary authority and public visibility on him: Nair's commentary on the importance of national literature appears in the local newspaper archives, and he also made a number of television appearances.[78] Nair is, in other words, a figure of the establishment. In contrast, Pugalenthi Sr has little public or archival presence. Despite the major influence that Pugalenthi Sr has in shaping Singapore's literary landscape, he only garners a brief critical mention in Koh Tai Ann's *Singapore Literature in English: An Annotated Bibliography* (2008), which notes Pugalenthi's incredible and bestselling output. The appearances he does make in the archives are often unflattering: a news story about him and his publishing company being banned from the Singapore book fair for not following rules, a news story about his publishing company's aggressive telemarketing, and reports of numerous disputes over salary put to the Ministry of Labour, to name some examples. Methodologically, postcolonial studies has emphasized subaltern histories and perspectives, but what Pugalenthi Sr and VJ Times represent in Singapore's literary history is the unseemly and less celebrated. Their anthologies represent a trend toward popular or commercialized literature rather than the formation of aesthetic sophistication. This is not to say that Pugalenthi Sr or VJ Times rejected institutionalized literary values wholesale. Rather, they operated within cultures of capitalism to cultivate a national literature and local reading public. In this way, Pugalenthi Sr and VJ Times also operate within a similar postcolonial capitalist logic as the state, even though the values they each espouse are somewhat opposed.

The height of VJ Times's anthological production coincides with what Ng Yi-Sheng describes as the 1980s to early 2000s "boom in local horror."[79] While Nair expressed some scorn for popularized literature, VJ Times clearly had no such qualms. Pugalenthi Sr edited four volumes of horror anthologies, starting with *Black Powers* (1991). VJ Times would go on to publish a number of single-authored collections as a part of its Nightmare series (1996–2003), including some written by Pugalenthi Sr himself. Although horror was already an established popular genre before the 1980s, as Ng points out, its boom during this period is striking for the sheer number of publications, with some even being adapted for local television.

How are we to understand horror's particular appeal at this time? Weihsin Gui notes the growing popularity of noir fiction, a genre adjacent to horror, in the twenty-first-century context of Singaporean writing and argues, "Imagining a grim world where hopes are relentlessly dashed and dark passions unleashed, noir presents a counterpoint to exuberant narratives of 'Asian Rising' while gesturing toward a more just and equitable society that is discernible but not yet achievable."[80] Gui also notes the critical propensity of gothic fiction, which has a shared aesthetic emphasis with horror in terms of affect and atmosphere, to "reject a Euro-American penchant for narrative cohesion and implicitly critique Singapore's biopolitical technologies of social engineering."[81] Certainly, a similar claim might be made of horror in the 1980s: it served as a counterpoint and challenge to the relentless state developmental discourses of the time. Writing more specifically about the ghost story anthologies from the 1980s and 1990s, Alfian Sa'at, on the other hand, argues that horror speaks to the appeal of Singaporean oral literature: "We tell ghost stories among ourselves not just to scare one another but also to bond. What cannot be explained can at least be narrated, and to be able to narrate in the presence of listeners—some of whom might just believe you—is a kind of reassurance that you are not going mad."[82]

Because a number of the ghost story collections were purported to be compiled from real accounts from ordinary Singaporeans, Alfian further argues that the popular ghost story collections "remove[d] the need for actual face to face transmission, making them accessible to all [and conjured] an imagined community of readers and storytellers."[83] The key point in Alfian's incisive commentary is the significance of how these anthologies position fellow citizens as storytellers because this gives us a different gloss on how to conceptualize imagined communities than is provided in Anderson's original formulation, which theorizes nationalism as a shared *reading* experience. Although the success of horror clearly indicates that there was a shared reading experience, ghost story anthologies also confer authority to Singaporeans for their "particular social networks" and the cultural insights—and warning—that such stories provide. When we further consider how the developmentalism of the previous decades produced a "style of politics on the part of the leaders that could only be called *pedagogical*,"[84] we see how horror anthologies offer new ways of imagining relations of power. What one might describe as pedagogical, others might pejoratively describe as paternalistic. This is certainly the case in Singapore, insofar as the state has always regarded itself as in the position of authority not just in terms of power, but in terms of actual knowledge. Such a vertical model of power and rhetoric was amplified and culturally rationalized during the Asian Values era, when Singapore drew on Confucianism to "support a paternalistic type of authority."[85] Although anthologies pedagogically situated Singaporeans as authoritative sources of knowledge of the supernatural world, these were not stories seeking to develop the reader as a national subject. Instead, they offered an enjoyable reprieve from state paternalism by providing alternative sources of cultural authority.

While Pugalenthi Sr's VJ Times cannot be credited with originating the horror boom of the 1980s and 1990s, their active participation in the cultural phenomenon attests to their attempts to build a national literature based on pleasure. In response to Alfian's social media commentary on Singaporean horror stories, Pugalenthi Sr writes, "A nation needs pop-literatures that entice and entertain a new generation. And it's from those readers that you will get a group that reads poems and other heavy fiction."[86] Although we might detect a developmental logic in Pugalenthi Sr's thinking that popular literature makes possible a readership engaged with "high" forms of literature, he also makes clear the importance of taking joyful, leisurely pleasure in "low" forms of literature. Such pleasure must be understood as a counterpoint to imperial ideas that cast literature as educational or virtuous as reproduced by state institutions and global institutions like UNESCO. In other words, Pugalenthi Sr forwards the notion that there is pleasure to be taken in literature independent of any institutional function. Of course, as with the correlation between the appeal of short literary forms and Singapore's burgeoning industrial modernity that I discussed earlier, this pleasure is not unfettered. It is still circumscribed by the working day and enabled by Singapore's increased wealth. Amid a literary landscape that emphasizes development, international legibility, and literary quality, however, Pugalenthi Sr's desire to cultivate the reading and writing of literature as a site of national pleasure is notable.

Perhaps unsurprisingly, VJ Times faced some public derision for its literary output. Certainly, one can easily imagine a critique of Pugalenthi Sr as opportunistically taking advantage of a profitable cultural phenomenon, one regarded as superfluous in the context of a burgeoning national literature. Indeed, Kirpal Singh worried that the trend of "ghost stories, sensational stories of one description or another," was overly prolonged and that he was "not assured that the direction we are taking is altogether wholesome or qualitatively better."[87] Such trends, Singh argues, were detrimental because they would preclude Singaporean literature from "mak[ing] the kind of international impact it deserves to make."[88] Regarding the appeal of genre fiction as "indulgence" and in contrast to "worthwhile and wholesome books" by writers such as Suchen Christine Lim and Catherine Lim, Singh calls for "real commitment" from Singaporean writers to "sharpen the focus, to express the deeper anxieties and experiences of a people."[89] Though he acknowledges that VJ Times's output is necessary when considering that a "society needs all kinds of books to satisfy different needs and cravings," it is clear that he subscribes to the idea that national literature must be serious in tone, consequential in impact, and internationally validated.[90] As illustrated by the prefatory material to many of their volumes, Pugalenthi Sr and VJ Times were well aware of such criticisms: "At this juncture, we would like to thank our ardent readers who have supported us throughout our strenuous growth. Though our books were frequently ignored or savaged by jealous critics, this new breed of Singaporean readers have boldly supported our books and our endeavour."[91] The choice to describe their readers as "bold" is notable for how it suggests a stance that goes against institutionally determined literary values. The conflation of "support" with "purchase" reveals a logic that consumerism can enact some kind of restorative justice—in this case, rectifying VJ Times's and Pugalenthi Sr's marginalized statuses—and also reveals postcolonial capitalist logics at work. There is a notable shift in context here, however. Though postcolonial capitalism tends to operate with a consciousness of colonialism mostly understood as foreign power, Pugalenthi Sr locates the colonial structure of power in the nationalized institutions and figures that perpetuate colonially determined literary values.

Pugalanethi Sr's publishing practices openly embrace the relationship between literature and cultures of capitalism. As remarks about VJ Times's prolificity and participation in Singapore's horror boom suggest, the disdain of what Pugalenthi Sr represents in Singapore's literary scene was often expressed as a problem of sophistication. This is, of course, unsurprising, as literature is so often associated with learnedness, worldliness, and the class marker of leisure time. In this way, we can read the criticisms of Pugalenthi Sr and VJ Times as a symptom of anxiety on the part of institutions and individuals that want to maintain a sense of literature as an autonomous domain, especially because this domain was understood as a mode of proving modern development. The anxiety surrounding maintaining literature as an autonomous site of sophistication was especially evident at the 1993 International Festival of Books and Book Fair, when Pugalenthi Sr was censured for violating the rules. According to newspaper accounts, these violations included "displaying unauthorised posters with special offer prices and comparing them with normal prices," "hawking their books, disturbing neighbouring booths," and "ignor[ing] the organiser's repeated warnings."[92] By promoting their books as desirable commodities rather than aesthetic objects of moral or developmental significance, Pugalenthi Sr and his associates drew attention to the book fair as a site of commerce. Moreover, by using boisterous techniques associated with street vendors, VJ Times essentially undid the association of books with sophistication, revealing books are like any other commodity and subject to economic desire.

In spite of the many volumes of ghost stories and pulp fiction that VJ Times published, it would be unfair to regard Pugalenthi Sr as merely a shrewd businessman or as someone who did not value literariness. His output of anthologies is especially substantial. VJ Times anthologies included not only different kinds of genres but also different levels of experience with literary craft and levels of investment in literature. *Motherland, Vol. 2* (1993), for example, includes a short-story thriller by Eddy Lam Yew Chiang called "Blood Lust" that draws on conventions of horror and detective fiction alongside a poem by Aleric Er called "Yonder" that employs elevated language and plays with spacing to achieve aesthetic effect. Similarly, *The Chrysanthemum Haiku* (1991) combines short thrillers with more abstract or idyllic poetry. In the volume readers can observe different levels of literary aspiration, with some pieces more personal, raw, and even juvenile and others reflecting a writer drawing on or experimenting with different literary and poetic styles. Some of the writers included in the volumes would go on to become noteworthy figures in Singapore's literary scene (e.g., Alvin Pang), while others now have little to do with Singapore literature. Perhaps the authors wrote their pieces on a whim in their youth, or perhaps they were taken by the back matter of a VJ Times volume that invited readers to submit their own pieces for publication.[93] We see in many VJ Times anthologies an assembly of both "high" and "low" literary forms and a compilation of mixed quality (an assessment I am making from an institutionalized perspective). The VJ Times anthologies, in other words, have what we can describe as a very uneven aesthetic.

The uneven aesthetic of these anthologies at once reflects the economic context in which Singapore literature is evolving and a nationalist ethos of generosity on the part of VJ Times. Already in 1980, a UNESCO development report noted that despite prevailing critiques that Singapore has ignored the arts in favor of economic development, the "cultural life and vitality to be experienced, notably at amateur and community levels, is remarkable for a young rapidly developing and urbanizing society."[94] Although amateur arts productions were flourishing, the report also noted that there was a real "need to establish a professional dimension to the arts in Singapore."[95] UNESCO was calling for art practitioners to be remunerated (i.e., the antonym of *amateur* is *professional*), but this call for professionalized arts is also an exhortation to *institutionalize* the arts. Before the internet, the production and dissemination of creative writing, perhaps more than any other art form, required institutional structures. Of course, the professional and material barriers to publishing amateur writing are not unique to Singapore, but writing in the context of a newly independent country poses particular challenges compared to writing in the context of the United States or the United Kingdom, where minoritized writers have some degree of access to established presses and publishers. The problem of publishing access was even more pronounced in Singapore because there were very few periodicals wherein English language creative writing might appear. Cynically, one could accuse VJ Times of taking advantage of Singapore's lack of a professional writing scene (as some have intimated), but I prefer to view VJ Times's anthological production as generous; that is, it is an inclusive form that inspires new aesthetic relations, whether literal or metaphorical, and that creates the conditions for local writing to appear during an era when, as Pang explains, "there were hardly any opportunities for publication: no journals, no e-zines."[96] Moreover, as we see throughout the many Singapore-focused volumes dedicated to Singaporean readers, VJ Times sought to remove barriers for fledgling writers and treated the anthology as a generative form in the name of a nationalized literary culture. As the front matter of the *Motherland* series declares, "Through the publication of 'Window of Singapore' series and other numerous titles, we have successfully launched more writers and poets than any other publisher in Singapore for the past five years."[97] The generative possibilities of the Singapore anthology meant forgoing institutionalized literary values.

With their immersion in locality, VJ Times's popular anthologies articulate a kind of nativist sentiment that turns inward, away from the global, in a similar manner to how the Asian Values narrative also turns away. But this turn away from the global is not of the same kind that we see operating in state discourse. The assertion of Asian Values by the state was still operating within orientalist codes of intelligibility, whereas there is very little evidence that VJ Times was seeking international legibility.[98] The popular anthology instead rejects normative, respectable ideas of the nation that perform development, modernity, or economic exceptionalism, opting instead for a conceptualization of the nation where Singaporeans take pleasure in each other as aesthetic producers. Those pleasures, the VJ Times popular anthologies insist, need not be restricted to literatures that have been sanctioned by powerful institutions. Indeed, the very content of these popular anthologies are not the kind lauded by Asian Values discourse. In other words, the state's and the popular anthology's turns away from the global are historically synchronized, but they are not in political consensus. Although the marginalized position that VJ Times represents within Singapore's national literary scene might suggest a politics of resistance, its popular anthologies were also operating with the logics of postcolonial capitalism in their reliance on consumerism. The history of Singapore anthologies in this period reveals the ways that the sociopolitical dynamics of postcolonial capitalism produce unexpected literary cultures and relations. In this case, the Asian Values era gave rise to a hyperlocalized cultural and literary phenomenon. Although this would seem to be the natural outcome of a state discourse that emphasizes cultural difference, anthologies offered relief from state developmental imperatives and the aspiration to global legibility.

CONCLUSION

After Singapore's post-1997 Global Asia turn, Singapore's anthologies reached new heights. With the exception of the ones given some support by the Singapore National Arts Council, anthologies have by and large been put out by private, independent publishers such as Ethos Books and Epigram. Even though there are more opportunities for individuals to make a living by writing and the global anglophone literary market allows for local and national literatures to gain international repute, the Singapore anthology continues to be both a generative and a generous form. Sing Lit Station, the Singapore Poetry Writing Month, and other such programs produce many anthologies. A number of anthologies also use prompts to generate new writing and thought experiments. Anthologies are also the grounds for transnational collaborations. Besides a number of Singaporean and Malaysian collaborations, there are also ones between Australia and Singapore, Italy and Singapore, Kerela and Singapore, and the Philippines and Singapore.[99] Anthologies not only provide the conditions for amateur writing; they also generate unexpected literary encounters and relations. Rather than frame the anthology as a national declaration of "what we are," the anthologies of the Global Asia period take on more experimental questions such as, "What do we look like in this configuration?"

In this chapter I sought to lay out a brief history of early postcolonial capitalism, the prevailing economic ideologies through which it is expressed, and the changing face of "the global." Postcoloniality, as read through this history of postcolonial capitalism, is not one homogeneous period. Already at stake before Global Asia were questions about how Singapore should be made legible. In the rest of this book, I investigate similar questions by turning to the contemporary genres of demographic compilations, coming-of-career narratives, and the princess fantasy, which all emerge after the 1997 Asian financial crisis. As I show, the formation and dynamics of Global Asia cannot simply be understood as postcolonial answers to the imperatives of contemporary, global capitalism. Rather, Global Asia also responds to the dynamics of postcolonial capitalism as laid out here.

Overseas Singaporeans and Their Uses

Population Aesthetics and Territorial Productions of Singapore's Global Asia Imaginary

Singapore's transformation into a global and cosmopolitan site has entailed a refashioning of the diaspora as a desirable and important population for the nation. A key form that emerged to represent and aestheticize Overseas Singaporeans as Global Asia's main protagonists, typically highly professionalized and anglophone subjects, is what I describe as the demographic compilation: a middlebrow collection of journalistic writing that depicts a population. Rather than describe a discrete, standalone form, "collection" here is used loosely to mark a unity among short pieces. Frequently though not always nonfiction, demographic compilations draw on the anthological form by portraying a certain population through a compilation of short pieces, often first-person accounts and sometimes short biographies. Unlike other terms that name human collectives (i.e., communities, multitudes), "demographics" is not based in a sense of belonging, kinship, or political commitment. Instead, it is based on recurring characteristics within a population and uses an organizing principle that recalls the administrative logics of colonialism and biopolitical governance.[1] The bulk of demographic compilations begin to emerge in Singapore around the turn of the twenty-first century, often as popular, ephemeral institutional texts. This was especially the case during "SG50," when the state and other institutions published demographic compilations to commemorate Singapore's fiftieth year of independence in 2015. Demographic compilations also appear as features in periodicals and as standalone trade books.[2] Some popular demographic compilations also perform the anthological impulse of presenting the "best of" or "most influential" of their demographic (e.g., *The Naysayer's Book Club*). Demographic compilations, however, tend not to foreground the editor's curation function through rank or cataloging logics because its rhetorical aim is to establish a demographic.

That a population like Overseas Singaporeans is aestheticized in service of a state's socioeconomic project is somewhat counterintuitive considering that populations are typically the grammar of administration and discipline rather than the site through which to cultivate ideology or values. Partha Chatterjee writes:

> Citizens inhabit the domain of theory, populations the domain of policy. Unlike the concept of citizen, the concept of population is wholly descriptive and empirical, it does not carry a normative burden. Populations are identifiable, classifiable, and describable by behavioral criteria and are amenable to statistical techniques such as censuses and sample surveys.[3]

Certainly, the administrative view of Overseas Singaporeans can be traced to a colonial inheritance of racialized, demographic logic that continues to shape governmental policy.[4] Though the "Overseas Singaporean" is not an overtly racialized category in the same way that the "Chinese-Malay-Indian-Others (CMIO)" label is, distinguishing Overseas Singaporeans as a population follows the colonial model of "differentiating between migrant groups."[5] Populations are not simply the stuff of colonial administration; they are also pertinent under the postcolonial governance of Global Asia. Aihwa Ong has observed the ways that populations in Singapore enable a system-level approach to neoliberalized governance: "Niches or nations of stabilized populations are drawn into flows; varied populations thus brought into interaction produce a baroque ensemble of diverse qualities."[6] Compared to the disciplinary control and statistical techniques of colonial-era or early postcolonial nationhood that approached governance with the fine-tooth comb of censuses, however, biopolitical governance is less interested in control through enumeration than in cultivating conditions so that various populations perform and produce certain outcomes.

Although the concept of populations is relevant under colonial and postcolonial governance, it has not figured significantly in aesthetic questions of how the nation is imagined. The population aesthetic in demographic compilations is a notable departure from the use of what Benedict Anderson described as the "national hero,"[7] the singular, exceptional protagonist in nationalist narratives. It follows that the Overseas Singaporeans' instrumentalist function in the demographic compilations in fashioning the national imagination complicates the idea of the national hero. Despite appearing as a deeply characterological genre, I argue that demographic compilations perform their ideological work through setting. This centering of setting stands in contrast to texts such as Lee Kuan Yew's *The Singapore Story*, where "character is crucial," as Philip Holden puts it.[8] Moreover, because populations are so conceptually attached to governance, we tend to forget that they have, as Emily Steinlight writes, "aesthetic force and narrative consequence."[9] Such forgetting is not helped, in this case, by the fact that state-produced texts such as the ones I examine here and in the book more broadly are typically read as transparently ideological rather than imaginative.

Later work of Anderson's "modern imagining[s] of collectivity" in forms of "unbound seriality" and "bound seriality" offers some important critical terms through which to clarify how such ideologically straightforward texts can still do imaginative work.[10] Building on his work in *Imagined Communities*, Anderson explains in *The Spectre of Comparisons* that unbound seriality is typified by the newspaper while bound seriality is typified by the census.[11] Whereas Anderson's earlier *Imagined Communities* tends to be known for its discussion of how print capitalism acts as a mediating force for national imaginings, he gestures in this later work toward the aesthetic force to which Steinlight refers, insofar as seriality is an issue of arrangement and thus form. Further explicating the implications of these different styles of imagined collectivity, Chatterjee writes, "[Unbound seriality] afford[s] the opportunity for individuals to imagine themselves as members of larger than face-to-face solidarities, of choosing to act on behalf of those solidarities, of transcending by an act of political imagination the limits imposed by traditional practices. Unbound serialities are potentially liberating."[12] Bound serialities, on the other hand, "are constricting and perhaps inherently conflictual. They produce the tools of ethnic politics."[13] Bound serialities, in other words, perform the work of social control. State-produced demographic compilations, such as the "Singaporean Abroad" series under discussion in this chapter, operate at the nexus of bound and unbound serialities.

The assumptions underlying the (national) imaginary possibilities and limitations of serialities point us to a formal problem of character in demographic compilations, a problem articulated by the distinction of round and flat characters. Because it functions as an instrument of disciplinary power and control, the bound seriality of the census removes the full complexity of its citizens, reducing its subjects to empirical description, as Chatterjee puts it, which flattens them into simple, unchanging, and indistinct characters. Indeed, populations are often represented as faceless crowds and masses, reflecting the scale of perception that accompanies biopolitical logic. Presumably, it is easier "to make live and to let die," as Foucault puts it, or to treat populations as part of a greater economic calculus than if they were to each be identified as an individual, that paradigmatic Enlightenment figure of the rational, modern subject.[14] Representing collectives as indistinct populations—a crowd, a horde, a mob, a mass, or a caravan—has long been a dehumanizing aesthetic strategy.[15] Moreover, in the context of nationalist narratives and Holden's point that "character is crucial," flatness would hardly seem a desirable quality or one particularly amenable to cultivating deep attachments to the nation. Nonetheless, as I argue through my readings below, flatness can generate national imaginaries. The population aesthetic of these texts expands Singapore's Global Asia imaginary and in doing so illustrates how populations function as a conduit for ideological power and not simply as a classificatory instrument for discipline and policy. The logic of populations, in other words, is not simply the administrative grammar of biopolitics, but, as Robert Mitchell argues, "the enabling frame for intense experience of hope and fear; fundamental judgments concerning what is beautiful and ugly, sublime and mundane; and our intuitive sense of how individuals are to relate to collectives."[16] If interiority is the aesthetic emphasis of postcolonial developmentalism, seriality emerges as the aesthetic emphasis of Global Asia.

After providing an overview of the ways that diasporic Singaporeans have historically been regarded both as a problem and as a solution for the national project, I track in this chapter the ways that population aesthetics negotiate the politics of the non-Singapore world and work in service of claims to Global Asia. Two of these claims are made in locally circulated demographic compilations: "Singaporean Abroad," a feature in the state-controlled *Straits Times* newspaper, and "50 Red Dots Around the World," a commemorative issue of *be movement* magazine on the occasion of Singapore's fiftieth year of independence. Both compilations feature Overseas Singaporeans in a far-flung and sometimes unexpected corner of the world, though they do so to very different ideological ends. As a cultural complement to the state's biopolitical governance and Global Asia agenda, "Singaporean Abroad" rehabilitates Overseas Singaporeans from being a problematic population for the nation and uses them instead to transform the territorial basis of the national imagination. In contrast, "50 Red Dots" critiques and ostensibly rejects the state's instrumentalization of Overseas Singaporeans for its Global Asia project. Ironically, such critique is made possible by the magazine's Japanese benefactor, the Japanese Chamber of Commerce and Industry. However, the magazine issue still embraces and operates within the logics of postcolonial capitalism. This example demonstrates how forms of what Weihsin Gui describes as "critical nationality" can still function within the terms of postcolonial capitalism.[17]

The chapter closes with a discussion of two short stories from Jeremy Tiang's collection, *It Never Rains on National Day* (2015), which features characters that perform exactly the kind of Overseas Singaporean ethos that the state seeks to develop among its citizenry. With its short-form narrative representations of Overseas Singaporeans, *It Never Rains* falls within the generic ambit of the demographic compilation. Like the others under discussion in this chapter, *It Never Rains* is a text that features Overseas Singaporeans in various locations around the world and is aimed at a Singaporean audience—even though Tiang is based in the United States, he published his collection with Epigram Books, a local press in Singapore. Loosely connected by repeated characters, the stories feature a number of different kinds of Singaporeans, such as a civil servant, a teacher, a writer, and an interracial couple, and the stories are set both in Singapore and abroad (e.g., in Zurich, New York, and Beijing). As I show, the story "Sophia's Honeymoon" critiques the demographic compilation's tendency to center on the climax of a capitalist success plot. Moreover, Tiang's stories call attention to the limits of the Overseas Singaporean's cosmopolitanism to overcome coloniality and to the

Eurocentric limits of readers who may interpret Global Asia's anglophone legibility as evidence of Westernized global capitalism.

COSMOPOLITANISM AND STATE ANXIETY

Since independence, the Singaporean state's relationship with cosmopolitanism
has been an ambivalent one. While the speech by Goh Chok Tong discussed in the
introduction makes clear that Singaporeans who have left the nation are regarded
as a problematic population by the state, his incendiary remarks were not entirely
consistent with how the state has strategically invoked Singapore's long history as
a port city with cosmopolitan subjects. As the historian Justin Tyler Clark writes,
"In the late 1960s and 1970s, PAP leaders had already invoked the concept of cosmopolitanism as less a project than an existing tradition."[18] In this line of thinking,
Singapore's cosmopolitanism is a feature to be celebrated because it proves the
success of government policies that managed difference, as Brenda S. A. Yeoh further explains: "The sense here is that Singapore is, as a legacy of its past, *already* a
cosmopolitan place, one that is home to a polyglot population and where the role
of good government is to mediate between groups divided by race, religion and,
increasingly, generation and technology as well."[19] This view of cosmopolitanism as
an existing tradition stands in stark contrast to Goh's speech, demonstrating how
cosmopolitanism's ever-changing function in nationalist discourse tracks with
the different permutations of postcolonial capitalism. Such shifting sentiments
shape whether Overseas Singaporeans are regarded as a problem or a solution for
the state. This in turn has further implications for how the world outside of Singapore is understood. In consideration of the shifting role Overseas Singaporeans
play in state narratives, I take on a geographic understanding of cosmopolitanism
similar to Yeoh's. "Cosmopolitanism must hence imply the presence of a geography, of places which are different from others," she writes. "Would-be cosmopolitans must thus learn to navigate a non-homogeneous landscape."[20] Overseas
Singaporeans, in other words, invite questions of how the presence of a global
geography acts as a mediating force between state and subject.

Even as Singapore's cosmopolitanism has been heralded by the state, it has also
been regarded as a challenge for establishing national legitimacy. When Singapore
was first instituting self-governance in 1959, a functional state apparatus already
existed in the form of the governing colonial infrastructure. Its nation was in a more
precarious condition, however, because Singapore did not have citizens. "Singapore's
population," as Michael Hill and Lian Kwen Fee write, "was made up of large numbers of immigrants who were non-citizens."[21] This was a problem for legitimizing an
aspiring independent nation-state as well as a problem for governance. "It was simply not tenable," Seng Guo Quan comments, "to have a big group of immigrants in a
state of limbo and thinking of another homeland."[22] One might say that the problem
was that Singapore had the capitalists but not the postcolonial nationalists.[23]

To address the lack of citizens and, moreover, to mitigate the problem of *other* national attachments, the government ran a three-month campaign known as Operation Franchise to register foreign-born residents as citizens, so long as they met character and birth or residency criteria.[24] Singapore's cosmopolitan population required state intervention in order to build the nation; it was a problem that required a solution. Newspapers at the time describe volunteers for the citizenship campaign needing to "help promote enthusiasm" among potential registrants and the need for "how-to-become-a-citizen propaganda."[25] That a citizenship campaign was needed at all complicates depictions of decolonization as a revolutionary, organic formation—in this way, we see again that Singapore does not represent a "ideal type" nation for postcolonialism.[26] Operation Franchise is but one convenient instance among innumerable historical developments that exemplify how cosmopolitan, diasporic populations coming into Singapore have been a governance issue. In drawing attention to this historical moment, I mean to supplement Clark's and Yeoh's historical discussion of cosmopolitanism by considering not only how cosmopolitan subjects have been central to the Singaporean state's presentation of the nation, but also how they have been a disruptive force.

After independence, the nationalist discourse of loyalty and belonging changed from a persuasive mode of empowering cosmopolitan migrants (i.e., Singaporean citizenship will provide autonomy from empire) to one of disapproving of cosmopolitan citizens. Until the end of the twentieth century, foreign education was the main impetus for leaving Singapore. For some, seeking a foreign degree was a reflection of class privilege or of postcolonial desire for the metropole. For others, it was a response to the limited space available at local universities.[27] Some Singaporeans who left were beneficiaries of organizations like the Colombo Plan, which offered scholarships for students to study in Commonwealth countries, such as Australia, New Zealand, and Canada.[28] Despite the educational motive, Singaporeans who left were a major source of national controversy. Notably, one of the earliest public critiques of diasporic Singaporeans I found did not come from the Singaporean state. A scathing letter to the *Straits Times* editor written by trade union leaders in 1971 deems Singaporean boys who left for education abroad as "parasites" and "draft dodgers" because they were asking for exemptions from the national army service requirement. "And where would Singapore be," they ask, "if the workers of Singapore decided that ours was a Government of the rich, for the rich and by the rich, and that our children are only good as cannon fodder to keep Singapore safe for social parasites?"[29] In an earlier, equally blistering statement to the press, the authors declare, "If the rich think they can send their darling children overseas while the sons of workers sweat it out to make Singapore safe for these namby-pambies to return and make money, we strongly recommend that the Government take only one course of action."[30] That action, the article states, was to take "one-way tickets out of Singapore to some other place."[31] While draft dodging continues to be a controversy today (Kevin Kwan's avoidance of National Service renewed such debates recently), these classed and gender-essentialist criticisms anticipate the ways that cosmopolitanism would be regarded as the "monopoly of [Singaporean] Anglophone elites."[32] Moreover, the binary drawn between the citizen performing military service and the citizen seeking overseas education reveals how nationalist belonging is idealized through a masculinized physical presence rather than ethnicity or ideology. Physical presence is a qualification for immigrant naturalization procedures in many contexts and thus not in itself unusual; here it represents a loyalty standard for already present citizens and is amplified by the valorization of the military. That the critiques of diasporic Singaporeans were voiced by trade union leaders reflects the nation's economic imagination at the time, which took on a more materialist emphasis because of industrialized manufacturing. Overall, critiques of cosmopolitan Singaporeans are also a rejection of the world outside of Singapore ("some other place") as unimportant for the national project.

As labor and human capital concerns came to the fore in the late 1980s and 1990s, censure of Singaporeans abroad was at its height—strongly voiced at this point by the state. Emigration and a so-called brain drain was put to Parliament as a national concern in 1987,[33] amplifying anxieties voiced as far back as the 1960s in response to scientists being drawn to work in other countries, particularly the United States, which had expanded the immigration opportunities available to Asians and was offering better resources and higher pay.[34] When members of Parliament suggested initiatives in 1991 to encourage Singaporeans abroad to come home, K. S. Yuen famously retorted, "These people have betrayed their country and are ungrateful. If they want to go, let them go. We shouldn't encourage them to come back."[35] Yuen's use of "ungrateful," while indignant and paternalistic, also indicates Singapore's changed economic status as a wealthier and politically stable nation. In contrast, Lee Kuan Yew's 1969 discussion of Singaporean "quitters" in the context of recent decolonization (rather than the quitters of Goh Chok Tong's 2002 speech) concedes that leaving for more economically secure nations was understandable even if it was not ideal from a governance perspective.[36] In other words, for Lee, the world outside of Singapore was regarded not only as a structuring force in terms of global order but as an extractive force in terms of Singapore's purported main resource: human capital. For Yuen, the world outside of Singapore is instead understood as a competing force; those who leave are thus characterized as having given into some kind of temptation because they rejected the opportunities the state has offered them in its rise to economic success rather than maintain their obligatory ties to the nation. Yuen's rhetoric aligns with the Asian Values economic ideologies of the time.

As I discuss in the next section, the state drastically shifts its view of diasporic Singaporeans in the 2000s. This change is marked by its formalizing of their identities as Overseas Singaporeans and its increasingly positive representations of them. Such celebratory depictions of Overseas Singaporeans as successful cosmopolitans certainly reflect Singapore's transition to the neoliberal, knowledge economy. However, these shifting representations are symptoms of how the nationals abroad are a problem to be solved and not simply the exuberant embodiment of the cosmopolitan, Global Asia ideal. Problem solving does not only operate through disciplinary or juridical power in this instance, but by recalibrating how Overseas Singaporeans are perceived.[37] This recalibration, I show, is part of the ideological work of population aesthetics.

THE CULTURAL PRODUCTION OF THE OVERSEAS SINGAPOREAN POPULATION

We must read state representations of the Singaporean diaspora as a mode of projecting ideals about cosmopolitanism as the state takes on a position of active production rather than belated capture with respect to its citizens abroad. This is not to say that the Singaporean diaspora is a complete fiction manufactured by the state. According to the 2020 census, there were 217,000 Singaporeans living abroad—about 6 percent of Singaporean citizens—up from 184,000 in 2010, which is about an 18 percent increase over a decade.[38] "Overseas Singaporeans" only became a formal term for state governance with the 2000 Census Act, however, which tracks all "persons who are not residing in Singapore,"[39] and it was first publicly reflected in state data in 2003.[40] Before 2000, the primary legal mechanisms for the government to trace Singaporeans who left was through exit permit regulations (a 1975 policy aimed at Singaporean boys and men for the purposes of ensuring their military service) and through the renunciation of Singapore citizenship.[41] State statistics and data before the turn of the century, in other words, present the diaspora in terms of loss, creating a scarcity narrative around its citizenry in the same way that natural, extractable resources often are depicted. In this way, the history of the Singaporean diaspora is quite distinct from other Asian diasporas in that it is not primarily read through presence, whether permanent settlements (e.g., Chinatown), established labor flows (e.g., plantation labor), or historical circumstances that lead to mass migratory movements (e.g., the Vietnam War).

Before the establishment of parapolitical structures and state agencies aimed at cultivating relations with Singaporeans living abroad, Singaporean students abroad often met in informal ways. For example, the Nonya Baba restaurant on Davie Street in Vancouver, Canada, in the 1980s and 1990s served as something of an unofficial community center.[42] It is in the 1990s that diasporic Singapore anglophone literature, as represented by the works of Boey Kim Cheng and Simon Tay, and diasporic community organizations also began to appear. Of course, diasporic community formation takes some time, which is perhaps why the Merlion Club in Melbourne was only established in 1990, even though student migration began after World War II. Internet communities were also key sites for diasporic Singaporean relations, as noted in works by Eunice M. F. Seng and Cherian George.[43] With the exception of these internet communities, Singaporeans living abroad were mostly identifying each other within localized, institutionalized pockets of universities and cities rather than as part of a larger transnational community or state-formed network.

Besides the formal naming of Overseas Singaporeans, the state's attitudinal change toward those who had left is reflected in a dizzying array of working groups, policy recommendations, and new government agencies that sought to salvage the damage caused by the state's alienation of its citizens abroad. Despite Goh's firm stance against Overseas Singaporeans, other government officials expressed more sympathy. Parliamentary discussions in the aftermath of Prime Minister Goh's controversial "stayers and quitters" National Day Rally speech illustrate a burgeoning consensus that Singaporeans abroad were at once a reflection of the nation's increasing wealth and of the conditions of global capitalism that demand more mobility. The policy report *Changing Mindsets, Deepening Relationships* (2003), published by the Remaking Singapore Committee, encouraged a more opportunistic view of its citizens abroad: "The number of overseas Singaporeans has increased substantially over the years. These highly educated and experienced overseas Singaporeans should not be viewed so much as a 'brain drain,' but rather 'brain circulation.'"[44] During this time, a number of nonprofit organizations and government agencies either formed or gained greater visibility as a result of the state's changed perspective on their citizens abroad: the Singapore International Foundation, Majulah Connection, the Overseas Singaporean Network, and Contact Singapore, to name a few. In 2006, building on a number of structures, programs, and outreach efforts put into place by these various organizations that all attempted to articulate a nationalist agenda in a global context, the Overseas Singaporean Unit was established.[45] It is around this time that state representations of the Overseas Singaporean begin to proliferate in newspaper series, YouTube videos, photography, heritage festivals, social media, business brochures, and political ephemera. By articulating Overseas Singaporeans as a distinct population, the state not only confers a new, official status on a group of Singaporeans, but it also transforms understandings of the group from representing national loss to representing national presence.

REFASHIONING THE TERRITORIAL IMAGINATION

"Singaporean Abroad" ran as a weekly feature in the *Straits Times* from 2009 to 2012, totaling over two hundred articles, and was the first of many state-produced demographic compilations about Overseas Singaporeans. Notably, "Singaporean Abroad" ended about a year after the 2011 General Election, after which, as Clark argues, the Singaporean state quieted its cosmopolitan discourse.[46]

Like many such demographic compilations, "Singaporean Abroad" presents short biographical sketches and interviews with Overseas Singaporeans about the cities in which they now reside. The cities range from well-known metropolitan centers (e.g., New York, Seoul, London, Mumbai, and Tokyo) to smaller and lesser recognized cities (e.g., Neuchatel, Switzerland; Astana, Kazakhstan; and Lappeenranta, Finland). Each article is a full-page story—and in some instances, even a double-page feature—complete with color photography. Though eight journalists wrote articles for the series, the structure and format of the stories were consistent. After each headline, the article begins with a small inset of what looks to be a self-selected headshot and a listing of the interviewee's name, age, occupation, and length of stay in the city where he or she now resides. Following a short blurb on the city and its history and how the featured Singaporean came to live there, each story moves into a transcript of interview questions and answers. The Overseas Singaporean is asked about the types of activities in the city that local Singaporeans might enjoy, the nightlife, the food, and how the city compares to Singapore. The "Singaporean Abroad" series draws on magazine and feature writing conventions and at times feels reminiscent of an alumni magazine's "see where they are now" section. As with the demographic compilation *Conversations on Coming Home* that I discuss in chapter 3, the language of "Singaporean Abroad" tends to be quite touristic—an effect that is amplified by the many advertisements for travel agencies and holiday packages that so often frame the articles.

In terms of its form, "Singaporean Abroad" typifies Overseas Singaporean representations produced by the state, although it is notable for appearing in a local, print newspaper aimed at an audience present in Singapore. For example, a number of features on Singaporeans living abroad appear online on the OSU webpage and social media feeds, either as links to the portal or as standalone stories. The OSU also distributed to its membership biographical pieces on Overseas Singaporeans in the digital magazines *Singapore Heartbeat* for Singaporean working professionals abroad and *Singapore Pulse* for Singaporean overseas students. Hypertextual, online publications provide a dynamic reading experience with linked references and interfaces that differs from the experience of reading print newspapers. Even while "Singaporean Abroad" manifests the new economic ideologies of Global Asia, that it appears in the "old form" of the newspaper—the very basis of Anderson's theorization of imagined communities—the series demonstrates how such old forms of nationalist imaginaries can continue to be revised and globally expanded.[47] Across the differences in media and audience, "Singaporean Abroad" and these other digital demographic compilations all instrumentalize a sentimental mode characteristic of nationalist texts to produce what Camilo Arturo Leslie describes as "map-mindedness," or "a multi-scalar sense of place that can be harnessed in the service of the political community."[48] This map-mindedness combined with sentimentality might simply seem to be another mode of reproducing the nation as an imagined community, but I argue that the flat aesthetic of "Singaporean Abroad" operates in service of producing the multiscalar sense of place for the Global Asia imaginary.[49]

Puccini's opera Manon Lescaut (above) is performed at the Sydney Opera House (above left), whose "sails" form the canvas for a light show.

PHOTOS: AGENCE FRANCE-PRESSE, ZUE, REUTERS

Harbour ardour

Sydney's harbour and outer reaches pack a wallop from wallaby-watching to a night out at the opera

Deepika Shetty

A ustralia's oldest and largest European settlement, Sydney, is a vibrant city built around a spectacular harbour.

It is often called the Harbour City and has the reputation of being one of the world's most dynamic cities. Two of its most iconic structures are the Sydney Harbour Bridge and the Sydney Opera House. The city hosted the first Olympics of the new millennium, and continues to host major international events.

Sydney is surrounded by nature and national parks, which extend into the suburbs and right up to the shores of the harbour. It is a place where people almost always seem to be enjoying the outdoors.

"A lot of activity is on the harbour or on the beaches. In fact, some of the best places to chill out is are at the harbour," says Mr Terence Yew, a commerce student studying for his master's at the University of New South Wales.

"Of course, you need to do other things too, like shopping in Paddington, exploring King's Cross and admiring the historic Rocks," he says.

GETTING AROUND

The best way to get around the place is...
By taking the buses or trains. Sydney's public transport consists of an extensive rail network, buses and ferries, a single light-rail line and a tourist-oriented monorail. Public transport can get you to nearly all of the city's attractions.

If you plan to rent a car, note that parking in the Central Business District is quite expensive. You can end up paying A$70 (S$85) per day or A$25 per hour at some places.

The best time to visit the place is...
All year round. Every season is special. Summer, from December to February, is the best time to enjoy Sydney's beachside outdoor lifestyle. Temperatures average 26 deg C and go on up to a high of 40 deg C.

In autumn, from March to May, you get clear warm days with mild nights. June to August is winter when it gets cool, not cold. At night, the temperature can dip below 10 deg C, but during the day it is a pleasant 14 deg C.

Spring, from September to November, is a great time to explore the city's attractions, bushwalking, cycling and visiting the great outdoors.

Your favourite stop is...
Rocks Market *(far northern end of George Street, open Sat and Sun, 10am - 5pm)*. You have to pass sandstone cottages and terraces with speciality shops, cafes and restau-

SINGAPOREAN ABROAD
IN SYDNEY WITH

Terence Yew
Age: 29
Occupation: Student
Length of stay: Seven months

rants to get to Rocks, one of Australia's most famous markets. Every visit here is an experience. You never know what you will find at the 150 stalls. I have picked up some exquisite metal and ceramic ware on my frequent trips here.

Which places really excite you?
Several, including the historic Rocks and the family friendly **Taronga Zoo** *(Bradleys Head Road, Mosman, tel: +61-2-9969-2777, www.taronga.org.au/. Open daily 9am - 5pm)*. At the zoo, you can come face-to-face with swimming seals as they peer through the glass windows of a simulated Submarine Research Station or a nursing wallaby.

Children always love to watch the cute penguins. The viewing windows for the penguins are at the bottom of a custom-designed pool in which they glide playfully through the water.

CULTURE

The entire city has so much to offer, where does one start?
The **Museum of Contemporary Art** in the city centre, near **Circular Quay** *(open daily 10am - 5pm, except Christmas)* is Australia's only museum dedicated to exhibiting, interpreting and collecting contemporary art from across Australia and around the world. It was covered with an "electric canvas" in May for two months as part of the Vivid Sydney festival. The museum facade was illuminated at night with an art display of lights.

SHOPPING

One cannot leave without visiting...
Paddington Bazaar, also known as Paddington Market *(St John's Church, Oxford Street, Paddington, www.paddingtonmarkets.com.au/. Open on Saturdays from 10am to 4pm)*. This is a busy church-yard bazaar with more than 100 stalls crammed with clothing, crafts, jewellery and souvenirs.

The best bargains are at...
Birkenhead Point The Factory Outlet Centre *(Roseby Street, Drummoyne, tel: +61-2-9812-8800)* is Sydney's largest factory outlet and offers the best of fashion, food and homeware. You shop in style at prices that are half what you would pay at a regular store.

The richest variety of products can be found at...
Pitt Street Mall, which is the main shopping stretch in the city like Orchard Road.

Do not leave the place without...
Trying **Pancake On The Rocks** *(www.pancakesontherocks.com.au/)*. The chain of restaurants has been around since 1975 and is a favourite destination for those who crave pancakes and crepes. They have several outlets but my favourite is at The Rocks.

The best breakfast is at...
Le Petit Creme *(118 Darlinghurst Road, tel: +61-2-9361-4748)*. Show up by 9am as the place gets packed around 10am. They serve the best eggs benedict in town, warm fresh brioche and an extra-tangy house-made hollandaise. I love the coffee here too.

The best lunch is at...
Bills *(433 Liverpool Street, Darlinghurst, tel: +61-2-9360-9631)*. You have to try its sweet corn fritters and roast tomato. My other favourite is the prawn and chilli linguine with garlic, ginger and lime. A meal for two here costs about A$50.

The best dinner is at...
Hurricane's Grill And Bar at Bondi Beach *(130 Roscoe Street, tel: +61-2-9130-7101, www.hurricanesgrill.com.au/)*. It specialises in premium quality Australian beef, pork, lamb ribs and chicken, which are marinated in special basting sauces from South Africa.

SUNDOWNERS

The best drinks are at...
World Square Pub *(Ernst & Young Tower, corner of George & Goulburn streets, www.worldsquarepub.com.au/)*. It has more

than 20 different kinds of international beers on tap, including Little Creatures, Tiger, Asahi, Beez Neez, Blue Tongue Lager, James Squire Golden Ale and Guinness. It is spread over four floors and is a great place for relaxing with friends.

What is the one must-try drink in town?
Tooheys Extra Dry, Sydney's signature beer which was launched in 1994. I like its smooth and mild taste.

What is the coolest place to chill out in?
Cockle Bay Wharf at Darling Harbour. Situated just minutes from central Sydney, this is one of the world's great waterfront destinations and one of Australia's major attractions. Several events and festivals are held here throughout the year.

The one place you always take your friends to is...
Lindt's Chocolat Cafe at **Cockle Bay Wharf** *(Shop 104-105 Cockle Bay Wharf, tel: +61-2-9267-8064, www.cocklebaywharf.com.au/venues/485/lindt-chocolat-cafe/)*. Locals call this cafe a "chocolate heaven" and it lives up to its name. Do not miss its melt-in-the-mouth almond meringue which has a creamy chocolate-based filling.

Is there a Clarke Quay equivalent?
Cockle Bay Wharf at Darling Harbour comes pretty close.

FURTHER OUT

What is there to explore?
The forested hills of the Blue Mountains, a Unesco World Heritage Area, offers clifftop views across gum tree valleys and craggy outcrops, as well as bushwalking and adventure activities. There are more than 200 bed-and-breakfast places in the various scenic towns here. From Sydney's city centre, it takes you less than 90 minutes to get here.

About 120km from Sydney are the Southern Highlands, where you will find Fitzroy Falls, a national park with little river inlets and cascading waterfalls.

One of Australia's finest surf locations is Newcastle, located on the north coast. It is also an industrial city. Newcastle Steelworks greets visitors driving into the area.

An hour's drive north of Newcastle is Port Stephens, with its pristine beaches and bottle-nose dolphins. This area is a dedicated holiday spot and resorts dot the white beaches with marinas offering boats for hire.

If you like wine, you should not miss Hunter Valley, an easy two-hour drive from Sydney. Fresh country air, old-world colonial guesthouses, 70 vineyards and some of the best restaurants in the state await you.

deepikas@sph.com.sg

On the outer reaches of suburban Sydney lies Ku-ring-gai Chase National Park (above left), one of many parklands earmarked for preservation. A female red-necked wallaby (above right) keeps watch as its five-month-old baby (called a "joey") soaks in the sun at Sydney's Taronga Zoo.

FIGURE 3. A page from "Singaporean Abroad." Source: *Straits Times* © SPH Media Limited. Reprinted with permission.

One of the most striking characteristics of "Singaporean Abroad" is that it presents the Overseas Singaporean as ordinary. This effect is achieved, in part, by the headshot that every story features. The pictures are candid and likely from interviewees' personal albums. When juxtaposed to the larger and often higher-resolution professional stock photography of the featured city, the headshots appear starkly commonplace. For example, a feature on Sydney, Australia, shows Terrence Yiew casually posing in a green T-shirt with his arm resting on a handrail, with the Sydney Harbor Bridge in the background. The resolution of the shot is not particularly high and the photo is neither glamorous nor remarkable: it simply memorializes Yiew's visit to a famous Australian landmark. Above the inset of Yiew's picture is a photo of the Sydney Opera House during an evening lightshow and an action shot of a Puccini opera. Below is a long shot of Ku-ring-gai Chase National Park and a closeup of a wallaby and her joey. The photography is crisp and shows impressive detail, such as the beading on the opera performers' extravagant costuming and the animated expressions on their faces. In another example, a feature on Andrew Chen of Bishkek, Kyrgyzstan, includes a small photo of him atop a snowy vista juxtaposed to wide-lens photographs of mountain ranges, the Chabysh festival, and a homestay in a yurt with locals. Again, the fairly plain, unsmiling picture of Chen dressed in black casually squinting into the sunlight stands in visual contrast to the photos of majestic landscapes and the deep reds and textures of Kyrgyzstani homes and fashion. Such visual contrasts between persons and places create the impression that Yiew and Chen are ordinary people, making such an elevated, noteworthy status seem attainable.

The elevated social status that Overseas Singaporeans enjoy in this series is emphasized by their function as tour guides for the cities in which they live. While the interview structure of the newspaper performs the effect of candidness, the respondents' answers are not especially revealing of their personalities. For example, in response to the prompt of "The best way to get around is . . . ," Alinah Aman of Muscat, Oman, answers, "By renting a car. Another great way to see what the country has to offer is by renting a boat and seeing the coastline and the numerous islands and waves along the way. Visit www.zaharatours.com to pick a tour that suits your style."[50] John Tan of Marrakech, Morocco, tells readers that the best time to visit is "between March and August when it is warm and sunny."[51] Despite the rather generic answers and apparent editorial intervention, the series ultimately represents Singaporeans living abroad as citizens to consult for their knowledge of the cities in which they reside. While the subtext of their tour guide function for residents of Singapore suggests that such citizens are worthy repositories of cultural knowledge, the framework of the series positions citizens at home with the upper hand, insofar as it serves their needs as potential tourists. Rather than being marked by their absence, lack of loyalty, or elitism, the Overseas Singaporean population is thus integrated into the national imagination because they offer value to the Singaporean living at home as the enabling medium for comprehending the world at large. Moreover, the Overseas Singaporeans in "Singaporean Abroad" facilitate the possibility of touristic pleasure, hailing the citizen-reader as consumers rather than politically interested subjects. Although such a transformation is consistent with Singapore's history of postcolonial capitalism,[52] what is distinct about the series is how it positions citizens in a consumptive role with respect to each other rather than with respect to the state.

Although flatness is an aesthetic trait of demographic compilations, it is obscured by the exuberance and characterological aspects of the newspaper feature. Each full-page, color feature of an ordinary, though celebrated, Singaporean performs a liveliness apt for global travel. Moreover, the series seems to be invested in character development because biography sets up such a genre expectation and because of the use of the interview. The question-and-answer format performs intimacy by suggesting an interest in personality and subjectivity. Despite all the characterological appearances of the demographic compilation, readers do not have a sense of character depth because there is no character interiority.[53] In fact, when read in the aggregate—that is, when it is continually read—"Singaporean Abroad" reads far less remarkably because its formulaic repetition becomes increasingly evident. While formulaic narratives can offer aesthetic pleasure, there is no sense that "Singaporean Abroad" is attempting to cultivate such a pleasure, nor does the substance of the interview ever really exceed the dulling effect of structural repetition. Although the formulaic repetition of each feature creates a relation of relevance by establishing a pattern, each feature has no bearing or effect on the others. For example, no transitions (i.e., "to be continued" or "next week") are built into the language of the articles. Flatness should not be mistaken for boredom or ideological insignificance, however. It is simply a different register that, in this case, generates map-mindedness by foregrounding space rather than time. Rather than a temporally organized progressive plot movement unfolding through the action or development of a major character—what we typically think of as narrative—we have a *spatially* organized narrative that relies on repetition through minor characters outside of Singapore. As the literary element that readers are affectively attached to, Anderson's national hero still holds formal significance. While for Anderson, the national hero's consolidatory function makes possible the imagining of simultaneous time within the bounds of the nation, the Overseas Singaporean as national hero serves as a device to map out Singaporean transnational connections in "Singaporean Abroad." Character is indeed crucial, to repeat Holden's observation about its formal role in producing nationalist narratives, but here character operates not through affective attachments, as often occurs with round characters. Instead, character is instrumentalized to facilitate consumerist attachments to space. The spatial and thus cartographic imagination that is created by "Singaporean Abroad" traverses vast geographic distances, from Askersund, Sweden, to Herrenburg, Germany, to Busan, Korea, extending the imagination of the nation beyond its state borders vis-à-vis the Overseas Singaporean. No longer is the nation imagined within its delimited territory. Instead it is imagined as a base from which the world can be navigated.

While "Singaporean Abroad" elevates the sociopolitical status of Overseas Singaporeans and expands the territorial imagination of the nation, it also serves as an enabling frame for a biopoliticized cultural imaginary that views the world in terms of surfaces. This surface view is part of the Global Asia knowledge project. Representations of difference are a preoccupation of postcolonialists, who long have grappled with the consequences of European depictions of non-European cultures.[54] The touristic depiction of the world focalized through the Overseas Singaporean resembles the imperial project insofar as the narrative form of the demographic compilation promotes a cartographic understanding of expansion. "The systematic surface mapping of the globe," Mary Louise Pratt writes, "correlates with an expanding search for commercially exploitable resources, markets, and lands to colonize, just as navigational mapping is linked with the search for trade routes."[55] When we recall that the state's eventual valorization of the Overseas Singaporean was prompted by the demands of global capitalism and a knowledge economy that depended on its citizens' ability to navigate cultural difference in service of reaching new markets, we understand that "Singaporean Abroad" is also a knowledge project motivated by capitalism. But even though "Singaporean Abroad" operates on cartographic knowledge of the world, it does not hold the colonial impulse of "totalizing classification."[56] For example, in an article about Copenhagen, Denmark, Ian Choo responds to the question, "Which places in the city excite you?," by saying, "Free concerts at the famous theme park Tivoli (Vesterbrogade 3, 1630 Copenhagen V, www.tivoli.dk) every Friday." Choo's answer appears generic because of how the language appears to erase his voice and how it does not perform insider knowledge. The editorial addition of an online information source further replicates the tourist markers that signify culture. Nationalist articulations outside the bounds of the nation, in this case, do not suggest a confrontational attempt to take over other sovereign places. Rather, they merely mark innocuous presence.

While we can certainly describe "Singaporean Abroad" as cultivating a "rootless" or "partial" cosmopolitan ethic in adherence to global capitalism, such an ethic also befits the perspective of biopolitical governance. Though populations are a central concept for biopolitics, Foucault calls attention to the significance of the "milieu"—nature, environment, and space—by illustrating how architectural design is the basis for manipulating populations to perform desired outcomes.[57] This is what Mitchell explains as the principle of a "plastic, sticky plane,"[58] or the malleable site onto which populations hold. Biopolitical governance treats the plastic, sticky plane as what Foucault calls "the target of intervention for power."[59] Though "Singaporean Abroad" does not represent non-Singaporean sites as plastic—after all, they are not sites that can be manipulated by Singaporean governance— they *are* represented as sticky. For Mitchell, "sticky" means that populations "can be embedded and held for some period of time" onto the plane.[60] Worked into Mitchell's notion of the sticky plane is the condition of possibility ("can be"), which is where the aesthetic and ideological work of "Singaporean Abroad" enters. Stickiness is produced by the Overseas Singaporean's touristic knowledge of non-Singaporean sites. "Singaporean Abroad" thus provides biopoliticized, cultural literacy to its audience by training them to know the non-Singapore world while also demarcating the Overseas Singaporean population's functionality for Global Asia.

On top of revealing the aesthetic education in biopolitics that "Singaporean Abroad" provides, the demographic compilation's flat representation of the non-Singapore world also offers insight into the rather middling cultural logics and power dynamics of Global Asia. Although the flatness of "Singaporean Abroad" might appear derivative of the colonial imagery of *terra nullius*, a significant difference is that the flat non-Singapore world is not imagined as empty. The demographic compilation is in fact well aware that the non-Singapore world is full. This distinction between viewing the world as empty and viewing it as full reflects very different capitalist perspectives. Rather than aspire to dominance, as with imperial ideology, Global Asia strategizes from a subordinated position within the global socioeconomic order and from a historical consciousness of colonialism. Instead of overthrowing existing sovereignty, this instantiation of postcolonial capitalism emphasizes a capacity to maneuver an already existing order of power. Whereas extractive capitalism relied on totalizing, classificatory knowledge to control non-Europeans, postcolonial capitalism emphasizes functional, surface knowledge to circumvent Eurocentric structures put into place by colonialism. By portraying the non-Singapore world as flat and maneuverable, the demographic compilation reassures its local readers that becoming part of the Overseas Singaporean population is not an uphill battle.

"Singaporean Abroad" expands the territorial imagination of the nation and trains local readers to view the world in terms of sticky planes. Furthermore, this reading of "Singaporean Abroad" also has broader methodological implications for how we read the power dynamics of postcolonial and contemporary capitalism. For literary and cultural critics, the significance of the milieu and plastic, sticky plane for biopolitical governance—not to mention the imaginings of the world outside of the nation—directs our attention to the element of setting. As a narrative element, "setting" typically refers to the social, historical, and geographic context in which action takes place. But when approaching setting as mired in and as an expression of power, we view setting as dynamic rather than inert. We can, in other words, read setting for its conditions of possibility. In the case of "Singaporean Abroad," the goal is not simply to identify elements of setting, such as the where or the when, but also to ask how setting shapes already unfolding action. In this example, "Singaporean Abroad" uses other settings to cultivate future action; the series conveys to Singaporean readers that they too can become valued citizens. It further serves as a reminder that power is not only legible through its oppressive or generative effects on subjectivity and thus character. By revealing how the aestheticization of setting is tied up in techniques of governance, "Singaporean Abroad" enables us to consider the representational politics of setting as well as its narrative function.

SINGAPOREAN CRITICAL NATIONALISM AND JAPANESE SOFT POWER IN "50 RED DOTS"

Since the publication of demographic compilations like "Singaporean Abroad," popular and literary representations of Singaporeans living abroad have increased. Some examples are a feature in *Female* magazine, "Home Away from Home: 5 Singapore Creatives Abroad Share Their Ways of Living" (2020); a lifestyle feature on houzz.com, "This Is Home for These Singaporeans Abroad" (2017); a YouTube video by DBS Bank, "Living Abroad: How Different Is It from Living in Singapore?" (2018); and a book on Foreign Service Officers, *Footprints on Foreign Shores* (2021). Many of these popular demographic compilations are ephemeral rather than continuous, but their proliferation suggests that state representations of Overseas Singaporeans have produced a positive feedback loop, influencing the ways that Singaporeans view the nation.

One critically notable Overseas Singaporean demographic compilation is "50 Red Dots Around the World," published on the occasion of Singapore's fiftieth year of independence by the organization be movement. A social enterprise described "as a movement to celebrate the courage to be," be movement maintained a "socially conscious publication" and a pop-up gift store that sold "a specially curated selection of artisanal, unique and creative products from around the world."[61] Cassie Lim, herself an Overseas Singaporean, began the be movement brand after a decade-long career in the media industry.[62] Though now defunct, be movement published six issues of its "bookazine," each focused on a particular city, with travel stories and features on people, businesses, and organizations deemed "inspirational." While "50 Red Dots" as a publication is unremarkable insofar as it was not particularly influential, it is significant for the ways it uses the demographic compilation as a mode of state critique and for what it reveals about competing layers of postcolonial capitalism.

In the SG50 issue, interviews with Singaporeans living abroad cohere around a common critique of the Singaporean nation-state as overly focused on economic achievement and blind to the class privilege generated by its wealth, critiques that Weihsin Gui would describe as expressions of "critical nationality." For Gui, critical nationality is a project of

> critical rationality motivated by a national consciousness that reveals, resists, and reconceptualizes the hypostasizing effects of *instrumental* rationality expressed through the determinate constructions of national identities. . . . [C]ritical nationality [is] open to what is nonidentical to it as it becomes imbricated with cosmopolitical and transnational cultural forms.[63]

From the perspective of critical nationality, "50 Red Dots" clearly seeks to resist state images of Singapore as Global Asia even as it draws on the formal conventions of state-produced demographic compilations. The full-color issue is sizable at 210 pages and comprises biographies of and interviews with notable Overseas Singaporeans. The cartographic presentation of Overseas Singaporeans as "50 Red Dots"—with "red dot" referring to the way Singapore is often represented on world maps because of its small size—conflates the Overseas Singaporean character with its overseas setting, much like "Singaporean Abroad." The interview questions put to the Overseas Singaporean in this case, however, are much more open ended and aimed at getting to know the person's life experiences and opinions on Singapore. In other words, the questions demonstrate a clear investment in representing Overseas Singaporeans as round characters. The use of caps, emoticons, and parentheses in the formatting and the repetitiveness of the answers suggest that many of those featured were interviewed via email and offered a list of fill-in-the-blank-type prompts. None of the specific questions or prompts is actually presented in the publication, and the responses appear to be uninterrupted streams of thought. However, a number of answers begin the same way: "Since moving away from Singapore . . . ," is prevalent, as are responses about whether Singapore is a First World nation. Readers can therefore deduce the use of standard interview questions.

While the form of "50 Red Dots" offers readers generic familiarity, there are some notable departures from state depictions of Overseas Singaporeans. For one, the Overseas Singaporeans are less sinocentric than those featured in "Singaporean Abroad," at least in what can be discerned from their names and from crude observations of phenotype. Moreover, while "50 Red Dots" retains the structure of presenting multiple, minor characters, these national heroes of "50 Red Dots" are represented as exceptional figures whose life insights are valuable. Success is not signified by a flourishing corporate career, as is the case in *Conversations* discussed in the next chapter, but by the work of LGBTQ+, disability, and refugee rights activists; social workers and musicians; photographers and poets; disabled athletes; and social enterprise entrepreneurs living abroad. "50 Red Dots" veers away from depictions of success that only validate citizens who facilitate Singapore's capital accumulation. The publication generally features those in occupations guided by altruistic principles rather than profitability.

My framework of critical nationality and my focus on this periodical's various contrasts with respect to "Singaporean Abroad" might lead readers to believe that I am now focused on the ways that Global Asia has been resisted by Overseas Singaporeans. While this is partially true, this interpretation does not reveal the full picture because a binary structure of state/subject overly simplifies the power dynamic at work. What my reading of "50 Red Dots" instead reveals is the different modes of postcolonial capitalism layered against each other: the Singaporean state, its subjects, and a former imperial occupier of Singapore, Japan. Although it is a local periodical, the "50 Red Dots" issue of *be movement* serves as a reminder that postcolonial capitalism is not particular to Singapore and, moreover, that it has transnational articulations.

The majority of the issue's interviews discuss how experience overseas facilitates realizations about the idiosyncrasies of Singapore's historical trajectory and governance. While it is not especially remarkable that such encounters with difference would lead to new sociopolitical perspectives, the interviews repeatedly critique Singapore as lacking empathy for the vulnerable. For example, Carol Tan comments:

> Heart-wise, I also felt too comfortable back in safe, clean, prosperous Singapore to contribute to drafting practical solutions for problems I didn't FEEL. . . . Many Singaporeans ignore the challenges that plague the majority of the planet's inhabitants. Either we assume that the rest of the world leads similar lives to us, or we jealously guard what we think we've earned.[64]

Similarly, Adrian Yap remarks:

> My concern for Singapore in the next 50 years is that if Singapore remains competitive, lacking genuine care for vulnerable groups, I fear that the gap in society will get wider and more people with special needs will never catch up with the majority. My hope is to see more Singaporeans show greater compassion and care toward our community members with their diverse needs.[65]

In interview after interview, the Overseas Singaporeans of "50 Red Dots" lament the lack of care Singaporeans have for others, a phenomenon that the interviews collectively locate in the emergence of Singapore's wealth. Moreover, many of the interview responses employ language that points to how Singaporean governance cultivates a lack of relationality among its citizenry.[66] The language of unfeeling, in other words, is used as a mode of critique.

The critiques of Singaporean culture and governance in "50 Red Dots" employ affective language, drawing on both discourses of human rights and local critiques of state mandates that compel its people to tirelessly work in the name of the nation. On the one hand, the desire for care and connection with the less fortunate that many express in "50 Red Dots" performs what Joseph Slaughter describes as a "humanitarian sensibility." As Slaughter writes, the notion of humanitarian sensibility, or "the voluntary assumption of responsibility to the other" as the "culmination of modern subjectivation,"[67] is tied up in ideas of human and personality development. Such ideas are very clear in the many interviews in the issue that narrate care for others as a moment of self-realization. While the critiques of Singapore as an unfeeling setting are generally apt for the humanitarian ethos of the Singaporeans featured in "50 Red Dots," their representation of humanitarian sensibility as being learned from the non-Singapore world aligns them with orientalist renderings of technocratic Singapore as "sterile" and "boring" (see chapter 4) or of Asians as inscrutable. Insofar as the critique is performed from a position external to Singapore using "techniques and a language borrowed from the occupier,"[68] and reproduces some of the orientalist discourse of unfeeling from the Asian Values era, we could view these Overseas Singaporeans as akin to Fanon's colonized intellectual. Their critiques are further reinforced by objections from Singaporeans weary from the "hard work" imperatives of the manufacturing economy. For example, Tam Wai Jia comments: "If I could change one thing about Singapore, it would be for Singaporeans to slow down and take joy in the little, simple things in life. When I am trapped in the rat race working 90 hours a week, I realized that while I worked more, I had less to give." Tam's reference to the "rat race" refers to Singapore's work culture and the state's emphasis on unending, efficient work. The very ways that many of the interviewees plainly link personality development with overseas experience to form their state critique reproduce privileged attitudes that view subjects of postcolonial governance as ideologically deluded.

Ironically, even though "50 Red Dots" emphasizes personality development and humanitarian sensibility as the basis of critical nationalism, many of the interviews reveal instrumental uses of state discourses for their *own* capitalist purposes and self-representation. Geoffrey K. See, for example, declares that "choosing this idealistic line of work is almost a rejection of the conventional success story Singapore culture often espouses and celebrates."[69] See's critical nationalism positions itself as politically opposed to the state, yet the interview reveals how he deploys Singapore's "Third World to First World" narrative for his social enterprise Choson Exchange: "How Singapore has developed its economy over the last 50 years is a story that underlies a lot of what we share with North Koreans."[70] Given that See's organization is essentially aimed at bringing capitalism to North Korea through cultural exchange, his use of the so-called Singapore Story is not surprising. In this simultaneous opposition to the institution of the Singaporean state and embrace of its discourse, See performs a contradiction that reappears in other parts of the issue. Darrell Ang, for example, strongly criticizes how Singapore's technocratic approaches to socioeconomic policy have led to the neglect of "history, culture, art, literature, and music."[71] Yet Ang still expresses regard for the ideologies that reinforce the very problems to which he calls attention, as illustrated by his self-representation using some of the language associated with the Asian Values era:

> Singapore, with its emphasis on discipline, hard work, thriftiness, independence and obedience—as well as filial piety—has given me strong fundamentals with which to grow as an adult in an ever-changing world. As a classical musician, one certainly needs discipline and diligence, and capacity to rely on oneself is every Singaporean's birthright.

Despite the issue's resonance with the commentaries on the increasing economic disparity in Singapore and the dehumanizing effects of manufacturing work, "50 Red Dots" asserts its own version of postcolonial capitalism through claims of exceptionality and oppositional politics—though in this case, that opposition is to the state rather than to colonialism and its legacies.

Further complicating a reading of "50 Red Dots" solely within a state/subject dynamic, however, is the way the publication is mediated by larger transnational forces and objectives. Notably, one of the key sponsors of "50 Red Dots" is the Japanese Chamber of Commerce and Industry (JCCI), Singapore. Like the many branches around the world, the JCCI in Singapore describes one of its main objectives as "promot[ing] and expand[ing] both trade and investments between Singapore and Japan."[72] Although JCCI primarily works with businesses, it has a registered charity, the JCCI Singapore Foundation, whose primary aim is to "support the development of arts, culture, sports, and education in Singapore."[73] Though such kinds of corporate philanthropy are not unusual, especially as JCCI is a guest organization in Singapore, the foundation's aims align ideologically with what is known as the Fukuda Doctrine, or the Japanese diplomacy strategy in the Southeast Asian region after World War II. Following its commitment to peace and in recognition of the atrocities of the Japanese Imperial Army, Japan took a soft power approach to ASEAN member states by funding infrastructural developments and cultural programs. In contrast to the Singaporean state, which is known for its political censorship and for its general disregard for arts and culture, Japan via JCCI via "50 Red Dots" is presented as a state invested in self-/free expression and personality development—values that are the basis of the Singaporeans' critical nationality in the be movement issue. An interview from "50 Red Dots" with Fumio Otani, JCCI president, reveals Japan's investment in Singaporean culture. In response to the question, "Where do you think Singapore could improve as a country?," Otani responds, "Since Singapore is quite young, there were not so many cultural activities that have taken root here in Singapore. So the culture part might be one area Singapore can grow a little."[74] Although Otani is careful to commend the Singaporean state for various socioeconomic policies and successes, his language of maturity and development echoes Cold War–era ideas of culture and the arts as a significant and necessary site of (national) development. The presentation of Overseas Singaporeans as round characters, or individuals with deep interiority, critical capacities, and developing personalities, is crucial for building Japan's appearance as a compassionate state facilitating critical nationality rather than as a patronizing, colonial state. The use of interviews with no clear interviewer further builds the impression that "50 Red Dots" is a publication supporting the free expression of Overseas Singaporeans. Moreover, among the interviews are features on the organizations that JCCI supports (the Singapore Disability Sports Council), the cultural exchanges they facilitate through study abroad initiatives, and Japanese companies (i.e., Nikon and Liang Court). When read alongside the interviews with Overseas Singaporeans, readers understand these Japanese organizations are working with and among Singaporeans, facilitating their needs and aspirations. Interestingly, in the features about JCCI or Japan, the interviewer presence returns, reassuring readers of Singaporean editorial control and thus agency. Ironically, the magazine's expression of Japanese soft power transforms the symbolism of the red dot into an evocation of the Japanese flag.

"50 Red Dots" simultaneously performs a critical nationalism of Singapore and an instrumental nationalism for Japan, a nation that formerly occupied Singapore. Japan instrumentalizes the aesthetics of Overseas Singaporean critical nationality in order to set up a relation of indebtedness and gratitude between it and Singapore. One of the cornerstones of postcolonial capitalism is the way it negotiates the impact of colonial history. "50 Red Dots" reminds us that the formerly imperial and not just the postcolony must strategize against a history of colonialism and, in this case, the violence that it unleashed. Like the Singaporean state's strategy of postcolonial capitalism, the Japanese state avoids overt ambitions of regional or global dominance, as evident in the Fukuda Doctrine. For this reason, Japan asserted its influence through programs that assist in Southeast Asian development and industrialization through their Official Development Assistance program, a strategy also evident in China's Belt and Road program. In other words, Japan facilitated Singaporean and Southeast Asian modernization, which was seen as part of national projects and not as colonial mandates. But now economic influence and assistance looks quite different, given Singapore's global economic standing.

While "50 Red Dots" does not go so far as to assert that Singaporeans should feel indebted or grateful to Japan and JCCI, it is certainly highly suggestive of this claim. The various features on JCCI-funded organizations in "50 Red Dots" emphasize opportunities accorded to Singaporeans that would otherwise not be possible, with the understanding that such opportunities are not simply about funding, but about state priorities. Japan, in other words, acts as the benefactor when Singapore does not. In this way, Japan sets up a relation of gratitude and indebtedness. Unlike the compulsory gratitude that might be demanded of new immigrants or of citizens (recall here Yuen's depiction of Overseas Singaporeans as "ungrateful"), "50 Red Dots" simply sets up the affective conditions for gratitude. These conditions are at once enabled by the reflective, critical nationalism of the publication and by the sentimentality of humanitarianism. In this way, the Overseas Singaporeans become the sticky plane on which Japan makes its power legible.

IMAGINING DENOUEMENT IN *IT NEVER RAINS ON NATIONAL DAY*

Like "Singaporean Abroad" and "50 Red Dots," Jeremy Tiang's short story collection, *It Never Rains on National Day* (2015), features a group of Overseas Singaporeans in various locations around the world (including some returned Singaporeans) and centers questions of nationalism, as indicated by the title of the collection. One could easily imagine the Cambridge-educated, New York City–based Tiang, who also translates Chinese into English and writes novels and plays, in one of the demographic compilations. While *It Never Rains* is not strictly a demographic compilation, the short story collection is its literary cousin insofar as it too is a compiled form and, in this case, featuring a population. Like the other demographic compilations under discussion in this chapter, the composite parts of the collection are differentiated by setting: Switzerland, Norway, Germany, China, Canada, Thailand, New York City, Singapore. Because the demographic compilation tends to present itself as a realist, journalistic genre, it can elide questions of narrative form. In this way, the *fiction* of Tiang's stories becomes the mode of critiquing the demographic compilation's form. In the context of "Singaporean Abroad" and "50 Red Dots," the two linked stories of the collection, "Sophia's Honeymoon" and "Sophia's Party," present a critique of the climax-centered narratives that so often accompany representations of Overseas Singaporeans.

"Sophia's Honeymoon" centers on Sophia, a Singaporean Chinese woman, and Nicholas, her white British husband, who are in Zurich for their honeymoon. Sophia and Nicholas are not only the most frequently appearing characters in Tiang's collection, this transnational, married couple that settled in Singapore are figured as the paragon of Singaporean success, both as individuals and as a couple. By virtue of her US education, readers understand that Sophia is of the social and economic class idealized by the Singaporean state. Sophia's husband, Nicholas, also possesses the proper social and cultural capital as a result of his background: "Thanks to an adolescence of ski trips and inter-railing, Nicholas is already au fait with Europe. . . . He speaks French, he likes to boast, with a Parisian accent."[75] Like the Overseas Singaporean, Nicholas is cosmopolitan, "familiar with global trends and lifestyles" and "comfortable working and living in Singapore as well as overseas."[76] Unlike the migrant workers who are seen as potential economic burdens to Singapore, Nicholas represents the kind of population that contributes to Singapore's capital accumulation, whether in terms of economic capital or the social capital signified by his whiteness.

By settling in Singapore with her husband, Sophia, moreover, proves that she is not the kind of difficult woman that the state anticipates. Sophia's socioeconomic background recalls controversial remarks in 1983 by Prime Minister Lee Kuan Yew, who asserted that highly educated women were not as marriageable and were not producing enough babies for the economy. As a result, the Singaporean government instituted tax incentives and other monetary incentives for women with university educations to have children and for low-income and undereducated women to be sterilized before the age of thirty after one or two children.[77] Not only were highly educated women considered less marriageable and less procreative, as noted in the *Changing Mindsets, Deepening Relationships* report, they were viewed as another avenue of population loss as "more female citizens, especially the better educated, are expected to marry foreigners."[78] Sophia both assuages the Singaporean state's anxieties and checks all the boxes for fulfilling Singapore's Global Asia agenda.

The story's focus on Sophia offers subtle cues indicating the ways that Singapore's particular history of postcolonial capitalism has shaped her understanding of success. As with the demographic compilations discussed in this chapter, the story performs an enumerative and cosmopolitan logic through the "process of elimination" that the couple goes through to decide on their honeymoon destination: "Not America—Sophia went to college there. They covered most of Asia during their brief courtship. Africa and South America will be perused later at leisure. Australia is, of course, not even in the running. This leaves Europe, which to Sophia means expensive chocolates and the novels of Thomas Mann."[79] The tongue-in-cheek narrative voice performs class privilege by reducing Europe to a consumerist association and a cultural detail likely culled from her schooling. On the one hand, such sanctioned ignorance—as a performance of Singaporean power and success—affectively mimics colonial privilege. On the other hand, the way that Sophia belies her class affectation with crude symbolism and the basic touristic knowledge of the non-Singapore world that "Singaporean Abroad" espouses also calls attention to the hollowness of the cosmopolitan Overseas Singaporean.

The Swiss setting of the story is particularly significant not only as a generalized symbol of European colonialism but also because it recalls an idiosyncratic detail from Singapore's history of postcolonial capitalism. For many years, the "Swiss standard of living" was touted as the developmental ideal toward which Singaporeans should strive (according to former prime minister, Goh Chok Tong, such a standard of living was achieved in 1994). The effect of the Singaporean state's grand portrayal of Switzerland clearly looms large in Sophia's imagination when she finds herself "astonished to discover such power and influence reposing in a place smaller by a factor of ten than Singapore."[80] Even though "Sophia's Honeymoon" is ostensibly about Sophia coming to terms with her role in her marriage to Nicholas and the new class privileges it affords her, the story also is about Sophia's arrival, as a Singaporean, to the scene of global capitalism. After all, Switzerland is a country that has signified First World development in Singapore, and it is known globally for its offshore banking. Thus, when Sophia gleefully "feels that Europe has spread itself before her feet as if she were a Henry James heroine,"[81] because of her association with Nicholas, her postcolonial capitalist success becomes shaded with an "Empire strikes back" narrative underwriting the story.

A consciousness of the structuring effects of metanarratives, whether received from the Singaporean state or from neoliberal ideology, pervades "Sophia's Honeymoon," as underscored by the mechanical imagery of the wedding industry. For example, the determinative and structural language describing Sophia's wedding as having "coalesced around her" emphasizes Sophia's position of passivity.[82] The passage continues: "Sophia submitted to the cake-tastings and gown-fittings, starting a machine that would not turn off until it had deposited her, winded and flushed, at the altar—where Nicholas awaited her, startlingly attractive in his new Hugo Boss suit."[83] What might have been represented as Sophia's agential actions are instead portrayed as her yielding acceptance to wedding conventions, as illustrated by the use of noun forms ("cake-tastings" that Sophia submits to) rather than the use of active verbs. When combined with the imagery of automated machinery, the passive grammar presents Sophia as a mere outcome rather than as an agent of her own success. Much in the way that the Singaporean state has produced metanarratives about what global capitalist success should look like, so has the wedding industry produced expectations and thus conventions about weddings.

In contrast to the demographic compilations that present living abroad as the defining climax of an Overseas Singaporean's life, "Sophia's Honeymoon" centers denouement. The implicit critique that "Sophia's Honeymoon" presents of texts such as "Singaporean Abroad" and "50 Dots Around the World," in other words, is that they instrumentalize partial narratives to achieve their ideological goals. Tiang not only uses the gendered metaphorization of Singaporean success through Sophia's marriage to capture the ebullience and performance of state discourse; he also uses it to comment on the disappointment that follows even when all expectations have been fulfilled. Narratively, "Sophia's Honeymoon" is the denouement of the broader narratives of Singaporean success. In this way, the title, "Sophia's Honeymoon," refers not simply to the celebratory vacation that she takes after her wedding, but to the waning bliss promised by achieving such success. That is, the story captures the *end* of a honeymoon period.

Sophia's gendered routines are a way for Tiang to draw out a critique of the cosmopolitan education that the state advocates in the context of Singapore's knowledge economy and Global Asia project. At first, the story seems to characterize Sophia's exercise and attentiveness to her appearance as a matter of vanity:

> She *knows* they make a handsome couple, and this is part of what draws people to them. . . . Sophia does forty-five minutes of Pilates every morning, and she never eats carbs after six. She *knows* what shades to wear to set off her honey-colored skin and straight black hair. They are the sort of couple one looks at and automatically begins imagining their beautiful children.[84]

Although Sophia is concerned about her body, the language indicates that the physical attributes she chooses to highlight are not only connected to her femininity, but to her coloring. Notable too is how Sophia frames her choices in terms of "knowing." Such declarative language would at first seem to connote Sophia's confidence in herself, but given how the story explores Singapore's image abroad, to "know" also signifies Sophia's ability to navigate her *audience's* desires. Sophia strategically aestheticizes herself to emphasize the interraciality of her and Nick's marriage, for that is what "draws people to them." With denotations of "striking," the descriptor "handsome" can also mean "contrast," or in this case, racial contrast. Although Sophia is, in her own right, a high-achieving Singaporean woman, she represents and expresses herself as the subordinated part of a couple, reassuring her audience that whatever power she holds is mitigated by white masculinity.

Tiang's story, however, also explores the limits of cosmopolitan education. Much in the way that Sophia's imagination of Switzerland is cut down to size during her honeymoon, so too is the assumed social benefits of Singaporean success. In another instance in which Sophia performs her postcolonial knowledge, she shares her prepared answers formed in response to European perceptions of Singapore. Sophia "is able speak glibly about the heat, the shopping centers, their adorable new flat in Tanjong Pagar with teak furniture imported from Myanmar. She is careful to emphasize how much of a financial hub it is, mindful that Nicholas suspects people of thinking he has relegated himself to a backwater."[85] Sophia's carefully constructed answers reveal that Singapore's economic success and rapid modernization have not afforded her social or cultural capital, and she must still perform her class privilege to signal her cosmopolitanism. Even though Sophia might be the exact kind of transnationally mobile, neoliberal subject that the Singaporean state so desires, Tiang illustrates how the Global Asia glamour of postcolonial capitalist success cannot easily overcome long histories of Eurocentrism.

Following Sophia's defensive encounters with Nick's Swiss colleagues who know little about Singapore, Tiang uses a metafictional technique to comment on Sophia's inability to decode the world that her cosmopolitan life was supposed to prepare her for: Zurich reveals the failures of her cosmopolitan education. Tiang first achieves this critique through the ekphrastic depiction of the opera Sophia and Nicholas attend. Though visually detailed in its description, because the narrative is focalized through Sophia, the reader has little sense of the opera's plot since Sophia herself does not know it ("She should have looked up the plot on the Internet,"[86] she chides herself). The description of the opera focuses on singers on the stage, but neither Sophia nor the reader understands what relations characters have to one another or how one moment leads to another. At best, Sophia can only triangulate meaning from the opera through audience reaction when, for example, "Nicholas nods appreciatively, as he does at a good volley at Wimbledon" or when her companions "are on their feet, applauding."[87] In a moment of frustration, Sophia decides to leave. Similar to her experience at the opera, Sophia is unable to interpret her surroundings enough to navigate the streets, which has the consequence that she is not able to find her hotel. She experiences slight relief when she stops at a McDonald's and finds comfort in the "universal" taste of the french fries.[88]

This is a subtle moment where Tiang also calls attention to the *reader's* inability to decode. While the story is sympathetic to Sophia, it also sets up a critique of her character because of her materialistic superficiality. One could imagine a reading that assumes the comfort that McDonald's offers Sophia as further evidence of her shallow cosmopolitanism, or even as evidence of her Americanization—after all, Sophia went to college in the United States. And though McDonald's is a well-known symbol of corporatization, it is also a nostalgic setting for a generation of Singaporeans that took advantage of the fast-food restaurant's tables and free air-conditioning as students. Even though everyone can communicate in English, no one can help Sophia find her hotel. She is panicked and with little hope when Nicholas appears out of nowhere. The story closes with the definite knowledge that "this time tomorrow they will be in Vienna."[89] As with the opera, Sophia's inability to navigate the Swiss setting is the failure of cosmopolitan knowledge. The main thing that Sophia can decipher is a corporate symbol of the global. But more than a critique of Sophia or her state-sponsored cosmopolitan education, Tiang points to the potential failure of a reader to comprehend McDonald's as a national symbol of home. One interpretation of "universal" taste can be read as the story's comment on how Sophia has conceded to the globalized power of McDonald's, as evidenced by the depiction of her shallow cosmopolitanism. Yet when Sophia marks fries as universal, she not only points to their global ubiquity; she also implies that fries are an experience she has had elsewhere. Given Sophia's worldly experiences, one can assume that she has eaten at McDonald's in many different countries. When also considering how Sophia is in a foreign country and her feelings of cultural alienation, we are to understand that the brief comfort she finds in the fries are somehow associated with the particularity of her home. Indeed, while wandering around lost, she makes clear that she desires the stability of being at home when she thinks that it is "as if she will never get back to the hotel, or Singapore, or anywhere that could be considered a place of safety."[90]

When assuming that McDonald's fries signifies a scale of identification operating outside of national particulars, readers are unable to fully grasp the depth of comfort Sophia finds in the throes of her panic. In this way, Tiang leads the reader toward an easy and potentially Eurocentric reading of McDonald's and then disabuses that reader by calling attention to the obfuscatory power of global signifiers when assuming neoliberalism or the United States as stable referents for the global. Ironically, if readers come to "Sophia's Honeymoon" for their own cosmopolitan education, one that is meant to train their imagination to make cross-cultural connections, we see how they can be limited in their education as Sophia is in hers.

If for "Singaporean Abroad" and "50 Red Dots," setting is the literary element through which to assert Singaporean, capitalist achievement, for Tiang setting is a way of imagining the full arc of state narratives that make a claim to Singapore's postcolonial capitalism. While it certainly leverages a broader political critique of Global Asia policies, *It Never Rains on National Day* also offers a formal critique: it repurposes the statist form of the demographic compilation to illustrate how state narratives are truncated. The remedy to the Singaporean state's instrumentalization of short literary forms is not the novelistic form or a clear narrative arc. Though there is an overarching logic in the arrangement of Tiang's stories, it is not one that is particularly obvious, nor is it progressive or linear. At times, some of the characters across stories appear to be the same ones, but we cannot always be sure. In one case, it is not initially clear whether the protagonist in the story is Singaporean, and we only figure out in a later story that he is. Thus, the population that

Tiang depicts in his story is one not simply defined by its status abroad or other demographic qualities, but by a readerly effort that draws connections between the various stories. Indeed, Tiang's collection calls for more accountability from the reader. Through the stories' arrangement, Tiang points to the claustrophobia induced by the Singaporean top-down model that shapes understandings of populations and instead advocates for a more organic connectivity that readers come to see on their own.

CONCLUSION

Despite their ideological differences, "Singaporean Abroad" and "50 Red Dots" perform an expanded Global Asia imagination for nationalist purposes through their representations of cosmopolitan populations and the non-Singapore world. In doing so, diasporic Singaporeans, a demographic figure with historical ties to colonial-era governance, are deployed as politicized cultural figures in service of Singapore's Global Asia project of postcolonial capitalism. We see how transnational identification does indeed complicate the "inside-outside dichotomy on which the nation-state is predicated," as Robert Young puts it, as the "cosmopolitan idea" represented by the non-Singapore world is deployed by and against the state to influence internal nationalist dynamics.[91] Tiang's short story "Sophia's Honeymoon" puts the cosmopolitan idea into question by calling attention to the politics of knowledge production and performance and thus displays the limits of postcolonial capitalism. My analysis of these texts problematizes the Singaporean state and its instrumentalist approach to the Singaporean diaspora for its economic ambitions. While such critiques of the state are fair, texts like "50 Red Dots" that in fact take up a cosmopolitan aesthetic and politics similar to that of the Singaporean state to perform a critical nationalism remind us not to reduce state power to only the repressive or disciplinary. Moreover, such a critique of state nationalism implicitly suggests that there is an authentic nationalism.

By way of closing, I turn now to the final story of Tiang's collection, "Sophia's Party," which is linked to the opening story. In spite of the state critique presented in "Sophia's Honeymoon," this second story performs a reparative reading of the Singaporean state by calling attention to the fiction of authentic nationalism that so often underlies critiques of state nationalism. "Sophia's Party" brings the elements of Singapore in Global Asia home, so to speak: in her flat in Singapore, Sophia is holding a gathering for her friends (many of them former Overseas Singaporeans) on the occasion of National Day, an event that "seems almost an anticlimax."[92] Sophia's Filipina domestic worker has been dismissed for the evening so that "the guests can be sure it was Sophia who cooked,"[93] underscoring how the national project of Global Asia is built on the erased labor of migrant workers. National Day presents a stark contrast to the occasion of "Sophia's Honeymoon," which is presented as the climactic point of Sophia and Nicholas's new marriage.[94]

Indeed, "Sophia's Party" acts as an inversion of "Sophia's Honeymoon": it is set at home rather than abroad, it is Sophia rather than Nicholas who shapes the power dynamic of the couple (in part because Nicholas has had heart surgery), and it is focalized through Nicholas rather than Sophia. Moreover, in this instance, Nicholas watches Sophia watch the National Day Parade, reversing how Sophia watched Nicholas watch the opera, and the story culminates in Nicholas's ruminations over the state of the marriage. All these elements make clear that "Sophia's Party" is to be read in relation to its opening counterpart. The final story is also understood as a cumulative point of the collection, not simply by virtue of being the concluding story, but because it brings together other Overseas Singaporean characters from other stories that have now returned. The final story connects the other characters from the seemingly unrelated stories in the collection through their friendship with Sophia.

Compared to the more tentative and vague description of the opera through Sophia's eyes, Nicholas's language in describing the parade appears precise despite his cultural outsider status; readers have a very clear idea of the scene that is unfolding. While Sophia was increasingly confused by not being able to follow the story of the opera, Nicholas *does* understand what is happening. Readers can thus comprehend what is happening by direct reference to what Nicholas is describing rather than having to triangulate meaning between Sophia and other characters as required in the opening story. Because Nicholas is presented as a sympathetic character to the reader by virtue of being the protagonist and having recently undergone a heart transplant, the narrative sets up Nicholas as reliable for his judgment. Although Nicholas's depiction of the parade might seem relatively objective because of its precision, the language reveals his judgment, whether when describing the "perfectly made-up face" of the host, Diana Ser, or when describing Singapore's multiculturalism as indicated by the "scrupulously diverse" performers.[95] That is, the National Day parade is overly curated and, therefore, inauthentic in the nationalist sentiment it represents. Nicholas's critiques are not unique but represent a familiar liberal disdain for military display or "the shameless manipulation of expertly-designed proselytizing."[96] Anyone with a healthy disdain for authority, the narrative suggests, should be skeptical like Nicholas.

Tiang's story does not contest that the National Day parade is an obvious attempt at ideological coercion, but it does call attention to the patriarchal and Eurocentric knowingness of Nicholas's various critiques. Nicholas finds himself bewildered by Sophia and her friends' lack of skepticism and indeed their earnestness in celebrating National Day, wondering why "Sophia, global traveller that she is, looks moved by the display" and why "the Singaporeans in this room [who] have spent a few years abroad" are so happy to consume state messaging.[97] Yet for all of Nicholas's cynicism—a sentiment that his readers might share—he admits that he finds aesthetic pleasure in the spectacle of National Day: "The camera picks out their firm arms, their rigid faces, and Nicholas feels his crisp European disdain of military matters melting around the edges. He thinks of himself as a pacifist, above the tinsel pomp of soldiers on parade, yet there is something seductively virile about these men in uniform, the regularity of them."[98] The passage suggests that the parade is so sublime that even the staunchest cynics give into the pleasures of the nation form. Moreover, it becomes clear that Nicholas's criticisms are to be problematized for their Eurocentricity, much in the way Tiang subtly problematizes a Eurocentric reading of McDonald's in "Sophia's Honeymoon." Nicholas's cynicism stands in contrast to Sophia and her friends' pleasure in each other's company and in the performance itself. When Sophia explains to Nick that her earnest engagement with the parade is "ironic," the story makes clear that she and her friends are not simply deluded nationalists. They are, in fact, quite clear-eyed about the ideological aims of the National Day parade. The story not only portrays Nicholas as unable to comprehend the fun Sophia and her friends are having with each other, but it also sets up critiques of state nationalism to ring hollow.

Moreover, "Sophia's Party" returns us to the original national tension between stayers and quitters discussed in the introduction to this book. While most of my readings have focused on the ways that diasporic Singaporeans are aestheticized through demographic compilations, Tiang's story draws attention to the ways that the stayers, as represented by the military, produce nostalgia as aesthetic pleasure for their viewers, the returned Singaporeans of "Sophia's Party," and even non-Singaporeans like Nicholas. National kinship in Tiang's formulation is about taking aesthetic pleasures in or with each other. In the final lines of "Sophia's Party," Nicholas finds himself cautiously hopeful about the state of his marriage, suggesting that the aesthetic pleasures of the parade, whether earnest or "ironic," are meaningful for the characters and not simply as an ideological force that stabilizes loyalty to the nation-state. Tiang's story thus compels us to consider how the state is not simply a sociopolitical administrative force but also an aesthetically mediating one that can produce unexpected effects.

3
―――

Coming-of-Career Narratives, the Postcolonial Work Ethic, and the Promise of a New Nation

At the opening of Isa Kamari's novel *The Tower* (2002), Hijaz invites the young clerk Ilham to join him on a strange quest to climb the stairs of the two hundred floors of the fictional 2000 Tower—Hijaz's architectural masterwork. Lured by Hijaz's promise to share his story, Ilham gratefully accepts the invitation, remarking, "I feel honored that you wish to share your story with me. For a long time I have been following your career."[1] As the two go on their journey, the story that Hijaz tells is not, as Ilham expects, about Hijaz's accomplishments in the architectural profession. Puzzled, Ilham comments, "From our conversations so far, you've emphasized life's questions more than your career," subtly illustrating how the career is assumed—and taken for granted—as the idealized mode of work.[2] For Ilham, "your story" and "your career" are interchangeable narratives. The novel draws a structural contrast between Hijaz's glamorous career trajectory, symbolized by the trek up the stairs, and his spiritual struggles living as a minoritized Malay Muslim man in Singapore, revealed in dream sequences and poetic interludes. While Isa's novel and oeuvre explore Islamic spiritual alienation in Singapore, the themes of *The Tower* asks readers to consider the problematic effects of making life legible through work and career success.

The Tower calls attention to the hegemony of what I describe as the coming-of-career narrative, a narrative form that literarily, ideologically, and thematically proliferated in the post-1997 Singapore literary and cultural imagination, as evidenced by the very range and number of texts in this chapter's archive.[3] Playing on the coming-of-age narrative, the coming-of-career narrative relates one's life story of personal growth as interchangeable with the story of work and career advancement. The focus on worklife in the coming-of-career narrative overlaps with the bildungsroman's traditional focus on middle-class socioeconomic development, particularly as it has been foregrounded in anglophone women's writing.[4] As Ilham's confusion in *The Tower* suggests, the logics of the coming-of-career narrative form are implicit in Singaporean discourse. Indeed, evidence of the narrative form can appear anywhere from state ephemera (see below), corporate-speak (job advertisements), and in casual conversation. Literarily, coming-of-career narratives build on a tradition in Singapore writing that uses work themes as a way of commenting on the socioeconomic changes that have accompanied the island nation's rapid modernization.[5]

Although coming-of-career narratives retain a focus on *Bildung*—variously defined as education, culture, formation, growth, or development, depending on its context—the subgenre distinguishes itself from the bildungsroman in a few crucial ways. Unlike the coming-of-age story, which focuses on the maturation process through a young person's move from childhood to adulthood in the context of the nation-state, in the coming-of-career narrative, the global, neoliberal economy dictates the processes that help form an ideal, mature, enterprising self. Work is the basis of maturity. For early German thinkers such as Schiller, Hegel, Goethe, and Humboldt, the links between the bildungsroman and the nation-state were explicit, because they theorized *Bildung* as the social processes of "self-cultivation" necessary to become a good citizen.[6] Whether the nation is an oppressive force or the structure in which individuals can realize their "self-culture," the bildungsroman has been regarded as insightful for comprehending the ideological workings of the modern nation-state. Notable too are the ways "social outsiders, primarily women or minority groups," have instrumentalized the genre to perform critiques of the nation-state.[7] Although often about protagonists who must adapt to rather than change society, the bildungsroman, as many scholars have shown, has been used to challenge societal structures because the nation is implicitly assumed to be the protagonist's main opponent. In the coming-of-career narrative, however, the "society" that shapes the protagonist's character is a *world* of many transnationally connected places, changing the terms by which we can understand the relation between determinative structure and the protagonist.[8]

The coming-of-career narrative's emergence in Singapore follows a broader trend in contemporary global anglophone literature that, as Kalyan Nadiminti observes, uses the developmental form of the bildungsroman to explore and critique the changing nature of work in the context of a neoliberalized, global economy.[9] Its proliferation in Singapore seems to further confirm Singapore's Global Asia status as a site that produces professionalized, corporate knowledge workers for the global economy and evidence of its exceptionality, especially when compared to other postcolonial economies in the region such as the Philippines that rely on, say, the feminized labor of domestic workers and their remittances. While certainly the coming-of-career narrative manifests the concerns of twenty-first-century work, my interest is in how this Global Asia genre grapples with, compensates for, and erases its own history of postcolonial capitalism.

While *The Tower* calls attention to the naturalization of coming-of-career logics in Singaporean culture, by describing his novel as part of his "reflections on Singapore at the turn of the century,"[10] Isa also situates the coming-of-career narrative in terms of economic transition—that of the 1997 Asian financial crisis—rather than, say, neoliberal ideology. At first glance, thematic emphases like capitalism as freedom, individualist enterprise, and citizens as consumers in coming-of-career narratives seem to evidence neoliberalism's ideological hold in Singapore through the influence of Western transnational corporations. Situating the narrative form in terms of economic transition, as Isa does, however, invites us to grapple with what precedes the form's emergence. And indeed, my analyses find the ideologically disparate, mixed-genre texts in this chapter consistently wrestling with the history of postcolonial capitalism through questions of work motivation, which leads me to investigate the nature of a postcolonial work ethic and its politicized logic. To think about a postcolonial work ethic, I argue, is to consider the pleasures of work and how such pleasures necessarily change over time. In the early history of Singapore, labor in the name of the developing nation helped spur decolonization movements, but the restructuring that took place under Global Asia means that nationally motivated work does not have the same force. Moreover, the Singaporean state's presence and governance are felt differently under Global Asia. To be clear, this is not an argument about whether the state plays a role in neoliberalism: it is now well established that despite neoliberalism's pro-market stance, state intervention is crucial for its functioning. But as I observe, there is a *seeming* retreat of the state in the texts under study. This paradoxical showiness of state retreat is itself a power move, one, I argue, that asks us to think about subject making at the institutional intersections of state and corporate entities rather than as the totalizing force of a singular institution.

Following a discussion of how work in postcolonial contexts has been understood as an aestheticized mode of protest against empire, I turn to Hwee Hwee Tan's *Mammon Inc.* (2001), a satirical novel critical of the state's cosmopolitan push following the 1997 Asian financial crisis. Tan's novel, which won the Singapore Literature Prize in 2004, has been taken as a contemporary text without much regard for Singapore's historical context or local politics because of its depiction of twenty-first-century, globalized, corporate work. But I show how even as it depicts the motivation and pleasures of neoliberalized labor, through subtle symbolic gestures, the novel portrays longer deleterious effects of governmental policies and campaigns that managed worker-citizens for a manufacturing economy in Singapore. While as a coming-of-career narrative, *Mammon Inc.* depicts how the pleasure of neoliberal labor unites employees with corporate management, my reading of the novel's climax illustrates that this pleasure does not operate in a historical vacuum. I show that comprehending the historical impact of Singapore's strong state on its citizen-workers is also at play in the self-pleasures of the coming-of-career narrative. The pleasure that the protagonist, Chiah Deng, takes in herself—as the site of her labor—is as shaped by neoliberal notions of human capital as it is by the postcolonial pleasures of agency.

While Tan's novel explores the politics of work motivation and pleasure as it relates to Singaporean subjectivity, *Conversations of Coming Home* (2012), a state promotional booklet that uses coming-of-career testimonies to recruit Singaporeans abroad to return, offers insight into the governing logics that *Mammon Inc.* sets out to critique.[11] *Mammon Inc.* teaches readers how the act of returning home to Singapore for family or sentimental reasons can be evocative of the Singaporean state's moralizing tendencies from the Asian Values era. Thus the challenge for *Conversations on Coming Home* is to present the act of returning to Singapore as part of a continuing developmental narrative, one in which "coming home" is not a neoliberal regression. As I show, *Conversations* attempts to recover transnational labor by reconstructing Singapore as both an imagined and a materialized setting operating in service of the coming-of-career narrative. I demonstrate how Singapore is presented as the ideal setting for a flourishing career in *Conversations* and further aligns returned Singaporeans with expatriates, revealing the logic of colonial social hierarchies at work in the cultivation of neoliberal ideology.

As a narrative form that values elite forms of work, the coming-of-career narrative is necessarily exclusionary. To understand how the values that undergird Singaporean coming-of-career narratives—namely, cosmopolitan, transnational mobility—play out among subjects that are brushed over in depictions of Singapore's Global Asia, I turn to *Ilo Ilo* (2013). Although Anthony Chen's award-winning feature film about a middle-class Singaporean Chinese family and their Filipina domestic worker has been heralded for its humanizing depiction of an Overseas Filipino Worker (OFW), my analysis focuses on the film's depiction of labor differentiation. While *Mammon Inc.* and *Conversations* depict Global Asia's obscuring of postcolonial state power, *Ilo Ilo* depicts how Global Asia's exceptionality is a mode of distancing and distinguishing itself from the Southeast Asian region. By announcing that it is not the Philippines, Singapore affirms its status as Global Asia. The racial and classed logics that undergird Singapore's dissociation from the Third World, as represented in the film by the Philippines, is where we again see Global Asia erasing a different marker of postcoloniality: that is, any inkling of Global South solidarity.

The chapter closes with brief readings of Troy Chin's graphic novel series, *The Resident Tourist*, which presents something of a post-career narrative, and a memoir/self-help book by the Filipina domestic worker turned corporate CEO Rebecca Bustamante, *Maid to Made* (2014). Chin's series explores what a Singaporean life narrative might look like when framed around the pleasures of "nothing," while Bustamante's memoir, on the other hand, invites questions about how Global Asia is ideologically reproduced outside of Singapore. Both texts provide insights for future critical directions.

POSTCOLONIAL CAPITALISM AND WORK

One of the earliest rallying cries to articulate work as a mode of liberation in Singapore came from Lee Kuan Yew in the context of its first independence from the British, when it was a part of the Federation of Malaya in 1957. Speaking then as secretary-general of the PAP, Lee declared:

> Merdeka is ours and with it the right to do what we will of our own country and our own lives. Let us all resolve to work hard together to build a happy and prosperous Malaya, to remove ignorance and poverty by education and production and to establish a more just social order where every man is judged on his merits and his contribution to society.[12]

Although Lee would not speak to Singapore as an independent nation-state until 1965, his address reflects a philosophy of work that would carry through to the years of Singapore's nation formation. *Merdeka*, the Indonesian-Malay word for "independence" and "freedom," was an important term during the pro-independence era and encapsulated an anticolonial sentiment that Lee situated in discourses of work. Working hard was to at once express *merdeka*, assert rights, and declare solidarity among fellow citizens. In Lee's logic, work is not taken as a political problem in and of itself. Work, to re-form Marx from *The German Ideology*, is posed as both the necessary and the inevitable postcolonial solution to the problem of colonialism.

Although the logics of the coming-of-career narrative appear so thoroughly neoliberal in terms of how it motivates work by encouraging subjects to think of themselves as human capital, the ideological effect it has in Singapore builds on a longer history of work under colonialism and postcolonial capitalism. To talk about a *postcolonial* work ethic, or the motivation and thus meaning assigned to work under capitalism in a postcolonial context, is to talk about labor's historical relationship to colonialism. For a number of historians of capitalism and postcolonial thinkers, colonialism is the violent, structural implementation of capitalism. As Frantz Fanon powerfully puts it, "Deportation, massacres, forced labor, and slavery were the primary methods used by capitalism to increase its gold and diamond reserves, and establish its wealth and power."[13] In other words, the history of colonialism is a history of exploited labor and what David Harvey describes as "accumulation by dispossession."[14] Thus when "postcolonial" is used to mark the aftermath of such a history, the notion of a postcolonial work ethic can appear, at one level, a politicized response to the violence of an extractive colonialism that took raw materials and labor.[15] Postcolonial work is no longer for empire's profit but for the now-independent nation. Working for the independent nation rather than colonial masters, in other words, makes the work ethic politically edifying. For the way that "postcolonial" suggests a response to or contending with the history of extractive capitalism—or at the very least, an acknowledgment of this history's legacy in the present—"postcolonial" is analogous to Rey Chow's theorization of "ethnic." "Postcolonial" too remarks on subjects "held captive in their specific histories" and "conceived of implicitly as proletarian, a resistant captive engaged in a struggle toward liberation."[16] Although Chow here is thinking about what notions of ethnicity mark *within* a nation, her language usefully captures the dynamic between a marginalized people and those in power. The notion of liberation especially resonates with early postcolonial nationalisms—as in the case of Lee's speech—that similarly situate work as a form of protest and as a form of redemption.[17] Fanon too captures the importance of work in decolonizing terms: "To work means to work towards the death of the colonist."[18] While here Fanon writes in the context of violence as a necessary mode of decolonization, like Lee, his use of "work" (*travailler*) frames an economic activity as political aspiration. In both Chow's and Fanon's thinking, in other words, postcolonial capitalist activity must be understood in relation to the history of colonial exploitation.

Despite the fact that the British Empire relied on the work of the colonies, the rejection of empire happens not through a rejection of work. The independent nation, as a structure of feeling, shaped the relationship individuals would have with capitalism.[19] Work was the mode through which to make the nation form whole, a solution through which decolonization was possible. Part of the motivation to work, then, was the moral imperative of national independence. The imagined collective experience of "work[ing] hard together" is the basis of a nation form appearing as a "project," as Balibar describes; work *forwards* the nationalist narrative away from its colonial past.[20] In this way, work was simultaneously politicized in its significance for postcolonial liberation and depoliticized insofar as it was not treated as a problem for the way work would entrench Singaporeans in a global system of capitalism. Lee's sentiments, as I later discuss, especially befit the manufacturing economy of Singapore's early years.[21] In the postcolonial context, in other words, what Chow describes as ethnic protest and ethnic redemption find their analogy in anticolonialism and national independence.

Articulating work as a nationalist response to the injuries of imperialism is problematic as it further entrenches capitalist labor as a pleasure principle. "Men and women, young and old, enthusiastically commit themselves to what amounts to forced labor and proclaim themselves slaves of the nation," Fanon wrote. "This spirit of self-sacrifice and devotion to the common interest fosters a reassuring national morale which restores man's confidence in the destiny of the world and disarms the most reticent of observers."[22] Despite the continuity of exploited labor, postcolonial work seems to heal the trauma of colonial labor exploitation. Developmentalism, as the prevailing economic ideology of the mid-twentieth century, would combine with the pleasures of postcolonial autonomy to provide further motivation to work. To quote Fanon again: "There is a widespread belief that the European nations have reached their present stage of development *as a result of their labors*. Let us prove therefore *to the world* and ourselves that we are capable of the same achievements."[23] Fanon here subtly points out that belief in the myth that work produces wealth obscures the history of colonialism that created the systematic foundations for continued Western capital accumulation even after the end of formal colonialism. Moreover, notions of economic development and underdevelopment are modes of thinking about historical difference and thus material wealth is necessarily tied up in the traumas of racial marginalization. Capitalist continuities between the colonial and postcolonial eras would be obscured by the promise of pleasure: the postcolonial pleasures of material compensation, hope, agency, satisfaction, and competence.

Fanon's emphasis on the *audience* for work, in addition to calling attention to the affective dimension of postcolonial work, shows how postcolonial work is highly aestheticized in a global context. While Fanon's comment about proving capability to "the world" indicates his awareness of the economic metrics used to evaluate the status of development in various nations, the idea that work can be "shown," or be looked at, suggests an aesthetic dimension to work that is also pleasurable. This is why, as Jini Kim Watson's theorization of the "new Asian city" illustrates, states of the so-called Asian Miracle nations were incredibly conscious of the aesthetic importance of performing their development through modern urban development. The idea of a global audience for work makes the postcolonial work ethic distinct from theorizations such as Max Weber's because rather than as an internal realization of spirituality or faith, the positive motivation to work is situated as partly external to the laboring body. Fanon's observations about the affective and aesthetic dimensions of a postcolonial work ethic provide the grounds for turning to literature.

Fanon's writing also makes clear the significance of the state for comprehending a postcolonial work ethic. While Fanon wrote of a particular concern he had of postcolonial nationalism going awry, he was also commenting on an emergent relationship between state and worker that was a global post–World War II phenomenon.[24] The way that the globalized, modern subjectivity of the citizen-worker combines with the imperative for Third World nations to develop is foundational to postcolonial capitalism. The highly entrenched sense of lag and desire to catch up would lead Kalyan Sanyal to describe postcolonial nation-states as "pre-committed to development."[25] Sandro Mezzadra points out that the citizen-worker form would facilitate the ideological depth of developmentalism by presenting "the generalization of wage labor as a condition for the full deployment of national citizenship (and therefore for the full achievement of sovereignty, which had fundamentally been at stake in anti-colonial struggles for independence)."[26] The citizen-worker subject, in other words, would yoke the affects of anticolonialism to a relation to the postcolonial nation-state by creating a nationalist system of valuing work.

Though, as Mezzadra reminds us, there is no single way of compelling labor, Fanon provides us the basic question we must ask of how a postcolonial work ethic is cultivated: How does the postcolonial state use colonial history and the idea of a global audience to compel labor from its subjects?

Given its ideological emphasis on individuality, such a question might seem irrelevant in the context of neoliberalism. Indeed, as Foucault explains, interventionist Keynesian policies, or the kind of policies that undergirded the developmental state nationalism of decolonization, was part of the "adversary and target of neoliberal thought, that which it was constructed against or which it opposed in order to form itself and develop."[27] Such ideological opposition is why the rise of neoliberalism is typically regarded as marking a historical break from forms of capitalism that preceded it. Moreover, as Foucault explains, neoliberalism as drawn from Theodore Schultz's and Gary Becker's respective works on human capital, brings in considerations of labor in distinctive ways.[28] Rather than quantify labor in terms of time or capital (i.e., classical economics) or understand the process of abstraction in the mechanics of capitalism (i.e., Marx), theories of human capital instead take on the perspective of the worker by asking, "What does working mean for the person who works? What system of choice and rationality does the activity of work conform to?"[29] Consequently, neoliberalism proclaims that "Homo economicus is an entrepreneur, an entrepreneur of himself[,] . . . being for himself his own capital, being for himself his own producer, being for himself the source of his earnings."[30] In other words, neoliberalism encourages an individual view of oneself as the capitalist enterprise against views that encourage a situated view of oneself as a figure of exchange within a broader capitalist system.

Though Foucault claims that neoliberal theories of human capital reflect "a complete change in the conception of this Homo economicus," many of its conceptual tenets are central to the experience of colonialism and, moreover, evident in the logic of colonial and postcolonial governance. For example, Foucault points to the eugenicist and natalist reasoning that shapes "the formation, growth, accumulation, and improvement of human capital."[31] Although Foucault sidesteps the racial underpinnings of such thinking—a seeming gesture to his awareness of the critiques of Schultz's ideas—in favor of familiar examples of human capital such as parenting, dwelling on examples from colonial history might have dampened Foucault's claims about neoliberal conceptions of human capital as "a complete change." As the narrator of Jamaica Kincaid's *A Small Place* wryly explains their resistance to capitalism, "Do you know why people like me are shy about being capitalists? Well, it's because we, for as long as we have known you, *were* capital, like bales of cotton and sacks of sugar."[32] While Kincaid is writing about the transatlantic slave trade and the Caribbean, she calls attention to a historical, postcolonial consciousness of being treated as human capital. In the British colonies of Southeast Asia, workers were racially hierarchized in terms of their ability to work, echoes of which resonate in Singapore's CMIO demography model and the phrase, "people are our only resource," so prevalent in Singapore state discourse. Such colonial histories have rightfully been critiqued for their dehumanizing effects, but less has been made of how such histories have produced enterprising, self-investing, postcolonial subjects who view themselves as capital because such subjects are so

often instead interpreted as the winners of neoliberalism. When Foucault discusses the role of mobility in the formation of human capital, it is again difficult
to not think of the ways that colonial and postcolonial subjects have moved to the
metropole using the very same calculations that Foucault describes: "Migration
is an investment; the migrant is an investor. He is an entrepreneur of himself who
incurs expenses by investing to obtain some kind of improvement. The mobility
of a population and its ability to make choices of mobility as investment choices
for improving income enable the phenomena of migration to be brought back
into economic analysis."[33] Indeed, such entrepreneurial postcolonial subjects and
self-investing migrants appear throughout contemporary and canonical postcolonial literature.[34]

   This is not an attempt to disprove Foucault but to bring in a more explicit
critical consideration of colonial and postcolonial histories of capitalism in the
production of neoliberal subjectivity. As I show, while the individualist pleasures
of the coming-of-career narrative may seem new and fitting for a neoliberalized
economy, it is a form that retains and renews a postcolonial work ethic. My readings illustrate how work motivation structured by the history of colonialism, postcolonial state power, and the global audience is still central to the Singaporean
coming-of-career narrative even as the narrative appears new and best suited for
neoliberalism. While newness has typically been associated with the aesthetic of
modernity, the novelty of the coming-of-career narrative remarks on the revi-
talization of work motivation and pleasure against a recent history of declining
work energy.

HISTORICIZING WORK IN SINGAPORE

For the way that it recalls the dynamics of early postcolonial capitalism in Singapore alongside its depiction of turn-of-the-twenty-first century corporate work,
Mammon Inc. provides a useful, generalizable historical frame for reading the various coming-of-career narratives in this chapter. *Mammon Inc.* is often described
as a lighthearted, humorous novel about the escapades of an upwardly mobile
cosmopolitan woman. Newly graduated, unemployed, and about to be deported
because of her expiring student visa, Chiah Deng begrudgingly agrees to interview with Mammon Inc., the largest corporation in the world. She applies for the
coveted position of "Adapter," in which she would help "the modern international
professional elite" gain social acceptance in the countries where they are posted.[35]
Readers follow the arc of Chiah Deng's foray into the "real world" after university
and her quest to pass the tests for the Adapter position despite her reservations
about pursuing a corporate career. Through the course of the tests and various
conflicts with friends and family, Chiah Deng comes to understand that the position would afford her and her family great financial benefits, and she agrees to take
the position at Mammon.

As a result of its multiple settings, *Mammon Inc.* has rightfully been situated in critical discussions of globalization and transnationalism, but such criticism has often focused on the global at the expense of the national. Reading *Mammon Inc.* biographically, Robbie B. H. Goh describes Tan as a "poster girl for the 'global' generation of Singapore writers" and suggests that as a result of her cosmopolitanism, Tan pays less attention to a Singaporean (i.e., national) sense of place compared to her local contemporaries.[36] Eddie Tay also frames the globality of Tan's novel in opposition to national context and argues that it reveals "that a subjectivity created via an appeal to national identification may no longer be a viable option within a paradigm of globalization."[37] In both examples, the global is an external structuring force that has the power to overwrite the significance of the nation. To a certain degree, this thesis might be true in terms of how much the novel's global status, as marked by its international publication, was grounds for its local celebration—an example of what Paul Nadal describes as "remittance fiction," or "a work produced abroad (as program fiction) and valorized at home (as national literature)."[38] The cosmopolitan nature and the appeal of Tan's novel on a global scale should not suggest, however, that the novel is not engaged with national particularities. To assume so can produce a false dichotomy of nation and globe and effectively dehistoricize and depoliticize the novel's global themes as they relate to specific material developments in Singapore.

In gesturing toward the work ideologies of Singapore's manufacturing economy while also portraying Singapore's engagement with neoliberal global capitalism, Tan's novel offers a number of clues that point to the longer history of postcolonial capitalism in Singapore. In the opening scene of *Mammon Inc.* Chiah Deng laments to her university roommate, Steve, "I feel like I don't fit in anywhere, like I can't connect. Like I'm a three-pin plug living in a two-pin world." Her revision of the idiomatic expression "a square peg in a round hole" indicates Chiah Deng's sense of alienation and confusion about her place in society in the twenty-first century, a time marked by the influence of electronic technology. Her language also reveals her cosmopolitanism. "Anywhere" for Chiah Deng is global in scope, as her knowledge of three-pin and two-pin plugs indicates. Indeed, as a Singaporean who has just completed a degree at the University of Oxford, Chiah Deng is keenly aware of the different cultural currents one experiences as one moves through the world without a proper connection.

Without consideration of the Singaporean state's overhaul of its manufacturing economy, Chiah Deng's plug metaphor appears to merely describe a globalized identity. Tay takes the plug metaphor as a comment on Chiah Deng's "transnational subjectivity that is, at the same time, transcendental" and states that the novel illustrates that it is difficult to "be a citizen of the world and at the same time remain loyal to local and specific national ties."[39] Such a reading can depict Chiah Deng's cosmopolitanism as unrooted while romanticizing it.

As a metaphor for her understanding of her place, or her lack of a place, in the world, Chiah Deng's plug takes on a different valence in an exchange with Draco Sidious, head of Mammon Inc. Explaining the tests that prove an applicant's aptitude as an Adapter, Draco Sidius hands Chiah Deng a plug: "We like to think of ourselves as being like a universal travel adapter. We enable our clients to go anywhere in the world, and plug into the power supply there." Slowly grasping the implications of Draco's explanation, Chiah Deng asks, "So you want me to become like a plug-and-play peripheral[,] . . . like one of those PCMCIA cards that you can just take out of the box and slot into any computer, anywhere?"[40] Mammon wants Chiah Deng to function as a connection between two-pin plugs and three-pin plug sockets and vice versa. Though the interchange may seem unremarkable because it is typical of the novel's humor, its language is also reminiscent of *Singapore 21*, a socioeconomic development report written in response to the 1997 Asian financial crisis, published two years before *Mammon Inc.*[41]

> The Singaporean of the 21st century is a cosmopolitan Singaporean, one who is familiar with global trends and lifestyles and feels comfortable working and living in Singapore as well as overseas. . . . They must be encouraged to explore foreign languages, literature, geography, history and cultures throughout their school years, so that they will grow up "*world ready*," able to *plug-and-play* with confidence in the global economy.[42]

Although Chiah Deng seems to use the meanings of "plug," the "PCMCIA card," and "plug-and-play peripheral" somewhat interchangeably, the metaphors point to different layers of the Adapter's work: the plug conceptualizes Chiah Deng as a conduit of power, the PCMCIA card as a conduit of information, and the plug-and-play peripheral as independently adapt*able* (i.e., hardware with software that is user-friendly and not in need of further user input). The plug metaphor and the PCMCIA card reference, moreover, dramatizes a changing global order, anticipating the Asian Century. The "two-pin world" references the United States, China, and many newly emergent Asian countries, and the "three-pin plug" references Chiah Deng's situation in the United Kingdom and Singapore's colonial heritage. The PCMCIA card also references the incredible success of Singaporean tech companies like Creative Technology, which needed to interface their products with many different international standards in the 1980s and 1990s. When taken together, the metaphors reveal the multifaceted significance of translators as intermediaries between changing interfaces of power, a hybrid role that has long, controversial roots in colonial history.

In the twenty-first-century context of global capitalism, Chiah Deng's job as a plug/Adapter also becomes a comment on immaterial labor. Noting the changes in economic paradigms over the history of capitalism, Michael Hardt writes that "providing services and manipulating information are at the heart of economic production."[43] Accordingly, Hardt argues, the nature of labor has changed and is

increasingly immaterial insofar as it is now a kind of labor "that produces an immaterial good, such as a service, knowledge, or communication."[44] Certainly, the very
notion of an Adapter, a consultant and assistant to the transnational elite, is exemplary of the immaterial labor that Hardt describes. But as the various referents
of the various plug metaphors suggest, the novel encourages a historical understanding of immaterial labor. As I later discuss, the novel depicts the pleasures
of immaterial labor not only as a comment on new economic paradigms but also
as an illustration of how such pleasures are a postcolonial, historical formation.[45]

The similarity of the language in Tan's novel and the *Singapore 21* report can be
read as an ironic relation that comports with the novel's broader efforts to satirize
and critique the Singaporean state. Even though I read the language of *Mammon
Inc.* as historically referential, slang and idiomatic language can easily be credited to the novel's globalized cultural milieu. Much like in the previous chapter's
example of Jeremy Tiang's writing, Tan deploys language that *seems* to evidence
the effects of global culture but is in fact historically resonant with Singaporean
policy and governance. The consistency with which a resonance occurs suggests
that *Mammon Inc.* is purposefully making a critique and calling attention to the
ways that Global Asia erases the history of postcolonial capitalism by misattribu-
tion. Thus, rather than read the novel's pop style and "mass-mediatized language
usage, one that reads easily, well and quickly, and is comfortable with the culture
industry,"[46] as evidence of Chiah Deng's or Tan's (Western) cultural literacy, I see
the language of *Mammon Inc.* as performing something beyond fluency: it is in
fact overwrought with pop culture allusions, caricaturing the Singaporean state's
ideal citizen as someone who is "familiar with global trends and lifestyles."[47] This
excess in language is akin to what Shashi R. Thandra describes as the postcolonial
aesthetic strategy of hyperbole, which ultimately has a critical function.[48] Read
this way, and as a reference to the *Singapore 21* report, the above exchange between
Chiah Deng and Draco Sidious repurposes the report's language. The report is
meant to be read as ambitious and perhaps even inspirational, but the grand-
sounding notion of "world ready" is ridiculed when Chiah Deng asks incredu-
lously if her job is to be the equivalent of a computer piece. While PCMCIA cards
were certainly crucial to computer connectivity in the early 2000s, Chiah Deng's
disbelief reveals the disjuncture between her perception of the Adapter's cosmopolitan glamour and Draco Sidious's unsentimental depiction of the Adapter's
instrumentality to power.

Chiah Deng's initial resistance to working at Mammon draws a throughline
between early and contemporary postcolonial capitalism in Singapore. Early in the
novel, she claims, "I didn't want to be a cog in some capitalist machine."[49] Within
the story world of *Mammon Inc.*, Chiah Deng balks at the idea of becoming a
corporate drone and attempts to resist Mammon's seemingly inescapable power
by refusing to become a mere function of a larger system. Again Chiah Deng's language, which could be simply interpreted as evidence of her trite or naive thinking,

FIGURE 4. A poster from the Productivity Movement, featuring Teamy the Bee / *"Bee" A Team,* ca. 1985. Poster from National Productivity Board campaign. Courtesy of National Archives of Singapore.

in fact points to the novel's broader political context, echoing some of the initial praise of *Singapore 21.* As a member of Parliament, Simon Tay, who commended the report, described some of the problematic economic rationalities of the manufacturing era as such: "In Singapore, we have been used to saying, 'People are our only resource.' This is an accepted truth. But part of the way this truth has been seen is that people become just a resource. That is to say, people become important only in so far as they give utility to the national good, the economic bottom line. . . . In this, there is a tendency to see people solely in an economic paradigm, as *cogs in a grand machine.*"[50] While Chiah Deng's sentiments might appear to register frustration with labor alienation and global capitalism as it is embodied by Mammon Inc., her invocation of "cogs in a machine" also captures a frustration that emerges from Singapore's economic history as it relates to work motivation issues from the manufacturing economy era.

When Singapore's economy was focused on industrial manufacturing, the government orchestrated a formal campaign known as the Productivity Movement, reflecting the kind of developmentalist-inspired work ethic that Fanon observed.[51] To promote Japanese management techniques and productivity concepts (e.g., teamwork, quality control circles), the state developed propaganda that included posters, television commercials with catchy jingles, a mascot known as "Teamy the Bee," pamphlets, and periodicals.[52] The Productivity Movement sought to equate "hard work" with what was known as "productivity will," or "the desire and drive to develop oneself for the growth of the company so that in turn, the individual will benefit from a stronger company and nation."[53] Work for transnational corporations was ultimately for the national good, and thus the government exhorted citizens to work endlessly, tirelessly, and precisely in its production of goods like hard disk drives and silicon computer chips. National Development Minister Teh Cheang Wan warned that Singapore would "stagnate and then fall behind if we do not increase productivity. And we, not being fortunate enough to be endowed with any natural resources, have nothing to fall back on."[54] Not simply relying on the liberation rhetoric, Teh emphasizes precarity by linking the nation's survival with its citizens' abilities to work productively. Arguably, the Singaporean state's emphasis on the nation's existential crisis is unique to the postcolonial world, reflecting the island nation's unusual path to independence. This period would also see a stronger celebration of urban modernity in political speeches—skyscrapers, Housing Development Board (HDB) complexes, subways—which would simultaneously function as an incentive to work hard as well as proof of the state's ability to effectively harness its citizens' hard work to create material rewards.

Rather than solely read the coming-of-career narrative in terms of its congruousness for the post-1997 knowledge economy, we might also read it as remedying the problems of living labor. Singaporean novels like *If We Dream Too Long* by Goh Poh Seng, set in 1960s Singapore, provide insights into the early labor history of postcolonial capitalism, a time when the state required workers for its industrialized manufacturing economy. The novel illustrates the disciplinary difficulties of managing what Marx described as living labor and, moreover, setting the conditions for the coming-of-career narrative to flourish. To put it a little differently: under contemporary postcolonial capitalism, during which the coming-of-career narrative emerges in Singapore, the nationalist state-driven developmentalism that Fanon speaks of does not quite have the same ideological hold on its subjects, though it will never completely disappear. The move from a developmentalist state-nationalist narrative to a coming-of-career narrative is not about the historical stages of capitalism but a comment on the vitalist nature of work itself.[55] For the protagonist of *Dream*, Kwang Meng, the industriousness of the manufacturing economy demanded of him resulted in a distinct lack of pleasure in work. This lack of pleasure would form the basis of the novel's critique: the industriousness advocated by the Singaporean state for the benefit of the corporation and thus the nation was not giving pleasurable meaning to work. While the colonial era work was exploitative, *Dream* suggests that the call to work by the postcolonial state is hollow because the work feels meaningless and boring. Certainly, as illustrated by Kwang Meng's petty attempts at resisting work, capital can neither discipline nor capture Kwang Meng's labor. This, combined with the novel's flat aesthetic, points to the diminishing motivational power of state-nationalist rhetoric. Singapore's urban developments, which were so often touted by the state as the gratifying achievement of hard work, provide no pleasure for Kwang Meng, who views their "seriality" with great apathy.[56] In other words, Kwang Meng's lack of pleasure in work is not only a comment on the industrial drudgery associated with a manufacturing economy but also a symptom of diminished energy that is inured to government appeals like the Productivity Movement and other gestures toward postcolonial independence.

Despite the exuberance of the Productivity Movement, state discourse of the time reflects an awareness of the problems of living labor and the difficulty of compelling work from Singapore's citizenry.[57] What Marx deemed the issue of living labor is what the Singaporean state deemed as the problems of "the individual" and their (Westernized) desires, problems that would become articulated as culturalist through emerging Asian Values discourse of the time.[58] Speaking then as a trade and industry minister, Goh Chok Tong affirmed that "workers are not mere cogs in the wheel of industry."[59] But as a speech by Acting Minister of Social Affairs Ahmad Mattar illustrates, the "cog effect" seemed part and parcel of the manufacturing economy.

> In this technological age, people are often seen as digits in the whole process of development. We are seen as factors of production and caught up in a whole social and economic process. . . . We are statistics for most purposes and except for some who make the public scene, the rest are just nameless and faceless. . . . People should be seen as individuals who have needs, feelings and emotions which have to be recognized. It is only when we show concern for people as people that we can hope to have a healthy population which can bring us to new heights in our nation-building. It is important that we nurture the healthy well-being of our people especially in a country such as ours where our only resource is human resource.[60]

Ahmad's worries about individuals and their emotional health stands out from the attitude of his colleagues, who typically foregrounded the needs of the nation and the corporation, with the individual mentioned as an afterthought. Despite Ahmad's more compassionate stance, his language comports with the economic bottom line: interest in the well-being of citizen-workers is ultimately in the interest of sustaining living labor. In fact, Ahmad's speech anticipates the kinds of twenty-first-century corporate management logics that would focus on employee happiness and well-being for the sake of better functioning in capitalist society.

Even as *Mammon Inc.* appears to engage the contemporary politics of Singapore's neoliberal milieu, Chiah Deng's use of the cliché "cog in a machine" to describe her resistance to corporate work invokes a longer history of state discourse on work. We will also see gestures to this history in the other coming-of-career texts I discuss later in this chapter. The pleasures that the Singapore coming-of-career narrative emphasizes respond to the problems of work motivation of the manufacturing economy. Certainly, the neoliberalized knowledge economy that Singapore transitioned to after the 1997 financial crisis emphasized new kinds of work and skills, namely, "social and intellectual capital," "innovation," and "creativity" for the purpose of providing highly specialized services to consumers and corporations rather than the ability to manufacture standard goods at large volumes.[61] In the transition to the knowledge economy, Prime Minister Goh appeared to promise new individualist pleasures for the Singaporean citizen-worker: "Individuals [would enjoy] satisfaction in being able to exercise innovation, [and] demonstrate initiative."[62] Moreover, the education reform aimed at the new work of the knowledge economy, Goh claimed, would allow an individual "the freedom to participate in improving his own life as well as his community and nation."[63] Although the novelty of such internal pleasures would seem to replace the inspiration of postcolonial independence, in view of the threat of declining modernity and the state mandate of productivity, such pleasures are, in fact, contending with the history of early postcolonial capitalism. In other words, the sort of individualist work pleasures that are typically read as neoliberal are also a corrective to the diminishing returns of developmentalism. In this way, the coming-of-career narrative has as strong a postcolonial gloss as a neoliberal one.

THE PLEASURES OF THE CAREER

Despite her previous reservations about corporate capitalism, Chiah Deng comes to accept the values of Mammon Inc. because she ultimately finds the labor rewarding. The reconciliation of Chiah Deng's values with Mammon's is true to the form of the bildungsroman narrative in that the protagonist reaches maturity the moment she is no longer in conflict with broader social structures, although in the bildungsroman the structure has typically been the nation, whereas in *Mammon Inc.* it is the transnational corporation. Chiah Deng's identification with Mammon Inc. illustrates what Colleen Lye via Kathi Weeks describes as a work ethic in which "employees' identification with management" remarks on the changing nature of post-Fordist work.[64] Because Mammon Inc. seems to have replaced the nation-state as the social structure shaping Chiah Deng's personality development, it is tempting to read Tan's novel as a commentary on a changed global political system in which the transnational corporation reigns. Indeed, depictions of the neoliberal era tend to characterize the transnational corporation as displacing the power of nation-state. Rather than the transnational corporation and the nation-state vying for ideological dominance, however, here the nation and the corporation operate in a symbiotic relationship. This relationship is most evident when we consider how the form of pleasure yokes the postcolonial with the neoliberal. Let us briefly turn to the passage in which this climactic moment unfolds.

For one of Mammon's tests, Chiah Deng must gain entrance into Utopia, an exclusive nightclub in New York City, ostensibly to prove her cosmopolitanism and ability to assimilate into unfamiliar situations. To prepare, Chiah Deng gives herself a complete makeover, going on an extreme diet and exercise program in order to lose weight and fit into an appropriate dress. After the final stage of her physical transformation, Chiah Deng looks in the mirror:

> For the first time in my life, when I looked into the mirror, my instant reaction was, "oh my God, I look so cool." I slid my hands down the sexy white-leather dress,

skin-tight against my finely honed body, which, for the first time in my life, bulged in all the right places. I never thought I could ever feel that way about myself . . . to be able to see myself and think—"Hello, cover girl. *Gen Vex* this month, *Vogue* the next."[65]

Here *Mammon Inc.* makes a powerful point about the pleasures of work. The satisfaction Chiah Deng experiences is in the product of herself as an aesthetic delight, as a commodity, and as her own person. In the critical vocabularies of the bildungsroman, one could describe the pleasure Chiah Deng takes in her person as a Lacanian moment of self-realization. This is certainly a valid reading, supported by Chiah Deng's repeated exclamations, "for the first time" and "I never thought," which both emphasize the internal experience of comprehension; the consolidation of the subject with social structure is an emotionally gratifying experience. The language of the passage, however, also points to Chiah Deng's tactile pleasure of what contains that pleasure: the bodily form of her self. While the bildungsroman emphasizes the *content* of the self through personality development and the internal voice made possible by the novelistic form, this scene reveals the significance of one's own *form* and one's externalized experience of it. In other words, if the climactic moment of the bildungsroman is the consolidation of the subject with broader social order of the nation, what we see in this scene is slightly different: the consolidation of the internal self with the external self, or the aesthetic experience of the self as subject and object.

The action and the setting of the scene, moreover, emphasizes how Chiah Deng's pleasure in her self (i.e., her body) is one that she experiences on her own (i.e, alone). The mirror, which conveys an external view of herself, and Chiah Deng's evaluation of her body as achieving gendered ("right places" to bulge) and racialized beauty standards (the white "skin" of the dress), suggests that the pleasure Chiah Deng takes in herself is, in part, determined by social norms. But the fact that this gaze is made possible by an object that Chiah Deng uses according to *her* needs, a mirror, foregrounds Chiah Deng's purposeful action. Chiah Deng deploys this social/external gaze in service of her own pleasure. She can see herself and enjoy herself in the way that an external audience does. The pleasure of the self is self-contained not just in terms of her body, but in terms of solitude: while alone, Chiah Deng finds emotional gratification from the development of her self-content, aesthetic enjoyment from her self-form, and scopophilic pleasure from the encounter with her self in the mirror.

On the one hand, we can read Chiah Deng's pleasure as a remark on the motivational power of the individualist ideologies so often espoused by neoliberalism, in this case by Mammon Inc. as the transnational corporation. As Chiah Deng's perception of her self-improvement deepens and her pleasure in herself grows with each passing test, Mammon Inc. is more effectively able to compel her labor because Chiah Deng becomes and sustains her own work motivation as a material object of pleasure. In this way, employee and management are united in their purpose. While it is true that Chiah Deng performs immaterial labor, it is hard to ignore how strongly the text emphasizes the gendered, material pleasure of her own body. Hardt explains that immaterial labor "results in no material and durable good,"[66] but the novel reveals that it is actually the producer of services that experiences the material good rather than the consumer of services. If under industrial or extractive capitalism material goods are typically understood within the purview of consumption, under informational and service capitalism, *Mammon Inc.* suggests, material goods have a labor function. Moreover, to use the parlance of neoliberalism, Chiah Deng's perception of her work as for herself can be described as that of individualism, or the orientation of labor, social actions, and behavior to the benefit of the individual rather than the community. The power of self-pleasure is abundantly evident in *Mammon Inc.* when she admits, "For the first time in my life, I had to admit that the bad guys were right all along. Mammon Inc. was right and I was wrong—money can make you into the person you've always dreamed of becoming."[67] The pleasures that Chiah Deng experiences and is able to generate for herself act as a positive feedback loop, which in turn distracts her from the effects of capitalist violence because Mammon Inc. appears as a catalyst for a better self.

On the other hand, the solitude of the mirror scene indicates a different kind of postcolonial pleasure that emerges from the feeling of agency, or the capacity to exercise free will. As Fanon points out in his critique of nationalized labor, the feeling and pleasure of agency—in his example, agency from colonial exploitation as articulated through nationalism—catalyzed capitalist developmentalism. The pleasure that Chiah Deng experiences in the mirror scene is formally akin to what Fanon describes, except that the structure in question is the nation-state. When we recall, as Tina Chen writes, that "agency is often paired with another term— 'structure'—the two understood as making up the dynamic between the choices and creative actions of individuals and the social, political, and economic structures within which they operate," we must then consider the ways Chiah Deng experiences the "feeling of structure" in the lead-up to the mirror scene.[68] In the rising action of Tan's novel, Chiah Deng experiences internal conflict about working at a "capitalist machine" that would enable her to support her family financially.[69] As Chiah Deng contends with the pressure to take care of her parents as they age ("You need to make a lot of money to give us, so Buddha will see that you're very filial," her sister Chiah Chen tells her), particularly as her father is suffering from worsening night blindness,[70] the feeling of structure that emerges in this moment is the institution of the nuclear family. Family is deeply imbricated in the national project, as the family is the site of what Teo Youyenn describes as "neoliberal morality" in Singapore, or "a set of institutionalized *relationships* and ethical *meanings* that link citizens to each other and to the state . . . [and] render the paradoxes embedded within state pursuits of neoliberalism inevitable, natural, and indeed *good*."[71] *Mammon Inc.* provides a slightly different and historical gloss on the notion of what exactly feels good about neoliberalism, however. As Chiah Cheng centers her family as the reason to pursue a career at Mammon, we see at play the neoliberal morality that Teo theorizes. But ultimately, this does not make Chiah Deng feel good, though in theory it is supposed to. Instead, she feels instrumentalized by her family since her labor is ultimately for *their* pleasure and the determinative force of structure is felt through her sense of obligation. Chiah Deng's family dynamics also invoke Singapore's Asian Values era, and Tan satirizes this history of exploiting traditional affects in service of its capitalist agenda through Chiah Chen's mixing of traditions (Buddhism is not known to espouse materialism; filial piety is a value more associated with Confucianism). Thus even as Chiah Deng registers obligation through the family, she feels the structure of the nation-state.

The mirror scene calls attention to how the self-form is central to the workings of individualism and agency, thus asking readers to consider the continuities between neoliberal and postcolonial work ethics. That we can read Chiah Deng's pleasure in her self as either indicative of neoliberalism's ideological hold or as her resistance to state-driven postcolonial capitalism more broadly illustrates how states and corporations operate in concert to compel labor from their subjects: in this case, neoliberalism offers a kind of pleasure in work that postcolonial subjects desire. Rather than read transnational corporations and nation-states as competing institutions, *Mammon Inc.* asks us to think through the intersection of their power. When Prime Minister Goh advocated educational reform that would promote the basic tenets of neoliberalism, this was not a concession of state power but a way of further obscuring it through the ruse of the global economy. The seeming erasure of the Singapore nation-state is evidenced in readings of *Mammon Inc.* that have tended to treat the "global" as an external structuring force that has overwritten the significance of the nation-state. *Mammon Inc.* illustrates the relative illegibility of state power and warns us to resist the critical desire to read capitalist power as emanating from a single sociopolitical structure or distinct historical period.

CAREER EMPLOTMENT
AND TRANSNATIONAL CAPTURE

While the temporality of the postcolonial nation has typically been discussed in terms of the colonial teleology of historicism or in terms of nationalism, *Conversations on Coming Home* reveals something quite different in the way it emplots Singapore as the career telos for the returning Singaporean's coming-of-career narrative. Emplotment—or the parsing of time into events and arranging them into a plot—is central for comprehending postcolonial critiques of developmental logics.[72] In the self-centric coming-of-career narrative, emplotment is conditioned by notions of life progression and conventional ideas about age identity. This is not to suggest that there are not broader determinative powers at work in career emplotment, but because the teleological workings of the coming-of-career narrative are premised on self-improvement—rather than national improvement or colonial superiority—structure recedes into the background.

The novelistic form of *Mammon Inc.* is especially useful for comprehending how emplotment constructs the career as life telos by illustrating how youth is a transient time of economic impossibility and impractical idealism.[73] The novel depicts youth as a life stage filled with pleasure and lack of (financial) responsibility. Youth and immaturity are made legible in the portrayal of Chiah Deng's and Steve's student life as fun and carefree or, as Chiah Deng puts it, "the perfect slacker lifestyle."[74] Chiah Deng muses over the things she would miss about her student life in England if she were to move back to Singapore for work:

> If I left England, there would be no more sleeping in on Bank Holidays, waking up just in time for the mandatory mid-afternoon Bond movie on telly. No more Saturday afternoons at the launderette, listening to the cricket on Radio 4 on our portable radio and fighting over who gets to read the TV Guide in the *Guardian* first. No more eating strawberries at Wimbledon, swept up in Henmania; no more intellectual slumming, nursing pints of Boddingtons while deconstructing Indiana Jones with reference to James Frazer's *Golden Bough*.[75]

As Chiah Deng performs her fluency with British contemporary culture, the passage portrays her student life as filled with entertainment and instant gratification. The repetition of "no more" indicates that life in the impending real world lacks pleasure. Also symbolically apt is how Chiah Deng says she will no longer be able to sleep in on bank holidays because her post-schooling life requires that she engage with the real world of global capitalism. This framing of youth as an inadequacy and as a finite surmountable *event*, rather than structuring ideology, makes it possible for the career to loom large as the inevitable solution and "coming." While the portrayal of youth as deficient has been a useful strategy of dismissal for justifying control, Tan's novel illustrates how the desire to transform oneself into a globally, economically viable subject is rooted in social constructions of age. The significance of a career is built on anxieties of economic survival and the pleasure principle of life progression. The ties forged between career advancement and life maturity are key for the coming-of-career narrative to appear and feel meaningful and essential for concealing broader structural forces like the nation or for justifying them, as in the case of Mammon.

The ideological work of career emplotment is especially evident in *Conversations on Coming Home*, a booklet I encountered while at Singapore Day 2012 in New York City.[76] As evidenced by the glossy booklet's length of fifty pages on heavy-stock paper, professional color printing, and sleek graphic design, no expense was spared in its production. If one were to construct a sense of the diasporic Singaporean demographic from *Conversations*, one would likely assume Overseas Singaporeans are predominantly Chinese. Functioning as a table of contents, the opening pages of the booklet feature a series of individual photos of the

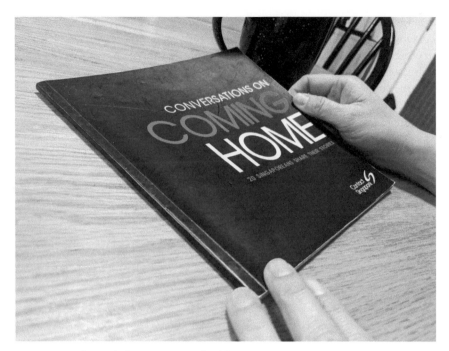

FIGURE 5. Author with the *Conversations* booklet.

returning, Chinese-passing Singaporeans. Although the names do not reveal those with mixed-race backgrounds, it is notable that none of the Singaporeans in the booklet have Malay or South Asian names—the major non-Chinese ethnic groups in Singapore. Underneath each photo we find the person's name, the company they work for, and where they lived before moving back to Singapore. As company names such as Goldman Sachs, Accenture, and Mitsubishi connote, these Singaporeans are highly skilled professionals. The booklet spotlights engineers, researchers, business managers, and legal interns, in addition to bankers. Overseas Singaporeans, according to this booklet, are synonymous with what Leslie Sklair describes as the "transnational capitalist class," or a global elite composed of corporate managers and professionals.[77]

The state's sinocentric racialization of coming-of-career narratives adds to the text's differential function.[78] Already coming-of-career narratives are selective by virtue of their limited articulation with professionalized work. Though the depiction of Overseas Singaporeans as primarily Chinese is likely true since Chinese constitute the largest demographic in Singapore and overall are in the best economic position to become professional, mobile, and cosmopolitan, *Conversations* is distinct from conventional state representations of Singaporeans. It is more typical to see representations of Singapore as a racially and ethnically diverse society.

Conversations thus invites questions of how and when the state deploys multiracial and multicultural inclusivity and why Overseas Singaporeans are, in this instance, represented as racially homogeneous. Certainly, the answer might simply be that the state has a clear preference for the kinds of Singaporeans they would like to return. But when considering how conscious the state tends to be about its global image and how *Conversations* is a text that circulated globally through Contact Singapore's programming and website,[79] the racialization of coming-of-career narratives, I would hypothesize, also serves a broader function of distinguishing Singapore's workers from others in the region, a point I discuss further in the next section. Indeed, the state's use of the coming-of-career narrative is one of the ways that it inscribes "First World" on its citizen-workers, which differentiates them from other modes of postcolonial labor and transnational mobility in the region, such as the Philippines, which bases its economy on feminized labor and remittance. In this way, *Conversations* reflects a state awareness that not all globalized forms of labor are equal.

By presenting the Overseas Singaporean as a classed and racial identity, the state is effectively generating the semiotic terms through which to understand Singapore as distinct from the rest of Southeast Asia (racially imagined as brown) and more firmly attaching itself to East Asia. When further considering how the Overseas Singaporean is subtly presented as a linguistic identity, or at least an identity with linguistic capability, Overseas Singaporeans are presented as distinct from other East Asians because they are anglophone educated. The cultural work of distinguishing Overseas Singaporeans thus feeds into the Singaporean state's broader goal of presenting Global Asia as an advanced stage of capitalist development, one that presents Singapore as having overcome its Third World roots of underdevelopment. In other words, the politics of representation in *Conversations* reflects the state's navigation of the racial politics of development on a global stage.

Much like the demographic compilations discussed in the previous chapter, the layout of *Conversations* follows a standardized format, and its repetition gives the impression that such Singaporeans returning home are a noteworthy population. Every profile is a double-page feature with one full-page colored photo and a second page dedicated to the story of the featured subject's decision to return. Each of the photos features a professionally dressed individual looking away from the camera against either a background that showcases Singapore's modern architecture or a "natural" landscape, denoted by trees. Not only does business clothing emphasize professional status; many of the returning Singaporeans are holding an iPad, a smartphone, a tablet computer, or a book. The presence of these commodities marks the subjects as modern, educated, sophisticated, in some cases technologically savvy, and thus embedded in a capitalist economy.

The coming-of-career narratives of these profiles are simultaneously stories of diasporic return, combining tropes of career ascendance with those of travel writing. However, the story arcs of these two narrative types are somewhat at odds.

In travel writing, the climax of self-realization typically happens during one's travels as a result of the protagonist's encounters with difference abroad. While the Singaporean state finds economic value in a cosmopolitan citizenry, so long as it wants to draw Singaporeans back home, it cannot present overseas experience as the climax of their citizens' lives. To do so would mean that the diasporic Singaporean's return home would run counter to the developmental logics of the coming-of-career narrative or appear as rather inglorious, particularly since the postcolonial home has historically been regarded as inferior with respect to the colonial metropole.

One of the ways that the booklet mitigates the return's connotation of regression is by choosing profiles that emplot overseas experience as an event in an individual's youth rather than as an identity like "Overseas Singaporean." In some of the profiles, the overseas sojourn is overtly portrayed as a youthful endeavor. The opening profile of the booklet, for example, reads:

> Debra Ma absolutely enjoyed her graduate school days at Boston University where she received an MBA in Finance and Strategy. She was inspired by the exchange of ideas within the diverse global student population. . . . Back in Singapore she is inspired in a different way—by exciting new architecture, fascinating heritage conservation and an equally international make up in her home city.[80]

Though seeking an MBA does not have the same connotations of youth in the way that pursuing an undergraduate degree does, the bio underscores youth through notions of fun ("absolutely enjoyed") and personal growth ("inspired"). Perhaps because of the booklet's rhetorical context, the description makes sure to convey that Ma's time abroad was temporally circumscribed but purposeful because she attained an advanced degree in a field that firmly connects her to the global economy.

In other profiles, the connotation of overseas experience as youthful is the result of the return to Singapore appearing as the "mature" event because of responsibilities for aging family members. Eileen Wong explains that her return was "propelled by the frustration I felt when my father fell ill and I was not there to support him in seeking the best medical care," and Alice Lim echoes the concerns about "parents who are getting older and whose health conditions are not ideal."[81] Such comments about family responsibility dovetail with ones that portray family as stable and territorially entrenched. For example, Lin Yan explains, "My family is here and I grew up here," language echoed by Dr. Vrizlynn Thing, who explains her decision to return to Singapore was because "my family is here."[82] Taken together, family emerges as the stable, durable referent that is in contrast to the transitory, temporally circumscribed experience of being overseas. Framing the overseas experience as an event rather than a defining characteristic, transforms overseas experience into the rising action of the Singaporean's career trajectory.

Though typically the protagonists of travel narratives experience self-realization as a result of their encounters with difference and newness, *Conversations* stresses that the newness is found at home, as evidenced by the constant praise of various urban, tourist, and recreational developments. While the developmental narrative of *Mammon Inc.* casts newness in terms of plot, *Conversations* presents its setting in a continuous state of newness. This is quite a departure from the generic conventions of the bildungsroman, which usually presents national setting as an unforgiving and immovable structural force as typified by the "individual versus society" formulation. By contrast, we see in Ma's profile, for example, that her continuing development not only relies on the temporal distinction of the present from her youth but also on Singapore's spatial distinction from its past in new urban developments. Singapore, with its "new architecture" and its increasing "international makeup" made possible by liberal immigration policies to attract so-called foreign talent, offers a distinct experience from what Ma remembers. Newness is even signaled through Ma's reference to "heritage conservation." Though "heritage conservation" would seem to be about the preservation of history and therefore not a novel experience, Ma is alluding to state initiatives to gentrify ethnic neighborhoods for tourism, thus transforming once-familiar sites into something new and different for the returned Singaporean. Indeed, throughout *Conversations* the returned Singaporeans extol the new Singapore they encounter. Chan Yan Neng comments, "Singapore's physical landscape has transformed and there are many new buildings and outdoor spaces. On weekends, I enjoy exploring the countless walking and cycling trails around the city and discovering new independent shops and cafes. I don't remember there being so much to do before!"[83] Wong Kit Yeng also commends Singapore for its new sites: "I like the new park developments such as Henderson Waves, the bridge that leads to Mount Faber. . . . I plan to visit the New ArtScience Museum as well, but have not had the time."[84] Ironically, as they reassure their readers of the unknown side of Singapore, Chan's and Wong's statements reveal a kind of pleasure more typical of colonial-era travel narratives—that of the undiscovered.

The simultaneous imagining of Singapore as new and as home in *Conversations* is where we can locate how the state is using tourist developments to reconfigure the role of the nation under Global Asia. Unlike in previous formulations, where state rhetoric would deploy the nation as a galvanizing political force or represent the nation as a site of state management (with all its disciplinary or authoritarian connotations), *Conversations* instead presents Singapore as the setting in which the climax of the coming-of-career narrative can unfold. While the notion of home retains sentimental value through family ties and cultural traditions in *Conversations*, its rootedness in the diasporic Singaporean's past is augmented by perceptions of newness. Newness is enabled by perspective gained by time away and then amplified by the new infrastructural developments of the island nation. But unlike the infrastructural developments of decolonization that Jini Kim Watson examines, newness is signified in *Conversations* through tourist attractions. Rather than present localized infrastructure such as housing, community centers, and neighborhood shopping centers, *Conversations* suggests an architectural performance that emphasizes personal pleasure rather than the national project of urban modernity. In chapter 4, I discuss how the politics of pleasure are central to the imagining of Singapore as contemporary and opposed to the nation as "lackluster" and "sterile" and in the broader context of orientalism. In this context of compelling labor from its citizen-workers, however, the booklet appeals to a classed preference for activities amenable to notions of work-life balance: outdoor recreation, cultural excursions, social interaction with new people. There are no depictions, in other words, of the Singapore "heartland," the residential estates in which the majority of Singaporeans live. By emphasizing the pleasures and the career opportunities that Singapore has to offer, the state reassures its subjects that they are not returning to a tiresome context where productivity must be maximized for the good of the country. Instead, Singapore will serve the pleasure of the self.

In fact, even though *Conversations* serves as state messaging to Singaporeans abroad, it is striking how muted the state presence is in the text whether by lack of reference to policies or governance or lack of economic nationalist rhetoric whereby returned Singaporeans portray their recently acquired skills or labor as a contribution for the nation. The foreword by Ng Siew Kiang, executive director of Contact Singapore, is devoted primarily to the agency's role in resettling returned Singaporeans using language like that of a CEO of a headhunting firm rather than a government bureaucrat. At best, Chan Yan Neng's profile mentions that "sociopolitical conversation . . . has become very lively with more people voicing their opinions through new channels for public debate."[85] The most direct comment on governance, in other words, is one that reassures readers about its lack of an oppressive presence.

This deliberate obfuscation in a state text indicates a changed dynamic, one in which the state's relationship to its subject is less direct and is rerouted through, in this case, the transnational, neoliberal corporation. The coming-of-career narrative, with all its presentist emphasis on self-making and self-pleasure that enables employee identification with corporate management, is a mode of concealing the state's past demands of endless productivity. *Conversations* presents the nation as a setting for work pleasure and as an atmosphere in which the ideal self can be realized. This text demonstrates how the Singaporean nation—as Global Asia—becomes a propulsive form in the background of the subject, symbolizing a potentiality that is apt to the coming-of-career narrative. The Singapore of early postcolonial capitalism, in contrast, shaped its subjects through containment aimed at galvanizing its subjects into the sociopolitical project of economic development. In other words, the nation of contemporary postcolonial capitalism is a space detached from the state that plays favorably to those performing certain kinds of labor.

Moreover, the particular kind of appeal being made to returned Singaporeans in *Conversations* is one that takes advantage of a postcolonial inferiority complex and citizen anxieties over Singapore's history of disciplinary governance. There have been long-standing local criticisms of how the state has oriented its governance to suit the needs of expatriates ("foreign talent," in government parlance) at the expense of its own citizens. But *Conversations* seems to promise returned Singaporeans that they can behave like foreigners and relish the kinds of pleasures typically afforded to expatriates and tourists, including more distance from the state.[86] *Conversations* appeals to the postcolonial subject's subordinate sense of being that has been further entrenched by the Singaporean state's treatment of expatriates and tourists. If the state's promise of the manufacturing era to hardworking Singaporeans was the reward of modernity, the knowledge economy promises the reward of foreigner privilege to cosmopolitan, professionalized Singaporeans.

THE DIFFERENTIAL POLITICS
OF COMING-OF-CAREER NARRATIVES

"A Worker's Journey," a poem originally written in Bengali by Sharif (Shromiker Pothchola) that was shortlisted for the Migrant Worker Poetry Competition in 2014, turns us back to the themes of the drudgery of work and cultural alienation that appeared in *If We Dream Too Long*.[87] "Journey," like "career," denotes a sense of traveling a long distance. But there is hardly any sense of progress or fulfillment in the worker's journey depicted in Sharif's poem. The speaker's desire in the first stanza "for a break in the rhythm" conveys how the worker's journey is endless and unchanging. In further contrast to the slow pacing of *Dream*, the repetition of the line, "I have to run, keep running," emphasizes the obligatory, physical nature of migrant labor. While "run" can denote the speed of movement, it can also refer to the state of being operational—a machine that is on—emphasizing how migrant workers are viewed as without human dignity. Beyond the assumed need for the money that comes with work, the specific obligation marked by "have to" is unclear in the poem, adding to a sense of purposelessness and drudgery. As the last lines of the poem underscore the speaker's sense of alienation ("At times I belong to this country / At times to that"), the final line ("I run, I have to run") shifts the obligatory meaning of "have to" to convey urgency and of "run" to mean "escape." Singapore, in this instance, is not the exuberant Global Asia where professional careers flourish but a "hellpit" for the migrant worker–speaker.

"A Worker's Journey" and the other submissions to the Migrant Worker Poetry Competition serve as an important reminder that accompanying Singapore's shift to a knowledge economy and its concomitant upward economic trajectory is the greater reliance on migrant labor to build the country's gleaming infrastructure. The underbelly of the Singaporean state's valorization of professionalized labor through coming-of-career narratives, and what is completely left out of

FIGURE 6. An *Ilo Ilo* poster from the Cannes Film Festival. Fisheye Pictures / Photo 12 / Alamy Stock Photo.

Conversations is the low-paying service sector and construction jobs—"unskilled labor," in other words—without which the state's drive to advance its knowledge economy would not be possible. In *Mammon Inc.*, Singapore's exploitation of unskilled labor is critiqued by Chiah Deng's roommate, Steve, in not very subtle terms: "Your whole economy is built upon the exploitation of the proletariat, and if there's justice in the world, the maids should start a revolution."[88] Although the state relies heavily on such migrant labor to build Singapore's infrastructure, run its service industries, and maintain Singaporean households, such workers are rarely depicted as desirable citizens or residents. Singapore has adopted laws designed to prevent "unskilled labor" from permanent residence, as well as measures that prevent their "mixing" with Singaporeans.[89] The pathways to residency and citizenships for such workers are limited at best, further illustrating the state's privileging of professional-technical labor as well as its efforts to denigrate the forms of labor—domestic or construction workers, for example—that maintain the country's infrastructure or ensure the efficient workings of middle-class and above households.

To further explore what *Conversations* leaves out and what *Mammon* gestures toward, I turn to Anthony Chen's *Ilo Ilo* (2013), a feature film about a middle-class Singaporean Chinese family and the relationship to their domestic worker. Set in Singapore in the aftermath of the 1997 Asian financial crisis, *Ilo Ilo* tells the story of the Lim family who decides to hire a Filipina domestic worker, Terry, to take care of their home and the son, Jiale, while the pregnant mother, Hwee Leng, and the father, Teck, are at work. Terry is at first treated very poorly by Jiale, a maladjusted ten-year-old and troublemaker at school. Eventually, Jiale takes to Terry and looks to her as a mother figure, and Hwee becomes increasingly jealous of Jiale's obvious affection for Terry. Because of the film's focus on the Lim's family relationship with Terry, *Ilo Ilo* is seen as exploring the ethical quandaries of how Singapore's economy relies on "unskilled labor" to sustain itself. Indeed, the Mandarin title of the film—"爸媽不在家" or "Father and Mother Not at Home"—poses the film as a family drama, lamenting the disintegration of the nuclear family, on the one hand, and honoring the new family intimacies that emerge with migrant labor, on the other. By making Terry an important figure within Singaporean domestic life, *Ilo Ilo* goes against the grain of typical, deprecating renderings of domestic workers in public discourse. As with the works showcased by the Migrant Worker Poetry Competition, *Ilo Ilo* critiques Singaporean labor practices and their attendant discourses that both minimize the importance of migrant work in Singapore and produce dehumanizing characterizations of such work. As Singapore has come under increasing fire for labor laws that enable abusive practices toward domestic workers, the film's humanization of domestic workers is no small matter and is particularly revealing of, as Joanne Leow puts it, how Singapore's neoliberal morality "is predicated on the exclusion and subservient status of migrant workers since it is a morality that is certainly not concerned for their well-being."[90]

While *Ilo Ilo* is not a coming-of-career narrative, it takes place in the aftermath of the 1997 Asian financial crisis and shows a strong awareness of the changing nature of work in Singapore during this economic transition. Rather than stage the oppressive power between, say, a professionalized worker and their domestic worker, *Ilo Ilo* depicts the ideological effects of valorized, neoliberalized work within the dynamics of *unvalorized* labor, which in this case also includes the middle-class Lim family. In other words, *Ilo Ilo* thinks through the in-betweenness of classed and migrant categories. Moreover, as the "English" translation of the film's title indicates—that is, *Ilo Ilo* rather than "Father and Mother Not at Home"—the film puts a regional frame on its depiction of work and highlights the politics of transnational mobility. As Alden Sajor Marte-Wood writes, "Destinations receiving Philippine labor—like Bahrain, Hong Kong, Singapore, and Saudi Arabia—become inextricably linked to the Philippines," and *Ilo Ilo* provides insight into the nature of those transnational intimacies.[91] To be clear, "Iloilo" is not itself an English word but is actually the name of a city in the Philippines. It is also the title used for English-speaking audiences. As a "strategically located" city that is "the center of commerce, trade, [and] finance" with "competent human resources" and a good "investment climate," Iloilo city has much in common with Singapore in terms of how it is represented as a Global Asia site.[92] Through the similarities in the economic trajectories of Singapore and Iloilo, Chen's film draws attention to the 1997 Asian financial crisis as a pivotal moment in differentiating transnational labor and the impossibility of political solidarity in the Southeast Asian region, a point that can get lost in the sometimes sentimentalist humanizing focus on the film and migrant workers more broadly.[93] *Ilo Ilo* gets at the implications of Foucault's claim about mobility as the necessary human capital investment by elaborating the social effects of only valorizing certain kinds of transnational mobility. In particular, Chen's film depicts the ways that domestic worker transnational mobility disrupts the power that nationally embedded middle-class Chinese families accrued during Singapore's manufacturing era and who now do not have the same ability to navigate a global economy. Mobility thus emerges as an organizing principle of social relations.

From its opening, *Ilo Ilo* presents domestic worker subjectivity in terms of mobility and immobility. Right before a scene when Terry emerges from a car at her new home, the film gives a brief shot of the windows of the home, an HDB building.[94] The camera pauses at the window of the HDB flat, showing a maid standing with her arms over a ledge and gazing wistfully into the distance. Her body language recalls that of a prisoner with her arms through a jail's bars. Later scenes repeat such imagery: in exchanges with a domestic worker next door, Terry's neighbor only appears behind the bars of her front door. The window shot then foreshadows a prominent theme throughout the film: by virtue of their occupation, domestic workers are immobilized, even imprisoned. In Singapore, where employers have to give maids just one day off a month, the employer's home as a prison is hardly metaphorical. The theme of immobility continues as Terry settles in with the Lim family: Hwee asks for Terry's passport under the guise of safekeeping, but in fact Hwee wants to prevent Terry from running away. While this is an ominous symbol of the curtailment of Terry's mobility, the passport also marks Terry's traversal of space. Moreover, the passport stands as a contrast to the highly localized space of the HDB flat that the Lim family lives in. Showing Terry around the flat, Hwee mentions that their phone cannot make international calls, so Terry must use a calling card and the pay phone downstairs to call the Philippines. The Lims' flat, in other words, has no transnational connections. In fact, *Ilo Ilo* suggests that Terry is better able to navigate the changes in Singapore's economy than her Singaporean employers as the more cosmopolitan subject. Terry is able to find a side job as a hairdresser, easily assimilating into Singapore's knowledge and service economy. On the other hand, Teck cannot find a job despite his fifteen years of sales experience (he gets passed over for a young, English-speaking man) and Hwee's secretarial position at a shipping company is far from secure. The Lims are stranded in the history of Singapore's industrialized, manufacturing economy.

As Terry's economic viability increases, so too does her status within the Lim family: Teck and Jiale become fond of Terry as the film progresses, a fondness that is symbolically marked in the way Terry increasingly wears the old clothes that Hwee gives her. In a poignant scene involving the breakdown of the Lim family car, the role that mobility plays in Terry's assumption of Hwee's social role becomes especially evident. After realizing that Jiale and Terry are too weak to push the car—and his wife, heavily pregnant, is not able to—Teck asks whether Terry knows how to drive. Terry does know, and as she gets in to steer, Hwee's face telegraphs her dismay. Hwee stands unhappily off to the side, unable to participate as Jiale and Teck push the car with Terry steering. The family is able to get the car working again, and it is clear that Hwee feels alienated from her family life, unlike Terry, who is able to use the car—the very symbol of personal mobility. Later, Teck decides to sell the car for scrap because of their financial woes. This happens at the same time that the Lims decide that they can no longer afford to employ Terry. Both literally and figuratively, the car represents the Lims' ability—and inability— to move. The loss of the car not only marks the Lims' increasingly dire financial situation and descent in socioeconomic status, but foreshadows their inability to navigate Singapore's changing economy.

As Terry's cosmopolitan capability and economic viability are posed as the most threatening to Hwee's matriarchal status, the film subtly suggests that it is the Singaporean state that will save her, even though it is the state that sets up the conditions for the devaluation of Hwee's economic subjectivity to begin with. Not only is Hwee alienated from her own family, but the film makes a point of Hwee's failed attempts to neoliberalize herself when she starts attending self-help motivational seminars only to later discover that the speaker she is enamored with is arrested for fraud. In contrast, Terry fits the state's vision of an ideal Singaporean citizen as the transnationally mobile, enterprising neoliberal subject. But Terry is a racialized, second-class citizen and will never be recognized as an ideal Singaporean. Of course, this is not a new insight: after all, migrant workers are codified as such in Singaporean immigration law. But what is interesting is how the film depicts Terry's second-class status. The film, instead of emphasizing Terry's abjection, shows how Terry is capable and resourceful and perhaps even uncritically celebrates her agency. Terry's neoliberal capabilities do not amount to any resolution or self-realization, however. Terry's narrative arc ends abruptly, after the Lims tell Jiale that Terry has to go back home. The film hardly dwells on Terry's departure: she is in the car with a sullen Jiale, and after he cuts a lock of Terry's hair to remember her, she is rushed out of the car to avoid another embarrassing spectacle with Jiale. Terry tells Jiale, "Learn to take care of yourself," and with that, she is gone. The Lim family power here is felt more acutely in their ability to dispense with Terry and end her narrative arc.

The film closes with Hwee giving birth, which is where she finally aligns ideologically with the state. Hwee's reproductive capability recenters her as a significant contributor to the state's efforts to increase Singapore's population and human capital through pronatalist policies. Just as the state's economic agenda alienates Hwee, so too does it restore her standing.

In this way, Terry is not presented as an existential threat to Singapore or even an economic threat but a more minor, social threat. Within the Lim family, Terry challenges Hwee's authority and plays an intermediary, bonding role between Teck and Jiale. When Teck and Jiale are in the waiting room during Hwee's cesarean section surgery, through shared earphones they listen to the song "Kahapon at Pag-Ibig" by Asin on a cassette tape that Terry left behind. As the English translation of the song's chorus reveals, the lyrics roughly repeat Terry's farewell to Jiale: "Take care of your life, because that is your only wealth." One could describe such lyrics as the very thesis of neoliberalized human capital.[95] Thus, in this scene, it is actually Terry who emerges as the nationalist, ideological voice of neoliberal morality in the Lim family, whereas Hwee reproductively maintains its biological, racialized infrastructure. It is this split—posed in the film as conflict—that stymies the potential for a coalition politics and does the work of labor differentiation.

Ilo Ilo at once calls for a nationalist recognition of migrant "unskilled" labor and exposes the conceptual limits of how that recognition can be performed. While the film usefully depicts how the elevation of workers like Chiah Deng or those in *Conversations* play out in other parts of Singapore's social hierarchy by examining the micropolitics of a middle-class family's drama, it grants Terry political agency only insofar as it articulates with the state's economic agenda. The humanization of Terry, the film warns, does not operate outside the terms of state discourse. Labor differentiation, *Ilo Ilo* reminds us, is not only performed through legal categories of citizenship or state representations of Singapore as First World, but through the perception of antagonisms as they play out in the politics of what Leow describes as the "absence and substitution" of Hwee by Terry.[96] Indeed, these social tensions are crucial for maintaining the distinction between kinds of transnational labor. By suggesting that Terry is the voice of neoliberal reason, *Ilo Ilo* demonstrates that postcolonial work—that is, capitalist labor in the name of national sovereignty—increasingly has an international dimension.

POST-CAREERS AND POSTCOLONIAL COLONIALISM

My aim in this chapter was to read for the interrelations of power between corporation and nation in an intuitively neoliberal genre, the coming-of-career narrative. As I show through my reading of *Mammon Inc.*, the pleasures of work derived from the coming-of-career narrative are as much a response to the strong state of early postcolonial capitalism as they are to the ideological workings of Global Asia. As *Conversations on Coming Home* further demonstrates, Global Asia works in concert with other capitalist forces to compel labor from its subjects. Recognizing the diminishing returns of a nation-motivated work ethos, the Singaporean state attempts to recruit its citizens abroad by representing Singapore as a site where the coming-of-career narrative can climax. The Singapore setting is made legible through the work pleasures and work-life balance it can offer. Moreover, by representing the nation as if it is free of a strong state and aligning returned Singaporeans with foreigners, the state appeals to postcolonial anxieties of inadequacy and desire for expatriate privilege. As a counterpoint to the class limitations of the coming-of-career narrative, Anthony Chen's *Ilo Ilo* illustrates the ways that the cosmopolitan, transnational labor—a characteristic of Singaporean career narratives—shape the social dynamics of undervalued workers. I close this chapter with readings of two texts that gesture toward future directions: Troy Chin's *The Resident Tourist* graphic novel series and Rebecca Bustamante's *Maid to Made* (2014).

Much like how *If We Dream Too Long* anticipated the diminishing returns of a strong, nationalist emphasis on productivity in an industrialized manufacturing economy, Troy Chin's autobiographical graphic novel series, *The Resident Tourist*, calls attention to the weakening of the coming-of-career narrative's ideological hold. Chin's novels remind us that even as the ideological power of neoliberalism vis-à-vis the coming-of-career narrative can feel totalizing, it is also vitalist, which is to say, its energies run out. *The Resident Tourist* (2007) depicts Chin's return to Singapore to pursue illustration of comics after giving up his music industry career in New York City. Throughout the novels, Chin is confronted by characters who question why he would give up his successful life in the United States, especially when he has no career plans in Singapore. While the kind of questioning Chin receives is not in itself peculiar, what is striking is how the disbelief at Chin's decisions are so often framed in nationalist terms. For example, using Goh's language, his childhood best friend, Kampong Boy, accuses Chin of being "a 'quitter' who has returned a nobody." He later goes as far as to accuse Chin of not being Singaporean enough: "That's the other thing, you're from Wharton, and what are you doing? Art. You're wasting your education. No Singaporean would do that."[97] The rebuke of Chin's art pursuits is framed in terms of impracticality: there is no clear professional career path for many Singaporean writers and artists. Without a clear coming-of-career narrative, in other words, Chin is not legible as a Singaporean.

Though Chin's career status ascends later in *The Resident Tourist*, after he wins the National Arts Council Young Artist Award, it briefly explores Chin's lack of legibility and what it means to tell a life story that is not emplotted according to a career telos. Chin embraces his "nobody" status by often representing himself without expression—his glasses cover his eyes—seemingly resisting the affective exuberance so often associated with neoliberal subjects who pursue passion projects for work. When asked about what his graphic novel series is about, Chin simply responds that it is about "nothing" as a way of countering the teleological narratives that demand meaning.

While the series offers an implicit critique of the coming-of-career narrative, the alienating effects of which are amplified by family and friends, Chin still longs for a more harmonious dynamic with the state as a condition of being home even as the series seems to embrace Chin's estrangement from Singapore as a "resident tourist." During a television broadcast of Singapore's National Day, Chin is struck by a line in the prime minister's speech: "Singapore is a city of possibilities." In response and with his trademark blank face, Chin thinks, "Somehow, I wanted to believe him *so* badly."[98] There is a curious reversal here from the other coming-of-career narratives this chapter discusses. The promise of work pleasure to Singaporeans in *Mammon Inc.* and *Conversations*, we recall, is based on the perceived retreat of the state. Feeling like a foreigner, in Chin's depiction, is a matter of feeling incompatible with the state rather than a matter of privileged status. Even as *The Resident Tourist* tries to imagine work narratives outside of conventional ideas of success, Chin's desire to experience consensus with the state points readers to the utopic postcolonial nationalist desires that continue to underwrite Singaporean experience, a desire that seems especially counterintuitive and critically significant. If neoliberalized work partially operates through the rejection of a strong state, what does this seeming nostalgia for a more omnipresent state suggest about how work ethic will change as postcolonial capitalism continues to evolve?

Bustamante's memoir, *Maid to Made*, also invites questions about how to comprehend state power in the Global Asia context of postcolonial capitalism. Her coming-of-career narrative is simultaneously a rags-to-riches story: working her way from her position as a maid in Singapore, Bustamante is now "made" as the founder of Chaire Associates and president of Asia CEO Awards. The book combines chapters dedicated to Bustamante's biography and chapters providing business advice, ostensibly based on her wealth and success. With chapter titles such as "What Real Success Means," "Obstacles to Success," and "You and Your Goals at Life," Bustamante's book is typical of the business self-help genre in terms of the advice she offers about goal setting, time management, motivation, and hard work. Much like the state's ideal twenty-first-century Singaporean, Bustamante's memoir performs her cosmopolitanism through her citations, which include (mostly Western) examples of successful people such as James Earl Jones and Abraham Lincoln.[99] Perhaps in an effort to be diplomatic to her potential Singaporean readers, the details of Bustamante's three-year stay in Singapore are rather thin. Readers are told that Bustamante's work as a maid in Singapore was "hard but fulfilling."[100] It is in Singapore, during her one day off a month, that Bustamante enrolled in an accounting course at the Singapore Institute of Management. When the opportunity to emigrate came, her employers initially refused to give Bustamante a reference, because "they were only upset to lose their cherished maid."[101] But even with such vague details, Bustamante's language reveals her time in Singapore as disciplined: her fulfilment is qualified with struggle, her time is restricted, and her economic mobility is hindered. What we can glean about Bustamante's experience in Singapore speaks to her subjectivity as "unskilled labor," which assumes a particular kind of power dynamic with the state in which she is marginalized and oppressed.

Though Bustamante's bootstraps narrative might simply seem like generalized neoliberal delusion, her business strategy and personal branding is strikingly Singaporean: she is an example of, as Gayatri Chakravorty Spivak has put it, "Singaporeanization."[102] As president of the Asia CEO Forum, Bustamante hosts an event that "promote[s] [the] Philippines as a premier business destination to global decision makers," much like how Singapore's economy gained capital by attracting multinational corporations with a promise of Global Asia.[103] Like Lee Kuan Yew's famous refrain of Singapore's "Third World to First World" trajectory, Bustamante tells her story of "Maid to Made" as a motivational speaker, relying on her status as an exceptional economic model for her business. Bustamante even frames her work ethic as nationalist, commenting that her time in Singapore inspired her to start a company that would counter the prejudiced behavior she experienced: "In Singapore, I heard foreigners say many negative things about Filipinos so I hoped that someday I could tell the world about the positive side of the Philippines and Filipinos."[104] For Bustamante, the formation of a transnational corporation is in the service of a nationalist project of positive representation.

Because low-wage, noncitizen workers are not the typical site for cultivating nationalist ideologies of postcolonial capitalism, what is unexpected about the Bustamante case is that it suggests a stronger ideological relation between state and noncitizen that goes otherwise uncaptured by biopolitical theories of neoliberalized governance.[105] Though Bustamante's self-help guide and interviews do not offer enough to deconstruct the process of interpellation, we have to assume that her ideological embrace of Singapore's economic doctrine had something to do either with her experience in Singapore or with her experience living in a Southeast Asian nation proximate to it. Though maid recruiting agencies in the Philippines represent Singapore as a favorable place to work, Bustamante performs a much more specific engagement with Singapore beyond general admiration, and in fact, she does not outwardly depict any approbation. Bustamante's assimilation of Singaporean state economic doctrine emerges from a relation of colonial dominance between state and noncitizen worker—that is, of racial hierarchy and Singaporean supremacy. Given this colonial dynamic in which we assume Bustamante absorbed state economic doctrine, her case invites us to ask: How does postcolonial capitalism colonize?

Most obviously, one could argue that postcolonial capitalism colonizes through the (Singaporean) family, but the humanitarian discourse that shapes the OFW's experience in Singapore is also key. As already mentioned, Singapore has been criticized for its treatment of migrant workers. Consequently, the state has allowed a number of parastatal organizations and government-organized nongovernmental organizations (GONGOs) into the country to support the needs of migrant workers. Some of these are considered more acceptable than others. For example, in Singapore's National Report 2021, a human rights review written as part of Singapore's obligation to the United Nations as a member state, three organizations are named as "invaluable partners in shaping the MW [migrant worker] landscape": the Migrant Workers' Centre, the Centre for Domestic Employees, and Aidha.[106] Describing their mission to "empower and provide opportunities for foreign domestic workers and lower-income women to transform their lives through sustainable wealth creation," Aidha appears as very ideologically attuned to the values of the coming-of-career narrative.[107] Indeed, the organization offers a number of courses with titles such as "Manage Your Money and Tech," "Plan your Financial Future," and "Start Your Business."[108] Such course titles have resonances with both Bustamante and *Ilo Ilo*. This is not to suggest that these humanitarian organizations are simple ruses for the state. But, as I have argued, state power works off of or combines with other institutions. Reading for the future of postcolonial capitalism will thus require further examination of how constellations of institutions work together rather than simply critiquing the totalizing power of one.

The aesthetics of postcolonial work, as they are reflected in the mirror scene in *Mammon Inc.* and in representations of labor differentiation in *Conversations* and *Ilo Ilo*, reveal both Singaporean and non-Singaporean audiences for Global Asia. *Mammon Inc.* and *Conversations* shows us how the totalizing force of neoliberalism shields the Singaporean state from accountability in the formation of capitalist cultures. This erasure of the state serves as reassurance to Singaporeans, who remember a stronger, disciplinary state from the decolonization and Asian Values eras. In the conflict between Hwee Leng and Terry in *Ilo Ilo*, we see how Global Asia relies on the dissociation of Singapore from the Philippines and how that dissociation is socially maintained among nonelite workers. Such a disassociation sustains Chinese racial privilege in Singapore and serves as a reassurance for a global audience. As Singapore announces we are not those "darker nations," to quote Vijay Prashad, Global Asia reassures onlookers that your best capitalist life in Singapore will not be disrupted by any Third Worldist solidarity politics. Taken together, *Mammon Inc., Conversations*, and *Ilo Ilo* elucidate how postcolonial erasure yokes the internal and external workings of Singapore as Global Asia.

4

The Princess Fantasy of Singapore

Shorter Histories and US Decline in Crazy Rich Asians

At the 2016 White House state dinner, Prime Minister Lee Hsien Loong presented President Barack Obama and First Lady Michelle Obama with a gift commemorating fifty years of US-Singapore relations: the "Dendrobium Barack and Michelle Obama." In Singapore, where the national flower is a hybrid orchid known as the Vanda Miss Joaquim, there is a history of "orchid diplomacy": orchids are bred for famous guests and state dignitaries, which have included Elton John and Aung San Suu Kyi.[1] In this case, the flower, created by the Singapore Botanic Gardens, is a cross between the Dendrobium Pink Lips, native to Barack Obama's birthplace of Hawai'i, and the Dendrobium Sunplaza Park, a hybrid orchid from Singapore.[2] Described by the Singaporean press as "vigorous and free flowering," the orchid's personality was symbolically apt for the Trans-Pacific Partnership free trade agreement that both nations' leaders were espousing at the time.[3] Moreover, the flower's mixed stock of Dendrobium Pink Lips and Dendrobium Sun Plaza Park symbolizes a heteronormative romantic relation that Singapore was projecting onto its US partner, one that reversed the typical gender dynamics of West and non-West relations. Through the suggestively named Pink Lips, the United States is feminized vis-à-vis Hawai'i (as Haunani-Kay Trask drily tells us, "Hawai'i—the word, the vision, the sound in the mind—is the fragrance and feel for soft kindness[;] . . . Hawai'i is she"),[4] while Singapore is masculinized by the Dendrobium Sun Plaza Park and its attendant associations with built space and modern construction. Indeed, the courting, wide-eyed tone of Prime Minister Lee's official state remarks—"I was struck by your focus, your informed interest in Asia and your desire to cement America's role in it"[5]—only affirmed the apparent budding romance between the two heads of state epitomized by the orchid.

This amorous relation is a clear pivot from the Asian Values era of the 1980s and 1990s. For example, in a 1994 *Foreign Affairs* interview with the former prime

FIGURE 7. Photo of the Dendrobium Barack and Michelle Obama. blickwinkel / E. Teister / Alamy Stock Photo.

minister, Lee Kuan Yew, Lee argued that the liberal, intellectual tradition that flourished in the United States after World War II was causing societal breakdown. Agreeing with the interviewer that he used to admire the United States, Lee went on to say that America's "failed social policies . . . have resulted in people urinating in public, in aggressive begging in the streets, in social breakdown."[6] Lee's comments were made at a time when the Singaporean state performed its national identity through, on the one hand, particularized interpretations of Sino-Confucian values and, on the other, occidentalist logics. Illustrating the latter point, Lee's emphasis on uncontained bodily fluids and invocation of masculinized images of homeless people roaming the street casts the United States as improper and undesirable. Despite the distinct political and economic circumstances in which Prime Ministers Lee Kuan Yew and Lee Hsien Loong were speaking, it is clear from their rhetoric that gender is crucial for comprehending the relations between the two nations.

This chapter investigates the dynamics of desire in the context of Singapore as Global Asia in mediating the politics of difference. Historically, racial difference has been wielded to justify the civilizing mission and extractive capitalism of colonialism. In the postcolonial Asian context, however, state leaders deployed difference from the West to claim autonomy and economic exceptionalism. As typified by Lee's interview, Asian Values discourse hardened binary differences between East and West in order to offer a culturalist explanation for so-called Asian Miracle economies and to fend off Western critiques of human rights records in Asia. The 1997 Asian financial crisis, however, marked the wane of Asian Values discourse in Singapore. One of the central investigations of this chapter, then, is how difference and thus desire have been reconceptualized in the post–Asian Values era, a time when Singapore's economic reputation is ascending and that of the United States is purportedly on the decline.

To address the question of how desire is reconceived, I turn to Kevin Kwan's novel *Crazy Rich Asians* (2014). Through the romantic travails of Nicholas Young and Rachel Chu—Singaporean Chinese and Chinese American, respectively—*Crazy Rich Asians* works within the familiar East meets West encounter but routes it through a postdiasporic context, in this case, Chinese. The breezily written novel, with its melodramatic plot and voyeuristic perspective into the lives of the obscenely wealthy of Singapore, made best-seller lists around the world and was adapted as a Hollywood feature film of the same title in 2018. For a number of local commentators, the *Crazy Rich Asians* film adaptation crystallizes some of the worst effects of Singapore as Global Asia. As the Singaporean poet Pooja Nansi puts it, the Hollywood adaptation's relegation of brown bodies to servitude is a "Singaporean Chinese man's fantasy of erasure of our multiculturalism," which is obscured in the reception of the film as a "win" for Asian Americans.[7] With its shallow chick-lit appeal, celebration of consumerism, and fetishization of wealth, Kwan's original novel too has been subject to much scrutiny, with many in the local literary community loath to have Kwan's work included under the label "Singapore literature." There is undoubtedly much to problematize about the politics of *Crazy Rich Asians*. Nevertheless, the novel, and the cultural phenomenon it generated, is significant for what it elucidates about Singapore's soft power and cultural capital and the workings of postcolonial capitalism over time.

My analysis centers on Kwan's novel and his presentation of Singapore in a chick-lit proximate genre that I describe as a "princess fantasy," or an unapologetically girly fantasy of being the center of attention, having all desires catered to, and being revered by all for her greatness. Much like male fantasies, princess fantasies are about power. But princess fantasies do not covet power and control in the male sense of domination. The princess fantasy is not a fantasy about becoming queen. Instead, the princess's power derives from her ability to attract and draw male subjects to her. The fantasy of being treated like a princess also suggests a desire for fantastical experiences of luxury, indulgence, and extravagance, for a Prince Charming to swoop in and save one from the doldrums or difficulties of one's life. The princess fantasy *feels* empowering insofar as the princess has all her material desires fulfilled by her ability to attract, but the patriarchal structure remains. The generic frame of the princess fantasy offers critical insights into the workings of

Global Asia with respect to the United States and, ironically, also explains the popular appeal of Kwan's work in the context of Global Asia. In this way *Crazy Rich Asians* is a complex text to read: the novel at once offers a critical commentary on Global Asia and history of postcolonial capitalism, is a beneficiary of Singapore's transformation into Global Asia, and, as the novel rose to fame, is constitutive of Global Asia itself. The criticality of *Crazy Rich Asians*, already quite subtle in terms of the writing, is further obscured by the fact that Kwan tends to promote his novel as an anthropological exposé of the Singaporean elite.

On the face of it, the princess fantasy simply inverts the gender relations between East and West as performed by (Prince) Lee and (Princess) Obama at the state dinner. Certainly, the princess fantasy relies on the passive female victim trope typical of what Cristina Bacchilega describes as the "Innocent Persecuted Heroine" fairy tale.[8] In doing so, it reinscribes the Occident's pleasure of the Orient to maintain the fiction of Western power. But more than a simple inversion where a masculinized Singapore dominates the now-feminized United States, Global Asia's appeal relies on a deracinated, "not quite" Asian masculinity. In this way, the princess fantasy shows how Global Asia's power is still mitigated by colonial histories of race, even as it instrumentalizes that very history of Western desire for power in order to accrue capital.

Crazy Rich Asians also makes a number of important historical points about Global Asia's power and the racialized politics of historical time. The novel illustrates the significance of US declinism for the production of the princess fantasy: the prince—manifesting in both character (Nick) and setting (Singapore)—saves the princess (Rachel and the United States) by bringing her to a site where heightened pleasures can take place. For Kwan's fictional princess fantasy, this has meant presenting Singapore as a place of strong affect with the use of melodramatic characters. Interestingly, Kwan's technique anticipates a state tourism campaign known as "Passion Made Possible" that emerged a couple of years after the publication of the novel. Both princess fantasy as novel and princess fantasy as tourism campaign counter Singapore's former image as a sterile, emotionless country. Through a reading of the novel's prologue—the infamous "Empire buys back" scene—I show that *Crazy Rich Asians* prioritizes shorter histories over the *longue durée* to comprehend the workings of postcolonial capitalism and how imperial critiques can maintain Eurocentrism. In doing so, I posit that *Crazy Rich Asians* reveals that a shorter view of new capital in Asia is necessary to undo a historicism that centralizes the British Empire. Like Jeremy Tiang and Hwee Hwee Tan in previous chapters, Kwan critiques how Singapore is typically read.

Finally, I argue that Kwan's princess fantasy calls attention to the role of setting in producing pleasure. If we think of the princess fantasy as articulating a kind of power over Western desires for the purpose of attracting capital, Kwan's novel demonstrates how this power is rooted in the aesthetics of Singapore's setting. Singapore as a setting of pleasure also, as I comment in the closing of this chapter, helps us understand what enabled some of the more controversial aspects of the Hollywood film adaptation.

THE PRINCESS FANTASY OF SINGAPORE

The first installment of the *Crazy Rich Asians* trilogy centers on the romance of Nicholas Young and Rachel Chu. It is summer break for the New York University professors (history and economics, respectively) and Nick's best friend, Colin, is about to get married. On the occasion of Colin's wedding, Nick invites Rachel to visit Singapore, his childhood home, to meet his family and friends. Rachel has no idea that Nick is a member of one of the wealthiest families in Asia and that he is expected to receive a large inheritance. The learning curve is steep for Rachel, who was raised by a working-class, single, immigrant mother, as she realizes who her boyfriend is in this cross-cultural, cross-class encounter. Staying fairly true to a conventional romance plot, Nick's family and friends serve as major obstacles to the couple's anticipated nuptials.

As postcolonial studies has taught us, the colonial encounter is a highly gendered confrontation of racial difference. As Anne McClintock puts it, "Gender power was not the superficial patina of empire, an ephemeral gloss over the more decisive mechanics of class or race. Rather, gender dynamics were, from the outset, fundamental to the securing and maintenance of the imperial enterprise."[9] Such gender dynamics manifest in an orientalist dynamic, as Edward Said writes: "She [the Orient] never spoke of herself, she never represented her emotions, presence, or history. *He* spoke for and represented her."[10] *Crazy Rich Asians* plays on these colonial, gendered histories of encounter and orientalist representations with a contemporary twist. The West is figured through Rachel Chu, an American, and Nicholas Young, a Singaporean. Racialized difference is here portrayed as geopolitical difference, since the couple are both ethnically Chinese. By positioning the US/Rachel Chu as the feminized, passive figure in this allegory of Singapore as Global Asia, *Crazy Rich Asians* invites a reconsideration of how the gendered dynamic of postcolonial difference is reconceived in the Asian Century.

Crazy Rich Asians uses a familiar, Cinderella-esque romantic plot, with Rachel serving as the unwitting princess protagonist of the novel. Like Cinderella, Rachel is the "undeserving victim [who faces] various hostile antagonists,"[11] and her "persecution stems from the fact that she is temporarily denied her true position through some calumny."[12] (Indeed, the Hollywood adaptation of the novel features Rachel in a blue dress, clearly riffing on Cinderella's ball gown in the Disney animated film.) As with so many fairy tale princesses, readers are reassured of Rachel's "goodness, patience, innocence, [. . .] and, most of all, beauty."[13] Rachel's "natural, uncomplicated beauty" is drawn in contrast to the "red-carpet-ready girls [Nick] had grown up around."[14] Rachel is innocent not only in the sense that she is naive; she also does not put any effort into manipulating her image. Such a depiction serves to emphasize the various injustices Rachel faces with Nick's friends and family and moreover stresses how little Rachel controls her circumstances, whether performed through her individual agency or her ability to manipulate her surroundings.

Through the gaze of Rachel, and all of her princess diminutiveness, the novel makes Singapore appear wondrously alien but in a way that emphasizes the setting's command over her. With the enumeration of hours of travel and the passage's attention to Rachel's first "glimpse" of Singapore, the description of Rachel's arrival in Singapore is reminiscent of that of a colonial explorer. Though her language draws on Western colonial tropes, the exotica of Singapore is also shaped by her ancestral knowledge: "She was in Southeast Asia now, in the realm her ancestors called the *Nanyang*."[15] Even for Rachel, who we may assume has familiarity with the region by virtue of being Chinese, the invocation of the Nanyang underscores the unknown of Singapore. The world she encounters is not what she expects: "But the view she could glimpse from the plane did not resemble some romantic terrain swathed in mist—rather, it was a dense metropolis of skyscrapers glittering in the evening sky, and from six thousand feet Rachel could already feel the pulsating energy that was one of the world's financial powerhouses."[16] Rachel's Westernized optic here does not reveal a hazy, indeterminate, malleable world waiting for interpretation and placement into history. The clarity of the sharp lines and bright lights represented by rigid skyscrapers asserts Singapore's modernity, denoting a masculinized authority over those who enter this world. The alluring phallic spectacle of Singapore is emphasized by "pulsating energy," offering a so-called money shot by uniting the masculine with the economic. The masculinized image of Singapore operates in sharp contrast to the "porno-tropics" of colonial-era writing that, as McClintock explains, feminized land for the taking.[17] Like a colonial narrative, Rachel's view of Singapore is based in an "erotics of ravishment,"[18] but if for Columbus types "ravishment" was a male power fantasy of "drag[ging] or carry[ing] away (a woman) by force or with violence," "ravishment" in the princess fantasy takes on its more passive definition of being "transport[ed] with the strength of some emotion; to [be] fill[ed] with ecstasy, intense delight, or sensuous pleasure; to [be] entrance[d], captivate[d], or enrapture[d]."[19] While colonial narratives express the "male bravura of the explorer, invested with his conquering mission,"[20] connoting a proximity because of the colonizer's aspirations to handle and master new lands, Rachel's initial encounter emphasizes distance and sensation in her ability to "feel" Singapore from six thousand feet above it. Like the porno-tropics, however, the eroticized overtones in the above passage are unmistakable and resemble that of sexual encounter.

High levels of pleasurable sensation compounded with Rachel's passivity (her lack of agency in determining the plot) enable everyday Singaporean scenes to transform into ones of excess and extravagance. After being picked up from Changi Airport, Rachel is whisked off to Lau Pa Sat, a hawker center "in the heart of the downtown financial district."[21] Though food tourism in Singapore is rather typical, that Rachel's first gustatory experience of Singapore is in the financial district emphasizes the significance of consumptive capitalism for the princess fantasy. As Rachel samples local Singaporean cuisines, her various exclamations ("Why doesn't it ever taste like this at home" and "Mmmm . . . heaven!") and excited reactions ("her eyes widened in delight") to the food make clear her ravishment.[22] The vibrant, endless descriptions of food in the grand, cathedral-like setting of Lau Pa Sat, combined with the emphasis on Rachel's passivity as Nick slides one dish after another onto the table, are evocative of the "Be our Guest" feast scene in Disney's *Beauty and the Beast*. While the princess allusion emphasizes the fantastical and otherworldly, the feasting also retains the eroticism of the porno-tropical financial scene, remarking on the sexualized relationship between consumption and pleasure through the eroticism of food consumption, or of foreign objects entering Rachel's body. Moreover, positioned as foreigners to Nick's Singapore world, readers are compelled to identify with Rachel, who also does not know anything about Nick's family history or Singapore. As the story proceeds, readers are put in a more knowing position, further increasing Rachel's passivity through her ignorance. The only willful action Rachel takes in trying to uncover Nick's background comes very late in the novel, after Rachel has been antagonized by Nick's family and friends over and over.

Though Nick's and Rachel's respective racial and gender identities counter the colonial expectation that such encounters are ones only between a white male (colonial) protagonist and a nonwhite (native) female, this gendered reversal, as it is figured through Nick, is not one in which he simply reperforms Western masculinity. The novel implies that such a simple reperformance is impossible in the racial context within and without the world of the novel. Before being introduced to Nick, Rachel's friend Sylvia warns her and thus the reader: "He's . . . Asian."[23] Sylvia's pause remarks on her hesitance, knowing Rachel's "no Asian guys" rule, but also suggests Sylvia's own surprise at how much the "curiously exotic" Nick defies her (and eventually, Rachel's) expectations of Asian men,[24] presumably because of their racialized assumptions about emasculated Asian men. Insofar as masculinity in the United States is typically coded as white, much of Nick's exotic appeal comes from his decidedly not white American subdued masculine manner: his "self-deprecating wit," "quiet masculinity," and "relaxed ease."[25] Further differentiating him from American masculinity, Rachel notes (and finds attractive) Nick's nostalgic colonial aesthetic: his "canvas jacket, white linen shirt, and faded jeans . . . reminiscent of some adventurer just returned from mapping the Western Sahara," and humor redolent of "all those British-educated boys."[26] Given the near-unlikelihood of "some adventurer" referring to an Asian mapping the Sahara (except perhaps the colonial assistant), we are to recognize that Nick's fashion marks him as a British white. Yet Nick is characterized as an emphatically attractive Asian man, as Sylvia assures Rachel that he "looks a bit like that Japanese actor from the Wong Kar-wai

movies,"[27] unwittingly positioning Nick as embodying both former colonial powers of Singapore. But Rachel's attraction to Nick focuses on his distinction *and*
proximity to whiteness, or what Homi Bhabha describes as "almost the same but
not white."[28] In this way, the question of difference is not simply that of the dynamic
between Rachel and Nick, but of how Nick's inter-imperialist desirability—British,
American, Japanese—is mediated by his racial proximity to whiteness.

But as much as Nick appears to be not quite/not white, so too is he not quite/
not Asian. Rachel finds that unlike the other Asian American men she has dated,
Nick does not flaunt

> how many generations his family has been in America; what kind of doctors his
> parents were; how many musical instruments he played; the number of tennis camps
> he went to; which Ivy League scholarships he turned down; what model BMW, Audi,
> or Lexus he drove; and the appropriate number of years before he became (pick one)
> chief executive officer, chief financial officer, chief technology officer, chief law part-
> ner, or chief surgeon.[29]

Rachel finds the stereotypical achievement-focused, status-conscious, enumerating Asian man unattractive. While the opening nativist sentiment signals Rachel's
critique of a certain kind of Asian American, the passage also invokes a critique
of Singaporean materialism—or what is locally joked about as the desire for the
"five Cs": cash, car, condominium, credit card, and country club—through a different five Cs, or "chiefs," in the passage's closing. Of course, for Nick, a character that
the novel emphasizes is of old wealth, the status that accompanies any of the possible Cs is of little concern. As the daughter of an immigrant mother who moved
around the country, seeking work at Chinese restaurants and eventually becoming
a successful real estate agent, Rachel embodies a rags-to-riches American dream
trajectory and represents the model minority myth. We come to understand that
Rachel racializes showy capitalist materialism as Asian, which is part of why Nick
and his ability to "fad[e] into the background" allows him to take exception to
Rachel's policy and be cast as not quite/not Asian.[30]

If conspicuous consumption remarks on an "old" way of being Asian, whether
one is concerned with assimilating to upper-middle-class US culture or shedding
a Third World image in favor of one of modernity, Nick represents a globalized
Asian that surpasses the kinds of highly cultured Overseas Singaporean that the
Singaporean state valorizes. Rachel is eventually impressed with Nick's ability
to recognize a Talking Heads song, "This Must Be The Place," as they walk by a
street performer: "She loved that Nick knew the song well enough to recognize
this bastardized version."[31] Even more than Chiah Deng of *Mammon Inc.*, Nick
has impressive cultural knowledge of the West, even recognizing variations of a
relatively obscure song. But unlike Chiah Deng, who needs to prove her skills
as an Adapter by demonstrating her ability to learn Western cultural norms and
then assimilate, Nick performs his depth of understanding of Western codes, not

just his achievement of them. This depth is "an implicit knowledge and procurement of knowledge that informs [his] consumption practices," or what Elizabeth Currid-Halkett describes as the knowledge of the (American) aspirational class.[32] It is Rachel's perception of their class alignment, in other words, that is the basis of her attraction to him. The *unattractive* Asian draws attention to the historical relationship between their race and desire to assimilate, racializing their aspiration. Nick's characterization as Prince Charming suggests that the attractive Asian is one who does not ostentatiously perform dominant culture but has already arrived.

While *Crazy Rich Asians* illustrates how the pleasures that the West takes in the East now assume a gendered dynamic in which the West assumes a passive role, it also reveals how such gendered pleasures are conditioned on a deracinated, "not quite" Asian masculinity. The gender reversal performed through the princess fantasy might appear as a campy remark on the rising power of Asia because the princess fantasy functions within a heterosexual matrix and hegemonic femininity. The princess fantasy is not only a depiction of the passive experience of pleasure; it is also Kwan's commentary on the circumstances that allow the West to find the East desirable even when the West is repositioned as feminine. In this instance, desirability is dependent on an erasure of materialist aspiration and assimilation of Western cultural knowledge. Both qualities are framed as some kind of transcendence of Asiatic race—a transcendence that is marked as sexually desirable—in the sense that Nick's behavior does not remind Rachel of histories that have conditioned Asian subjects to economic ambition.

THE PRINCESS FANTASY: WHY NOW?

Although the fantasy of unfettered consumption and meeting Prince Charming is likely appealing at any historical juncture, the princess fantasy and its broader associations with being saved has a particular historical resonance when considering the economic decline of the United States and Singapore's function as an offshore financial center that literally saves money for corporations and the elite. As Jed Esty writes, "The 2020s will be the last decade when the US economy is the largest in the world,"[33] and the fantasy of being "saved" or brought to a fantasyland to indulge in consumption without the worries of accruing more debt is especially comforting after the 2008 financial crisis.[34] Indeed, Kwan uses subtle and snarky humor to comment on the power of Asian capital in reference to US economic decline (itself a major factor that plays into the novel's very appeal in the United States). For example, during a minor scene at Peik Lin's house, children are chided for not finishing their food: "Aiyoooooh, finish everything on your plate, girls! Don't you know there are children starving in America?"[35] Kwan repurposes a well-worn, racialized American dinner scene phrase to cast America as the new Third World Africa, a scene further ironized by the fact that said children are eating McDonald's McNuggets, food emblematic of US corporate and cultural influence.[36]

Also significant is how Rachel and Nick's love plot begins in New York City, the financial center of the United States, in "Autumn 2008," when the global financial crisis began and US public debt began to increase substantially—a pivotal year in American declinism that "revealed the fragility of American prosperity."[37] The context of the couple's desire for each other, in other words, is one where the West's position has weakened. The least subtle reference to US economic decline happens well into the story, when Alistair Cheng embarrasses his family by announcing his engagement to Kitty Pong. In an attempt to ignore the announcement, Victoria Young and Cassandra Shang turn to Rachel.

> "Now Rachel, I hear you are an economist? How fascinating! Will you explain to me why the American economy can't seem to dig out of its sorry state?" Victoria asked shrilly.
>   "It's that Tim Paulson fellow, isn't it?" Cassandra cut in. "Isn't he a puppet controlled by all the Jews?"[38]

The brief exchange echoes some of the same patronizing, Third Worlding sentiments of the earlier McDonald's scene: Hank is carelessly referred to as Tim, the complexity of the largest economic crisis since the Great Depression is reduced to an offhand remark, and a conspiracy theory on the "real" problem of the United States is offered. The humor behind many of the jabs at American economic decline takes on the same kind of "Empire strikes back" logics also apparent in the opening of the novel when the Leongs buy the Calthorpe Hotel and seem invested in stereotype critique. But they also make a pointed gesture at the new global order in which *Crazy Rich Asians* is situated, poking fun at a certain kind of imperial nostalgia represented by writers such as Tom Plate and Thomas L. Friedman. For them, Singapore represents a time when the United States too was a gleaming beacon of modernity made possible by "good governance," as Friedman puts it.[39] If we are to consider the broader emergence of the "princess industrial complex," which Peggy Orenstein suggests is a post-9/11 phenomenon, the princess fantasy of *Crazy Rich Asians* appeals to an American desire for innocence during an era when the global reputation and safety of the United States are perceived to be at risk.[40] Indeed, the *New York Times* describes the allure of *Crazy Rich Asians* as an escapist novel "after a year of heavy news—the Boston Marathon bombing, [and] nuclear threats from North Korea."[41] Whether ongoing national anxieties stemming from 9/11, the 2008 financial crisis, or the latest national crisis, *Crazy Rich Asians* offers needed relief.

While the novel appeals to some idea of Singapore as an imagined safe haven for the indebted and the spurned, Singapore as a haven becomes more literal when we contemplate its role in the offshore economy, something that *Crazy Rich Asians* also gestures toward. We might recall Peik Lin's comment to Rachel, that "Mainlanders feel that their money is far safer here than in Shanghai, or even Switzerland."[42] The Singaporean state makes plain its accommodation of transnational corporations and the wealthy through its safe harbor accounting practices whereby capital gains and profits from investments or real estate are not taxed.[43] Less discussed is how the "stable image" that Peik Lin refers to also benefits foreign investors who are looking to put their money into emerging markets such as Vietnam's real estate. As Kimberly Kay Hoang writes, "Emerging markets are characterized by weak formal institutions, limited information access, widespread corruption, and high levels of distrust."[44] Hoang finds that foreign investors in Vietnam often "had majority ownership structures set up in Hong Kong or Singapore" because they mitigate perceptions of risky investment.[45] In this way, the princess fantasy articulates with the Global Asia image through their mutual emphases on safety, whether affective or financial.[46]

While the very success and cultural phenomenon of *Crazy Rich Asians* epitomizes how the desire for Global Asia that the princess fantasy produces is partly the outcome of global economic rearrangements, it is also the historical outcome of Singapore's attempts to counteract its image as a sterile, lackluster destination. Already in 1997, and in response to the financial crisis, the Singaporean government began to voice concern about the nation's dull national image and its implications for capital accumulation. Singapore's economic trajectory led to its less flattering reputation as a "sterile and antiseptic" city as a result of its authoritarian government and relentless corporate work culture.[47] This reputation is best encapsulated in a piece by William Gibson who critiqued Singapore as an overly curated, "relentless G-rated," "Disneyland with the Death Penalty" in a controversial 1993 piece for *Wired* magazine. Citing an exchange with a taxi driver, Gibson's essay portrays Singapore as a function of corporate capitalism.

> [Taxi driver:] "You come for golf?"
> [Gibson:] "No."
> "Business?"
> "Pleasure."
> He sucked his teeth. He had doubts about that one.[48]

Later that same year, Singapore's reputation for punitive rule grew as the story of the caning of an American teenager, Michael Fay, for theft and car vandalism circulated in the US media. Also contributing to Singapore's image of sterility has been Singapore's poor performance on various "gross national happiness" indicators, where Singaporeans were reported "as the least likely in the world to report experiencing emotions of any kind on a daily basis" and Singapore was rated "the least positive country."[49] Apparently noticing that Singapore's sterile reputation had economic consequences, Lee Kuan Yew declared, "We need to be a cosmopolitan Asian city for all peoples from the world over—Americans, Europeans, Arabs and Asians."[50] Part of Hong Kong's "buzz," Lee argued, was that its "foreign exchange dealers and share brokers, foreigners and locals alike socialise much more at lunchtime and after office hours in bars and restaurants than they do in

Singapore. When they fraternise, they exchange confidential information."[51] For Lee, in other words, cultivating successful markets meant generating fun, social spaces of consumption.

Consequently, there began a pronounced developmental focus on leisure, recreation, and entertainment—the infrastructure of Global Asia. Many of these developments took place under the aegis of tourism, following Fanon's predictions that the national bourgeoisie's wealth would grow as a result of the Western bourgeoisie, "who come to [the nation] for the exotic, for big-game hunting and for casinos. The national bourgeoisie organizes centres of rest and relaxation and pleasure resorts to meet the wishes of the Western bourgeoisie."[52] The newly reformed Singapore Tourism Board in 1997, for example, took the lead in revitalizing a number of attractions, including the so-called ethnic enclaves (i.e., Chinatown and Kampong Glam), shopping, nightlife, and museums.[53] Such plans worked in conjunction with other initiatives such as the Ministry for Information and the Arts' *Renaissance City Report* (2000), which proposed strategies to shape Singapore into a "global arts hub." Though many of the large-scale infrastructural developments had clear touristic aims, there was also an effort by the state to cultivate leisure among its citizenry. For example, in 1991, the Land Transport Authority commenced the construction of the Park Connector Network (PCN), biking and walking paths that linked parks throughout Singapore.[54] While the construction of the PCN was also for the benefit of "healthy lifestyle" state-led initiatives, such developments are examples of recreational infrastructure that we associate with the professional, yuppie demographic. Together with the gentrification of older housing estates, Singapore's urban spaces make possible pleasure as well as business, unlike the city that Gibson encountered in the 1990s.[55]

In his seeming awareness of the Global Asia transformation that was taking place in response to its previous reputation as sterile and boring, Kwan's princess fantasy offers a humorous corrective by portraying Singapore as a setting in which strong affects can take place. No longer defined by Gibson's "white-shirted constraint," "humorlessness," and "conformity," the characters in *Crazy Rich Asians* perform a range of extreme emotions: we observe Eleanor's calculating determination to prevent Nick from marrying Rachel, Eddie's intense jealousy of Leo, Kitty's drive to be associated with the wealthy and elite, Colin's depressive episodes, Charlie's unrequited love for Astrid, and so on. Kwan's characters suggest that Singapore's setting is no longer restrictive or determinative, that people are able to fully experience and express an array of emotions. Not only do such high emotions seem to counter Singapore's reputation for sterility, but they also contest orientalist stereotypes about Asian inscrutability. There seemed to be, at least at one time, a desire on the part of Kwan to challenge the status quo when it came to Asian representation. For a Western readership, the seemingly critical work that the emotive characters perform against stereotypes may feel especially novel, even though Asian melodrama is hardly new.[56]

Curiously, a few years later, Kwan's representational work in *Crazy Rich Asians* would dovetail with Singaporean state initiatives. The affective emphasis on Singapore as a site of unrestrained emotion foreshadows the Economic Development Board and Singapore Tourism Board's 2017 campaign slogan, "Passion Made Possible." The campaign sought to create a national brand that emphasized "Singapore's attitude and mindset: a passion-driven, never-settling spirit of determination and enterprise that constantly pursues possibilities and reinvention."[57] The emphasis on storytelling and passion in the campaign directs tourists to see Singaporeans as emotional affective beings and to indulge their own (consumerist) passions. One has to wonder whether the emergence of "Passion Made Possible" was coincidental or whether, given the wild success of the novel and film, the Tourism Board took the princess fantasy of *Crazy Rich Asians* as a blueprint.

THE SHORTER HISTORY OF *CRAZY RICH ASIANS*

Crazy Rich Asians critiques interpretations of Singapore's economic success as continuous with and enabled by British colonialism. Contra *longue durée* approaches to the history of capitalism, I advocate a midlevel scale of reading Singapore in a way that accounts for more recent national history. In doing so, I mean to emphasize an account of postcolonial capitalism that treats power's effects as not predetermined by colonialism.[58] In foregrounding the postcolonial rather than colonial status of Singapore's capitalist formation, I am rejecting historicist, potted narratives that lock the events of British colonialism and the rise of a complicit, draconian postcolonial state as the key, determinative episodes that explain the workings of postcolonial capitalism, or the Asian Century. Such historicist readings appear in both popular and academic responses to the novel and the film. In the popular realm we see a desire for Singapore's history to remain in the frame of a mythical past and accessible only through the native informant. In the academic realm we see recourse to a history that emphasizes the determinative effects of colonial or global (often coded as Western) institutions on postcolonial state formation. In their inability to grapple with the politics of the novel's presentation of contemporary Asia, both responses reflect the limitations of Eurocentric historicist interpretations of the novel.

As evidenced by the popularity of both the novel and the film adaptation, *Crazy Rich Asians* has been well received by Western audiences. Part of the novel's sellability, as a *Vanity Fair* journalist suggested in an interview with Kevin Kwan, has something to do with its exotic appeal to the Western reader. "I get the sense," Lauren Christensen comments, "that the appeal of the book isn't all about wealth, though—a book called *Crazy Rich Europeans* simply wouldn't have the same allure."[59] Christiansen's observation is well taken: though the "wealth porn" of Kwan's novel is pleasurable, the "Asians" of the title and the exotic difference that they represent have been key to its success. While it would seem intuitive to turn to orientalism as an interpretive framework, the twenty-first-century, neoliberal context of power is very different from that of Said's theorization, something that Kwan seems keenly aware of in his thinking about both his novel's subject matter and its audience.

Notably, Kwan once formulated the selling points of his book—racial difference and cultural distance from the West—as an issue of historical time. In interviews that took place after the novel became a best seller, Kwan tends to frame his book as an exposé of the affluent, as it is based on his childhood growing up in Singapore and on his own family's wealth. But earlier interviews reveal a more thoughtful framing of *Crazy Rich Asians*:

> It just really felt to me that there was a gap in terms of the sort of book we were seeing about Asia in America. There really seemed to be only two genres within fiction: historical fiction set in Asia, of the Amy Tan variety for instance, and then the contemporary stories about Asian-American assimilation. It seemed like nobody was really writing about Asia now.[60]

While Kwan here is not quite fair to the American literary scene regarding contemporary Asia, he is correct insofar as US audiences tend to seek a particular imagining of Asia that maintains US superiority. Historical fiction and "Asian-American assimilation" narratives are interested in the pastness of Asia, and because of this, *contemporary* Asia is incomprehensible to the West. For Kwan, writing about contemporary Asia means dealing with its ascendant economic status: "There's so much emphasis on the economic might of China, of Southeast Asia, Asian 'Super Tigers' [sic] and things like that. But nobody was really looking from the perspective of a family story, of these individuals."[61] Kwan's "but" is key: his comments call attention to how contemporary Asia is rarely understood outside of economic discourse, a discourse that has been mostly framed with respect to Asia's threat to the West. By manifesting Singapore's rapid modernization and economic ascension in themes of generational difference and familial tensions, Kwan is able to depict exactly how acute such changes were in Singapore. Family dramas are also, of course, a familiar genre for Asian representation in the West—something that Kwan demonstrates awareness of in his mention of Amy Tan. In this way, we see Kwan contending with the representational challenges of depicting Singapore and making contemporary Asia legible to his Western readers.[62]

In their representations of Singapore to the West, both Kwan and the Singaporean state have a stake in a *contemporary*, transpacific Global Asia. The contemporary remarks on the representational politics of historical time emphasize coexistence with the West and perform a decolonial move even as it is, in this instance, in the service of global capitalism. Subtly distinct from what C. J. W.-L. Wee terms the "Asian Modern," or "East meets West [whereby] centre and periphery, old and new, are conjoined," my emphasis here is on the definition of *contemporary*: "belonging to the same time, age, or period; living, existing, or occurring together in time."[63]

Wee's Asian Modern, on the other hand, with the word *conjoined* stresses different elements together in a particular setting, akin to what Mary Louise Pratt describes as a "contact zone," or "social spaces where disparate cultures meet, clash, and grapple with each other, often in highly asymmetrical relations of domination and subordination."[64] Insofar as the Asian Modern encourages contact between East and West, the Singaporean state enabled a performance of modernity that demonstrated Singapore is no longer regarded as a precolonial society of "primitive people" who are "shy, timid, [and] shunning contact."[65] While the performance of the modern and of the contemporary both respond to histories of colonialism and reflect different modes of postcolonial capitalism, the mode of the contemporary underscores intimacy beyond the encounter; it is an affinity, or a rapport, that moves through time. It is no surprise then that the contemporary is narrativized through a love plot.

This distinction between the contemporary and the modern is the difference between an economy driven by neoliberalism and industrial modernity. As Watson has written in *The New Asian City*, some of the qualities that distinguish the era of the Asian Modern in terms of socioeconomic initiatives are a developmental emphasis on catching up to the West, a more entrenched sense of difference between East and West, and an emphasis on urban development and language ability. In other words, under the modern great importance is assigned to developing and showcasing Singapore's infrastructure to prove that it is *functional* for global capitalism. Under the contemporary, however, there is a stronger sense of being on par with the West and the possibility of exploiting white American nostalgia for its global standing, what Esty describes as declinism. To be clear, the colonial histories of being subordinate to the West are still at play. With the contemporary, we see a shift in the Singaporean state's socioeconomic focus from infrastructure to affect, or from the "hard" to the "soft," or still yet, to use some of the conceptual terms of the previous chapter, from the material to the immaterial.[66] As I discussed earlier, this is why we see in Singapore more of a pronounced focus on recreational infrastructure and one's ability to "play," alongside perceptions of it as a model city/state.

Popular reviews of *Crazy Rich Asians* interpret its family drama as a critique of the elite and the moneyed. That is, the humor of the novel is a class critique. As the blurbs in the book tell us, *Crazy Richs Asians* is satirical: "Both a deliciously satiric read and a Fodor's of sorts to the world of Singapore's fabulously moneyed, both new and old" (*Daily News*); "[A] winning summer satire" (*Vogue*); "It's impossible not to get sucked into this satirical novel" (*Glamour*). Many of the reviews published in the Western media see Kwan's novel as critiquing the invisible, elite, old money world of the diasporic Chinese through satire. One reviewer, for example, describes *Crazy Rich Asians* as "a story about competitive wealth, tradition and hypocrisy told with an expert satirist's combination of affection and astonishment."[67] Indeed, the satire is conveyed by the novel's very title. The focus on issues of class and race thus tends toward attention to character, especially since the exaggerated, humorous aspects of the novel, such as the outrageous protectionist tendencies that the Singaporean Chinese elite have against outsiders and the insatiable desires of those seeking entrance into high society, are central to the novel's plot. The Youngs, for example, are so secretive about their wealth that one of their gigantic mansions, Tyersall Park has been erased from satellite views on Google Maps. The Youngs' wish for intense security and privacy is an attempt to ward off characters such as Kitty Pong, whose drive for wealth and status spans the narrative across the trilogy.

Though Kwan depicts the insular, classist, xenophobic world of the affluent through parodic characters, his critique of class is often fleeting and subtle. For example, a passage about Eddie Cheng's servants explains, "[T]hey employed two Filipino and two Mainland Chinese maids (the Chinese were better at cleaning, while the Filipinos were great with the kids)."[68] While the passage portrays the extent of Eddie's wealth by enumerating his possessions, the parenthetical also acts as a racialized rationale for the domestic labor the Chengs employ. Because this passage is attributed to Eddie by way of narrative focalization, Kwan portrays the racialized logics as problematic, like Eddie, one of the most over-the-top, status-conscious characters in the novel. But Eddie is ultimately treated as a sympathetic character, who acts out as a result of feeling parental neglect. These jabs at class hierarchy are thus subdued by the fact that class difference is maintained throughout the trilogy and moreover understood as surmountable differences in taste and consumptive practices rather than of labor or class oppression. At best, a comment appears in the final installment of the trilogy on the untenability of maintaining an invisible, family-centered, old money world of wealth, favoring instead a corporate model to preserve class structure. One might read this as nostalgia for the social structures of old money or as a realpolitik observation of changing, neoliberalized class structures. Perhaps it is both. Either way, Kwan seems to take class hierarchy as a given and is uninterested in offering a round critique of it, focusing his critique instead on how various characters navigate and maintain class structure.

Treating *Crazy Rich Asians* as a satire of class can problematically stabilize the world Kwan depicts and has the effect of transforming the novel into an anthropological work. In other words, the novel's popular reception reveals a Eurocentric understanding of satire. The exaggerated details that appear in the service of class satire begin to feel possible if not plausible: the opening hotel scene of the novel feels reminiscent of the kind of wealth and power that Chinese property investors wield on the west coast of North America, for example. It is not even clear that the characters that appear as caricatures can really be sustained as such: the overbearing Eleanor, for example, is treated as truly domineering by other characters, to the point that her husband cannot live in the same city. Details of the novel that seem like evidence of satire, in other words, paradoxically appear as gestures toward realism. Satire is always risky because it may be read as true by audiences who do not understand the joke, but the risk involved in *Crazy Rich Asians* is not simply one about genre.

As evidenced in later interviews with Kwan, the *Crazy Rich Asians* trilogy is most appealing to Western readers when they are assured that its criticality is based on an anthropological exposé of the affluent. In an interview anticipating the publication of the last work in his trilogy, *Rich People Problems*, Kwan declares, "There's very little in my book that's made up. Everything's actually drawn from observation and reality. I don't have the imagination to dream up plastic surgery for fish. I really don't."[69] What is notable is how Kwan discredits the possibility of his own artistic creativity, reinscribing the issues that Chow describes as "the dichotomy between the 'realpolitical' non-west and the 'imaginative' West.[70] In spite of his earlier aspirations to present a story about "Asia now," or the economic rise of Asia, Kwan takes recourse to his own past to explain the trilogy, vaguely appealing to an exoticized notion of history. Given the entirety of the *Crazy Rich Asians* phenomenon, we can take Kwan's framing of the novel as a marketing strategy that also suggests that popular audiences are not ready to be sold on a novel billed as about contemporary Asia because they desire an orientalized difference between East and West and are willing to read historically so long as it maintains this difference.

The illegibility of contemporary Asia appears not only in popular responses but in US academic criticism as well. When the novel *is* treated as thinking historically, Singapore is viewed as overdetermined by large, global forces. Anne Anlin Cheng points us to the residues of colonialism in the novel and film backdrops as registered by the Black and White Houses and "the tony British accents sported by this parade of beautiful people."[71] Cheng rightfully points out that the film perpetuates a Singaporean state myth about the modernizing forces of Chinese settlers, eliding the history of collaboration between Singapore's upper class and colonial power. Grace Kyungwon Hong also notes that Singaporean wealth, as part of what she describes as the global model minority, "cannot but reference colonial and racialized pasts."[72] Both Hong and Cheng, moreover, are conscious of the ways the novel is politically mired in the ascendance of Asian capital as it is figured through diasporic, affluent Asians. Hong observes that the novel "sets various modes of value against one another" and "attempt[s] to suture old and new histories of Asian racialization and capitalization."[73] For both thinkers, in other words, *Crazy Rich Asians* is an allegory for twenty-first-century global capitalism, a phenomenon that emerged from the structures of British colonialism.

Both are, of course, completely valid readings. But reading Singapore as an allegory for global capitalism often takes on a historical narrative that casts the British Empire and a complicit authoritarian postcolonial government as its main actors. For example, Hong describes the "true object" of the series as "a description of the consumerist behaviors and tastes upon which the Singaporean lifestyle is based," concluding that the novel is a treatise on consumerism as a governing ideology of the PAP.[74] Although Hong's analysis is invested in comprehending Kwan's novel on the transnational scale of "interconnected global ethnic Chinese capitalists,"[75] when she turns to the national, her reading of the Singaporean state potentially reproduces depictions of Singapore as a nation with a despotic government and deluded citizens.

So what history does *Crazy Rich Asians* point us to? Let us turn back to the beginning of the novel. In the famous opening scene, readers are introduced to the Leongs and the Youngs, powerful, rich Singaporean Chinese families, during a standoff with a racist hotel manager, Reginald Orsmby, who refuses to honor the Young family's reservation of the Lancaster penthouse suite. Ormsby, who has no idea about the degree of wealth (or the degree of vindictiveness) that the "disheveled" and "dowdy" Leong and Young family women hold, snarkily suggests that they find a place to stay in Chinatown, making clear his race-based disdain.[76] Ormsby's prejudiced attitude is out of place in the context of 1986 London, to the extent that Felicity Leong muses that she "hadn't seen this particular brand of superior sneer since she was a child growing up in the waning days of colonial Singapore, and she thought that this kind of overt racism had ceased to exist."[77] With no other place to stay, Felicity Leong places a call to her husband, Harry Leong, who in turn makes a quick call to the hotel's owner. When the Leongs and Youngs eventually return to the hotel, Ormsby quickly learns with great horror that the Leongs have bought out the Calthorpe and Felicity is its new owner. The prologue closes with Felicity firing the hapless manager.

Part of the satisfaction of the prologue's "Empire buys back" revenge fantasy is in the way that it asserts the new world order of the Asian Century that the crazy rich Asian families represent by overturning the power dynamics of East and West. In one kind of reading, postcolonial capitalism here reperforms the territorial logics of colonial power for the purposes of vengeance; our perverse pleasure hinges on the East/West binary, even though, or precisely because, the power dynamic has changed. The passage gestures toward the politics of colonial mimicry as Ormsby observes Felicity's overbearing Chineseness alongside her "Thatcheresque perm and preposterous 'English' accent."[78] Rather than reinscribe Felicity's postcolonial subjectivity as "almost the same, but not quite," Felicity's reception as a woman who is mimicking the colonial becomes a source of ironic pleasure for the reader because of the way she eventually dispenses and displaces Ormsby.[79] Colonial mimicry is not simply a sign of difference or a symptom of deference to colonial culture, but a means of enhancing revenge.

The prologue serves as more than just a wry commentary on how such figures like Ormsby have no place in the new world order ushered in by Asian capitalism, or, as Hong cogently argues, the "narrative of Asian capital's ascendance cannot quite evade the specter of racism and colonialism."[80] Very subtly, the prologue also has readers consider *how* to read this specter, calling attention to how the history of postcolonial capitalism is obscured by modes of reading (and their consequent pleasures) that privilege East/West or colonizer-colonized conflict. The prologue states:

> Anyone else happening upon the scene might have noticed an unusually composed eight-year-old boy and an ethereal wisp of a girl sitting quietly in a corner, but all Reginald Ormsby saw from his desk overlooking the lobby were two little Chinese children staining the damask settee with their sodden coats.[81]

This passage shows how the narrative continues to be viewed through Ormsby's racialized perspective, emphasizing both the dominance of Ormsby's Western gaze and the difficulty of moving away from its pull. Despite their exceptionality as marked by descriptors of "unusually" and "ethereal," Ormsby can only see soggy Chinese children ruining furniture. By calling attention to what is *not* being noticed, that these two soggy children—Nicholas Young and Astrid Leong—are nonetheless "unusually composed" and "ethereal," our attention to the conflict in the prologue is problematized because it assumes the importance of British colonialism. The prologue's critique of binary difference is not its faulty logic but the way the drama of binary difference centralizes British colonialism as the specter in the story of postcolonial capitalism and at the expense of recognizing a post-1997 history that is symbolized by Nick and Astrid, who go on to become Overseas Singaporeans par excellence (as a respected fashionista in Europe, Astrid, like Nick, proves herself deeply versed in codes of Western culture). Spivak once warned that "placing colonialism/imperialism securely in the past, and/or by suggesting a continuous line from that past to our present," can "sometimes serve the production of neocolonial knowledge."[82] Or as Andrew Liu of *n+1 magazine* puts it, "There isn't a smooth path from British colonialism to 21st century Asian capitalism," and the *longue durée* of capitalism can actually reinstall Eurocentricism if shorter histories are not also accounted for.[83]

As my reading of the "Empire buys back" scene suggests, the answer to what history readers see depends on what readers assume is the show of "economic might" that Kwan speaks of in his interviews. Read from the perspective of Felicity Leong, who is incredulous at Ormsby's hostility, the 1986 context in which the scene unfolds is a temporal remark on the hotel manager's "backward and residual white animus."[84] If we are to situate the 1986 context as part of Nick and Astrid's childhood, however, 1986 can be read as the historical marker of the Overseas Singaporean's nascency. It was not only the year that Singapore experienced its first post-independence economic recession; it is also the year that Singapore began slowly developing its economy for modern services, away from a manufacturing economy. At this point in history, Singapore was around the corner from its Tiger economy status. Singapore was not regarded as economically significant and was but one nation among many in the post–British Empire world vying for a place in the global economy. But we might say that 1986 marks the beginning of a knowledge economy that would become more pronounced after the 1997 Asian financial crisis and more culturally evident after 2008. Interestingly, the jump in time from the 1986 prologue to the novel's post-2008 present tempts us to gloss over the centrality of 1997 for understanding Singapore as Global Asia—a potential critical and subtle remark on Kwan's part. While Kwan's writing certainly invites a number of different kinds of readings (which has given him latitude in terms of how he can represent the novel), the opening indicates a consciousness about Singapore's history of the present as well as the politics of the West's reading of the East.

Assuming that the power effects of British colonialism are "negative," as Foucault puts it, or oppressive centers the question of power through East/West conflict. Nick and Astrid, on the other hand, remind us of Foucault's injunction that "power produces."[85] In this vein, we recognize that the historical effects of British colonialism on Singapore have generated Overseas Singaporeans as a new subjectivity that navigates different systems of power. Their newness does not mark a clean break from history, however; Nick and Astrid are there with their mothers, after all. The oppositional politics toward colonialism, as embodied by Felicity Leong's postcolonial revenge, are situated as but one historical thread in the broader condition of postcoloniality.

Allusions throughout *Crazy Rich Asians* centralize the shorter history of constructing Singapore as a safe haven for foreign capitalist investment rather than the longer history of British colonialism. One of the most common critiques of the prose in *Crazy Rich Asians* is its stilted dialogue and thus unrealistic, flat characters. Hong, for example, notes that dialogue such as Peik Lin's explanation of Singapore to Rachel, "We're the most stable country in the region, and Mainlanders feel that their money is far safer here than in Shanghai, or even Switzerland," does not sound like realistic banter between old friends.[86] Rather than read the stilted dialogue as a reflection of bad writing, we should read it as a symptom of the novel reckoning with the specter of state power but circumventing the issue of reproducing an orientalist depiction of an Asian despotic government. In other words, Kwan avoids making *Crazy Rich Asians* about state power. The example of stilted dialogue that Peik Lin parrots is likely eerily familiar to Singaporeans, who, since independence, have faced state aspirations to "stability" in the name of global capitalism. In this respect, it is more useful to think about the stilted dialogue as giving voice to the authoritative discourse of the Singaporean state.[87] Although Singapore's reputation for stability (which amounts to safety for foreign investment) is touted by the Singaporean government and accepted by many international economic and political organizations, what clues us into the particularities of the voice of the Singaporean state is the reference to Switzerland, which holds an idiosyncratic symbolic significance in Singapore. As with Jeremy Tiang's short story discussed in chapter 1, the reference to Switzerland, the exemplary nation in the eyes of the Singaporean government since 1984, alludes to the former prime minister Goh Chok Tong's exhortation to achieve a "Swiss standard of living."[88]

In fact, it is the Goh family that gives voice to the kind of Singaporean state rhetoric typical of Prime Minister Goh's tenure throughout the novel—and their names are plainly the same. Of the various families in the novel, the Gohs are represented as part of the nouveau riche who built up their wealth "out of sheer sweat and tenacity" against the odds of their Hainanese ancestry, a relative disadvantage compared to the Straits Chinese or Hokkiens.[89] According to Peik Lin's father, Wye Mun, "Singapore was a meritocracy, and whoever performed well was invited into the winner's circle."[90] While the notion of meritocracy can be traced to Singapore's independence era under Lee Kuan Yew's leadership, the particular logics of monetary reward for hard work and ability is a cornerstone of Goh's incumbency.[91] In a passing exchange with a family friend, Dr. Gu, a minor character, Peik Lin, assures him that his daughter's and grandson's life decisions (which Dr. Gu disapproves of) are a sign that "they are being *creative*,"[92] which again links the Goh family to the socioeconomic policies associated with Goh Chok Tong, who promoted creativity in the name of the knowledge economy.[93]

Readers are made to understand that the Gohs' nouveau riche class identity is tacky in the ways that they revel in their wealth and the Trumpian, Vegas-like aesthetic of their home. The Gohs clearly believe that this is the lifestyle they have earned and that the government's policies have made their wealth possible. This is not a subtle aspect of the novel. Wye Mun, who is "always on the defensive whenever anyone criticized the government," even goes so far as to repeat one of the Singaporean state's most deeply entrenched myths of its exceptional progress in the transition from "Third World to First World": "Think of how they've [our politicians] transformed this place from a backward island to one of the most prosperous countries in the world."[94] Given how Kwan's trilogy sets up "a value system of morality and discernment (and discernment *as* morality),"[95] there is a clear judgment imposed on state authoritative discourse that perpetuates the myth of Singapore's economic success when it is voiced by one of the most garish and tasteless families in the novel. State discourse is not positioned as a voice of reason, or as an oppressive force, but as that which does the work of concealing shorter histories of postcolonial capitalism.

While the novel might be critiquing upwardly mobile diasporic Chinese families like the Gohs for buying into and perpetuating state discourse, it also calls attention to the ways that those outside of Singapore reproduce such narratives. In the opening of the novel, when Rachel considers the idea of visiting Singapore with Nick, she thinks, "As an economist, she certainly knew about Singapore—this tiny, intriguing island at the tip of the Malay Peninsula, which had transformed within a few short decades from a British colonial backwater into the country with the world's highest concentration of millionaires."[96] The repetition of language between Rachel and Wye Mun unifies an outsider to Singapore with a local, giving Singapore's success story transnational coherence. The narrative's Eurocentric versus meritocratic appeal demonstrates the wide-ranging function the myth has for different subjectivities.

With a wink and a nudge, Kwan calls our attention to how only certain histori-cal versions of Singapore are palatable to Western and perhaps even Singaporean readers. When giving Rachel a tour of Tyersall Park grounds, Nick tells her about its historical significance for Malay culture and its roots in the Majapahit Empire:

> "'The Last King of Singapura.' Sounds like a movie. Why don't you write the screen-play?" Rachel remarked.
> "Ha! I think it'll draw an audience of about four," Nick replied.[97]

What this exchange suggests is that Singapore's ancient, indigenous history is not only of little interest (and it certainly was not in the Hollywood adaptation of the novel), but the master narrative of Singapore's Third World to First World develop-ment as spawned by British Empire is actually a transnational source of pleasure. As I have discussed, such a *longue durée* conception of Singapore's development is also at the expense of interrogating the particularities that emerge with attention to a shorter history of Singapore's economic arc. The next section considers what the concealment of history makes possible for Western fantasies of the East.

PRINCESS FANTASY, READING SETTING

Another implication of the princess fantasy for reading postcoloniality in the context of the Asian Century that *Crazy Rich Asians* draws out is the role setting plays in pleasure. The melodrama, stereotypical characters, and stilted dialogue of the novel direct our critical attention to characterological approaches, and while Kwan's characters provide entertainment, they are not the main draw of the novel or the basis for the phenomenon *Crazy Rich Asians* has become. Rather, consum-erist pleasures are built into the setting itself: setting is not simply the backdrop or the stage on which character development takes place; it instead replaces character as the affective mode through which readers connect to the narrative. Reviewers and critics have frequently noted that Kwan's writerly strengths do not lie in char-acter development. Nonetheless, they marvel at the "guilty pleasures" that readers derive from the "expository nature of the novel."[98] The passage where Rachel first visits Tyersall Park provides a good example.

> The "living room," as Nick so modestly called it, was a gallery that ran along the entire northern end of the house, with art deco divans, wicker club chairs, and otto-mans casually grouped into intimate seating areas. A row of tall plantation doors opened onto the wraparound veranda, inviting the view of verdant parklands and the scent of night-blooming jasmine into the room, while at the far end a young man in a tuxedo played on the Bösendorfer grand piano. As Nick led her into the space, Rachel found herself reflexively trying to ignore her surroundings, even though all she wanted to do was study every exquisite detail: the exotic potted palms in mas-sive *Qianlong* dragon jardinieres that anchored the space, the scarlet-shaded opaline glass lamps that cast an amber glow over the lacquered teak surfaces, the silver- and

lapis lazuli-filigreed walls that shimmered as she moved about the room. Every single object seemed imbued with a patina of timeless elegance, as if it had been there for more than a hundred years, and Rachel didn't dare to touch anything. The glamorous guests, however, appeared completely at ease lounging on the shantung silk ottomans or mingling on the veranda while a retinue of white-gloved servants in deep-olive batik uniforms circulated with trays of cocktails.[99]

Emblematic of Kwan's writing in the trilogy, this passage evinces a suppression of character in favor of setting. Not only are characters entirely secondary to the setting itself—if not simply *of* the setting in the case of the nameless piano player and the "glamorous guests" lounging around—the language actively restricts Rachel's interiority and any emotional performance. Using the social mores of the world as a plot device, the narrative flattens Rachel as she tries to "ignore her surroundings" and *not* engage the setting through touch. The overwhelming design of the living room cows Rachel into silence, effectively anesthetizing her and erasing her personality as she becomes part of the grand scene. As Rachel attempts to ignore her surroundings, the narrative continues for the reader's pleasure. Certainly, Rachel's lack of affect instructs the reader of the magnificence of the scene, but our understanding of the setting has little dependence on Rachel's interaction with it. With the exception of the seating and the infrastructure of the building itself, the lack of interface has to do with the fact that very little of the setting actually has any use beyond scopophilic pleasure.

Much of the awe and pleasure from Kwan's elaborate settings come from its presentation of "exquisite details," which in this case depict enormous wealth by means of the objects that make up the setting. The passage does not simply portray an accumulation of objects; it emphasizes order among "sensuous, trivial, and superfluous textual presences."[100] The narrative moves our gaze through the scene, pausing on the furniture in the room and the views outside it. The grandness of the scene derives, in part, from contrasting scales that make up the setting of the living room: the details of filigree, batik, and Qianlong designs are juxtaposed to the openness of the veranda, parklands, and grand piano. The mathematical contrast of minute design and empty space marks the scale of the Young family's wealth and power through labor (commodities valued for their artisanal craft) and territory (command over space). This aesthetic of contrast is further constructed through the arrangement of Eastern and Western objects: the art deco divans with shantung silk ottomans, the tuxedo-clad piano player next to the batik-wearing servers, the Qianlong porcelain alongside opaline glass. The wealth that brings these contrasts together to construct the seemingly nonremarkable scene (for people of a certain world) denotes both a command over setting and an organizing logic whereby wealth is able to overcome cultural difference.

East/West aesthetic details are also idealized through the Leong family home. Resonating with Rachel's experience of Tyersall Park is Annabel Lee, Araminta's mother, who offers one of the few passages viewed through someone other than Rachel, in this case, her experience of the Leong family home. Like Rachel, Annabel is an outsider to the Singaporean Chinese elite social scene, though she herself is incredibly wealthy. As she has been lauded by *Architectural Digest* for her "Edward Tuttle–designed house,"[101] we understand that Annabel is a discerning woman, so her awe signals the aesthetic magnitude we too should experience as readers. As with Tyersall Park, the Leong family home operates with East/West contrasts: Pimms cocktails served on Selangor pewter trays; orange blossoms alongside Ru ware from the Northern Song dynasty; and Peranakan-style opium chairs.[102] Although we are privy to a prolonged and rather animated internal commentary by Annabel, it seems that Annabel does not engage with the social scene at hand. At best, she thinks, "Oh look, Eleanor just waved at me,"[103] but otherwise there is no social interaction. Again, we observe how the narrative favors details of setting by flattening Annabel's character, even though the writing *seems* to signal character depth through the internal monologue marked by italics. The internal dialogue, however, is simply a mode by which to, as Annabel expresses it, soak in "every minute detail of the way these people lived,"[104] and to bask in the aesthetic pleasures of the setting.

Kwan's privileging of setting over character development is at once his resistance to the assimilatory pressures of the Western gaze and his way of attracting it. The novel's favoring of setting over character development works against notions of difference derived from personality and personhood.[105] Given Kwan's apparent scorn for Asian American assimilationist novels and Asian historical fiction that either capitulate to the Western gaze's demand for likeness or maintain its demand for binary difference, we might read Kwan's minimalist gestures toward Asian self-representation as deliberately avoiding characterological emphasis rather than as inadequate gestures.[106] We can also read the emphasis on setting as a technique of postcolonial capitalism, a way of profiting off colonial desire. Kwan's elaborate depictions of setting are closer to what Anne Anlin Cheng describes as "ornamentalism," or the processes that render Asian femininity ornamental and Asia as ornament. The way that Cheng describes the 2015 Metropolitan Museum of Art exhibition, *China: Through the Looking Glass*, which appeared a mere two years after the publication of *Crazy Rich Asians*, could also apply to a number of Kwan's settings: "Opulence and sensuality are the signature components of Asiatic character; that Asia is always ancient, excessive, feminine, available, and decadent, that material consumption promises cultural possession."[107] Cheng's language also describes the rhetoric of the Singapore tourism campaign "Passion Made Possible." Reading the details of Kwan's setting as ornamentalism, however, still assumes the inherently masculinized ethos of the West in the East/West dynamic. Given the economic context that *Crazy Rich Asians* points us to, I have suggested that we read the West as increasingly feminized, not simply as a way of figuring the West's economic decline through gender identity, but the implications of that decline for how we understand orientalist desire.

The elaborate detail of Kwan's settings asserts a command over women, not by oppressing them, but by overwhelming them—that is, by overcoming mind or feeling—with pleasure. There are resonances here between the effects of the princess fantasy and what Achille Mbembe describes as the aesthetics of superfluity, which is "premised on the capacity of things to hypnotize, overexcite, or paralyze the sense."[108] Certainly, the details in Kwan's novel maintain the Orient as a site of pleasure and fantasy for the colonial explorer, but they are not in service of a male fantasy of domination. Taking pleasure in Singapore's setting would seem to position the Western subject as one in power because of the agential denotation of "taking." Such is the illusion of the princess fantasy. But in the soft power context of Global Asia, pleasuring the princess—the West—is the means by which to draw in capital.

The emphasis on Singapore as setting performed through detail is not idiosyncratic to Kwan. In a 2019 episode of *The Bachelor*, a TV show where women compete for a bachelor's affections, contestants were flown to Singapore. As if taking its cue from *Crazy Rich Asians*, Singapore is presented to the women (the princesses) through sweeping aerial views of the city and through the luxury of their Fairmont hotel suite.[109] The sound track is punctuated by various excited exclamations, but when the women enter the suite, they are awestruck and silent, reminiscent of Rachel's initial visit to Tyersall Park. Like the wider views of the "verdant parklands" seen from the Tyersall Park living room, the camera offers impressive cityscape views from the suite's balcony. "I've never been in a hotel like this," one of the contestants tells us as the screen cuts to an interview. "From our room you can see all of Singapore." The women walk through the suite single file, marveling at modern furniture with various ethnic touches, tropical houseplants, Chinese brush paintings, and art deco light fixtures. Like the women of *The Bachelor*, viewers are treated to the details of Singapore's setting: this world will bring you all that you need. In its seeming accommodation to the needs of the Western gaze, Kwan's writing is hardly subversive, at least in any critically satisfying way. The subversion of the West under postcolonial capitalism does not operate by a neat inversion of East/West binaries (though the opening of *Crazy Rich Asians* might tempt us to believe so). In other words, the assertion of power over the West is not a mimicry *of* the West's power. To assume so is itself a Western fantasy. What *Crazy Rich Asians* in fact demonstrates is how postcolonial capitalism operates with a long historical consciousness of the workings of colonial pleasures and uses those pleasures to its advantage.

While it is through setting that we can read a subtle assertion of power through its ability to overwhelm, the details of setting also aesthetically assert difference from the West through cosmopolitan craft: Singapore has taste and style. Recalling here the state project of overhauling Singapore's image of sterility, the emphasis on style—as sterility's antonym—is unsurprising. Given the colonial history of Singapore as the "crossroads of the East," as well as the emphasis on East/West difference in the Asian Values era, the reemergence (and continuation) of East/West aesthetics is not especially novel or contemporary. There are, however, some distinctions in the way that East/West aesthetics are asserted after 1997. Historically, Singapore as a site of East/West encounter served as validation for

British imperialism's civilizing mission and as proof of Singapore's modernity in an ever-globalizing world, whereas the East/West aesthetics of Singapore in *Crazy Rich Asians* emphasize the ability to synthesize unruly elements. Bringing East and West together in an aesthetically pleasing way is a matter of good taste and deliberate design. In admiring the East/West aesthetic in the novel, readers credit the (unknown) designer for their craft as a sort of invisible hand, validating the designer's power.

The novel upholds the contrasting aesthetic of East and West as ideal and as distinct from the aesthetic presented by Eddie's and Peik Lin's family homes, both of which assert wealth through their performance of conspicuous consumption and their accumulation of Western objects. While in Tyersall Park readers are overwhelmed by magnitude through an aesthetic of contrast, magnitude in Eddie's home is about enumerated excess: "five bedrooms, six baths, more than four thousand square feet, not including the eight-hundred-square-foot terrace," "two Filipino and two Mainland Chinese maids," "five parking spots," club memberships at the "Chinese Athletic Association, the Hong Kong Golf Club, the China Club, the Hong Kong Club, the Cricket Club, the Dynasty Club, the American Club, the Jockey Club, [and] the Royal Hong Kong Yacht Club," and "more than seventy timepieces from the most esteemed watchmakers"[110]—all made even more special when we consider Hong Kong's limited space as one of the densest cities in the world. Unlike Tyersall Park's brandless, eclectic aesthetic, Eddie's style is insistently old European, with a "Biedermeier-filled" home designed by the "Austro-German decorator Kaspar von Morgenlatte to evoke a Hapsburg hunting schloss."[111] Similarly, we see in Peik Lin's home markers of old Europe: a "frescoed replica of Fragonard's *The Swing*," "Venetian mirrors and candelabra," "two versions of the *Venus de Milo*," and "a heavy Battenberg lace tablecloth and high-backed Louis Quatorze chairs,"[112] but the overwhelmingly gold coloring throughout the home invokes a Vegas-Trump aesthetic. By virtue of Eddie's performances of wealth and Peik Lin's family's unapologetic nouveau richeness, readers understand that the wealth performed by these two families is comically regrettable, especially when compared to the Young family's presentation. They are objects of disdain not only because of their over-the-top presentation of conspicuous consumption but also because they signify wealth through the mindless accrual of Western objects, which in turn reveals an inferiority complex with respect to the West.

CONCLUSION

As I show in my reading of *Crazy Rich Asians*, attention to Singapore's shorter history of postcolonial capitalism can counter the hegemonic effects of *longue durée* master narratives, but it requires a reading practice that lets go of colonial binarism in favor of a more generative, rather than disciplinary, account of power. Moreover, as I showed in my discussion of the princess fantasy, the changed global order of the Asian Century does not result in a simple inversion of how power is asserted. Instead, postcolonial capitalism works with a consciousness of that history of power by capitalizing on colonial desires and US declinism in the production of Global Asia.

I close here with a brief rumination on the Hollywood adaptation of *Crazy Rich Asians* (2018), a wildly successful film that generated much controversy over its representational politics for Asian Americans. While the film was celebrated for featuring a number of Asian American actors and actresses, its critics expressed ambivalence about the class politics of the film and how it might reaffirm a classist respectability politics in the United States. In the context of my discussion of the novel in the context of Global Asia and US declinism, the film adaptation adds another dimension, perhaps unexpected, to the perception of Singapore as a haven: it is not only a site of fantasy for capitalist consumption without debt or a safe harbor from corporate taxes and regulation; for Asian Americans, Singapore is an affective refuge from US histories of racialization. But what is most interesting to me about the film, which I understand as an American interpretation of the novel, is what its accommodation of the Asian American gaze indicates about Singapore as Global Asia. Certainly, we can and perhaps should hold accountable the director and scriptwriters, who had no concerns about putting in "ethnic" details that were clearly directed to an American rather than Singaporean or Southeast Asian audience. For example, in a tender scene that was described by one *HuffPost* reporter as an example of a "culturally nuanced moment"[113] and celebrated by other writers as especially meaningful for the way it speaks to how "many immigrant families stay connected with their heritage,"[114] Rachel sat down at a table with the Young family to fold dumplings. This was not a scene that came from the novel. Such dumplings (*jiaozi*), however, are unlikely to be part of the culinary traditions of the Chinese diaspora that went through Southeast Asia, since most of the migrants came from southern China rather than the north where such dumplings originate.

My point is not to quibble about authenticity. Rather, my question concerns how the screenwriters, director, and cast—many of whom are sensitive to racial and cultural representation—could transform a novel that is, in my reading, centrally about Singapore into a film about, as the director John Chu puts it, "how it feels for an Asian-American to go through a cultural identity crisis when traveling to Asia for the first time."[115] In other words, what is it about Singapore that allows for the Asian Americanization of the *Crazy Rich Asians* film? Is the current Hollywood adaptation imaginable had Kwan's novel been set in other Global Asia sites like Hong Kong, Kuala Lumpur, or Seoul?

I think the answer is no. We could read the imposition of details like the dumpling scene as reflecting a colonial mind-set of *terra nullius*, where Singapore is nothing but an empty stage for Asian American fantasies to play out, or as reflecting the American privilege of ignorance, where Singapore is imagined as a racial enclave like a US Chinatown. But I would suggest that the very possibility of making the film about Asian American experience demonstrates the power of Singapore's anglophonic legibility, a legibility that produces desirability and, in this instance, is mistaken as evidence of Singapore as *not that* different—or, apparently, not different enough to precipitate the careful cultural and historical sensitivities of those we would typically assume to be concerned with the racial politics of representation. Even though Singapore and Asian America are diverse in manifold ways, Singapore's anglophonic legibility allows for an inter-imperial, transpacific coherence of sinocentricism: the dynamics of Chinese privilege in Singapore with the Chinese American representational hegemony in the Asian American context. Thus, what is especially revealing about the film adaptation is how the Singaporean state's work to craft its dehistoricized and decontextualized Global Asia image now has transpacific affective investments, further entrenching and exceeding a state-produced dominant narrative.

The sinocentric excess enabled by Singapore's anglophonic legibility, however, is potentially a threat to Singapore's national interests. Certainly, Singapore as Global Asia has served the class interests of Singaporean Chinese, and only time will tell how such racialized privilege will interact with China's expanding political and economic clout. Much like we saw with the Overseas Singaporean Unit, China has established the Overseas Chinese Affairs Office, also aimed at "winning the hearts and minds abroad."[116] Such attempts at ideological influence may be a challenge in Singapore, given local xenophobia toward recent migrants from China, or perhaps recent conflict between the US and Russia will facilitate China's efforts. Either way, the rise of China does not necessarily portend the end of Singapore as Global Asia, but it certainly suggests that Singapore's anglophonic legibility is risky business in the face of ongoing global rearrangements of power.

Conclusion

In the long course of writing this book, "Global Asia" has begun circulating more strongly as a term. As with the Singaporean state's branding of the nation, "Global Asia" in the corporate world—Global Asia Alliance Consultants, Global Asia Trading Company, Thrive Global Asia Pacific, Global Asia Exporters, Global Asia Holdings, and Global Asia Material Companies, to name but a few examples— signals cosmopolitanism and readiness to manage the demands of global capitalism. The corporate brand of Global Asia means that the very term "Global Asia" accrues meaning and value through circuits of finance. More familiarly for readers of this book and as briefly mentioned in the introduction, "Global Asia" and "Global Asias" name academic subfields. As the fields of Global Asia and Global Asias becomes more prevalent, we also see the development of new university programs and research centers, which in turn, confer and accrue intellectual value. Although corporate and academic manifestations of Global Asia are often politically at odds, all renditions materialize as institutional formations. Institutions generate, organize, and systemize value. This is not to suggest that institutions are always suspect or problematic, but as Stuart Hall once warned, institutionalization is "a moment of extraordinarily profound danger."[1] This leads me to ponder, what is that danger with respect to Global Asia?

Thinking about the politics of institutionalization with respect to Global Asia brings me to the case of the soon-to-be-closed Yale-NUS College, a collaboration between Yale University and National University of Singapore. YNC's conception as a liberal arts college began as a part of "higher education trends driven by Asian entry into the so-called global knowledge economy, manifesting in high government investment in research and higher education."[2] With its highly touted Common Curriculum in which students engage "Asian as well as Western materials,"[3] and the assertion YNC was an educational institution that would be able "to feel the buzz of societies on the move, to respond to the zeitgeist, the issues, the priorities of a rising continent"[4] and was *not* simply "a carbon copy of Yale in New Haven,"[5] Yale-NUS College was part and parcel of what I have outlined in this book as Global Asia. It is an institution both producing and constitutive of Singapore's soft power and cultural capital.

With no warning or prior discussion, the National University of Singapore President, Tan Eng Chye, President of Yale-NUS College, Tan Tai Yong, and founding president of Yale-NUS, Pericles Lewis, announced on August 27, 2021 that the Class of 2025 would be YNC's final class.[6] The details on the reasons behind the closure are murky, but various think pieces and investigative journalistic articles speculate that the purported problems of financial stability or of capital fundraising do not tell the entire story; rather, it is YNC's controversial policy of academic freedom—a policy not extended to NUS itself—that is under fire because it goes against the state's history of controlling free speech.[7] Whatever the true rationale behind YNC's impending closure and however justified, when considering that the "[Singapore] education ministry provided capital funding for Yale-NUS's infrastructure and matched donations to its endowment fund,"[8] the liberal arts college is ultimately a state institution. This is to say, regardless of the exceptions to free speech that YNC was able to take through its association with Yale, YNC is ultimately subject to state power. Certainly, the sudden nature of the closure and the lack of clarity around the reasons why it was closed are characteristic of authoritarian governance.

From the view of authority, the problem with institutions of soft power is that they do not always operate according to plan. Cultivating creativity, even in the name of producing neoliberal entrepreneurs for the global economy, can be risky for a state attempting to curate certain economic or political outcomes. Reflecting on his experience, Shawn Hoo, a Yale-NUS alum, writes:

> For all of us who were, unbeknownst to us, experimental subjects—alumni, students, faculty, staff—Yale-NUS was a place where, we were led to believe, we could truly build a community of learners who studied a curriculum we actively wanted to shape; for all of the well-considered criticism of our cloistered elitism, a real place where we wanted to find out how academic inquiry could meet social engagement; a physical home where residential living can be innovated on with policies such as gender-neutral living (a first on Singapore campuses); a true opportunity to find our place in the higher education landscape in Singapore, in Asia, for the World—or so our vision used to go.[9]

On the one hand, one can detect a tone of resignation in Hoo's language, one that understands how he, as a Singaporean, is subject to the vagaries of disciplinary power. Yet Hoo also emphasizes the joy that he and his classmates found in living and working together as creative, intellectual, national subjects. I have heard similar anecdotes from faculty about the pedagogical pleasures they have working at the college when forming a liberal arts curriculum in Singapore. Like many of the writers under study throughout this book, Hoo's account emphasizes pleasure. It also demonstrates how, in practice, YNC students, staff, and faculty exceeded the ideological confines set out by a state institution of Global Asia. Hoo's remarks and the literary and political contestations of Singapore as Global Asia under study throughout this book teach us that although Singaporeans, as potential agents of Global Asia, are subject to the whims of institutional power that may promote and dispense them as necessary, it is by underscoring the memory of pleasure, no matter how fleeting, that the possibilities of new, political futures are forged. In this way, we might regard pleasure as a counter-authoritarian form, one that allows for freedom from state instrumentalization.

The case of YNC is instructive for how it stages a conflict between harder and softer forms of power. Indeed, this book challenges the Eurocentric modes of reading that follow narrow conceptions of power in diagnosing Singapore as solely disciplinary, forceful, or coercive. However, future directions to consider, as illustrated by the YNC example, are the contexts, continuities, and contradictions among manifold forms of power, in Singapore and beyond. One of the priorities of *Becoming Global Asia* has been to foreground the question of soft power in the context of Singapore. This should not be mistaken as a dismissal of the real oppression and marginalization of those who do not easily fit within the exuberant story of Singapore as Global Asia: the non-Chinese, the non-anglophone, the migrant workers, the queer, the elderly, the disabled, the working classes.[10] On the contrary, it is precisely by bringing soft power to the forefront and situating authoritarian, disciplinary power through what I have described as a "feeling of structure," that I have produced a nuanced account of power in Singapore. By examining Singapore's soft power we are more able to understand and to challenge the systemic array of cultural, political, and socioeconomic forces that the modern state marshals to its various ends. State power over the nation is global.

To illustrate this point, *Becoming Global Asia* has offered a critical account of Singapore's emergence as a capitalist haven with an outsized influence on the global cultural imaginary in the historical context of postcolonial capitalism. Genre has been methodologically central to this book. The emergence of major and popular anthologies, demographic compilations, coming-of-career narratives, and the princess fantasy at particular historical moments of economic change—state developmentalism, Asian Values, and Global Asia—reveal the cultural capitalist logics of their moments. My close readings of the texts and genres of Global Asia further elucidate how such cultural logics are not only responding to global economic imperatives by, for example, cultivating a cosmopolitan, diasporic citizenry, but also negotiating historical layers of postcolonial governance and evolving economic conditions within Singapore and beyond. The emergence of careers as a pleasurable mode of work, as I discuss in chapter 3 for instance, is as much a manifestation of neoliberal corporate ideologies of individualism as it is a rejection of the developmental postcolonial state. Insofar that "genre" refers to literary typology and to a mode for creating expectations for how literary objects should be read, it has also been significant for thinking about Singapore as a problem of interpretation.

As a project of soft power, Singapore as Global Asia has involved changing the city-state's image and narrative while also shaping the terms for how it is read. Whether through major anthologies that draw on colonial organizing logics to make claims to modernity or through demographic compilations to prove Singapore's global influence through its cosmopolitan populations, one way that postcolonial capitalism operates is through an appeal to anglophone legibility in the global cultural imaginary. Singapore's legibility—and thus desirability—rests on what Jini Kim Watson describes as the "loose signifier of 'Asia.'"[11] Its looseness does not suggest that Asia has no meaning, but rather that Singapore can make claim to Asia and take advantage of Western desire for Asia, as we saw with the Hollywood adaptation of *Crazy Rich Asians*. As my discussion of coming-of-career narratives and the princess fantasy show, however, that legibility cannot only be attributed to the state even if the project of legibility begins there. Limiting understandings of Singapore to expressions of state power, as I have argued, does not capture how Global Asia is accorded a transnational coherence. Certainly, new questions will emerge about Singapore's anglophonic legibility with the rise of China. How will Global Asia morph with considerations of Singapore's sinophonic legibility?

By articulating postcolonial capitalism as a mode of recognizing the shorter though heterogeneous period of what historically constitutes "the postcolonial," this project has also aimed to take up the question of how the field of postcolonial studies should engage with the contemporary capitalist moment. Because the field of postcolonial literature has recently been transformed into global anglophone literature, my preservation of "postcolonial" might appear nostalgic.[12] But in expanding our critical view to sites that are not typically marked as postcolonial—or, shall we say, not legible in postcolonialism's canon—my book has aimed to push at the field's discursive limits and at how it typically uncovers and analyzes the working of power. While the field of postcolonial studies has been concerned with contesting the ongoing legacies of imperialism, and rightly so, this book has been more interested in thinking through the ongoing legacies of postcolonial nationalism in our political present.

Engaging questions of what that legacy looks like in our contemporary moment has meant grappling with the dynamics of US empire and thus the transpacific, which until the recent rise of China, have arguably been the most significant economically structuring forces of the global order. While, generally speaking, transpacific studies has been offered as a mode of rehabilitating parochial tendencies in Asian American and Asian studies produced by disciplinary silos and nationalist methodologies, *Becoming Global Asia* demonstrates how transpacific studies can produce new research directions for postcolonial studies to consider. Given the Cold War, it is almost impossible to disregard the transpacific in the Southeast Asian context. But if the transpacific continues to be a contested, interimperialized space with global effects, postcolonialists would do well to consider how the transpacific might change how we theorize "the postcolonial." In this way,

I join Jini Kim Watson and Gary Wilder's call to be "Neither simply *for* nor *against* postcolonialism, and instead to "think *with* and *beyond* postcolonial theory about political contemporaneity."[13] As *Becoming Global Asia* has shown in the Singaporean context, the postcolonial is becoming increasingly appropriated and exploited for capital gain. Consequently, we must revise, expand, and multiply our notions of what postcoloniality looks like.

NOTES

INTRODUCTION: GLOBAL ASIA, A WAYWARD POSTCOLONIALISM

1. David Lamb, "Singapore Swing: Peaceful and Prosperous, Southeast Asia's Famously Uptight Nation Has Let Its Hair Down," *Smithsonian Magazine*, September 2007.

2. "GDP (current US$)," World Bank, accessed January 25, 2023, https://data.worldbank .org/indicator/NY.GDP.MKTP.CD?most_recent_value_desc=true&year_high_desc=true.

3. Philip Holden, "Postcolonial Desire: Placing Singapore," *Postcolonial Studies* 11.3 (2008): 345–61, 345.

4. This narrative is also part of the title of Lee Kuan Yew's memoir, *From Third World to First World: The Singapore Story* (Upper Saddle River, NJ: Prentice Hall, 1998).

5. Christian Caryl, "Africa's Singapore Dream," *Foreign Policy*, April 2, 2015, https://for eignpolicy.com/2015/04/02/africas-singapore-dream-rwanda-kagame-lee-kuan-yew/. See also "Three Places That Dream of Becoming Africa's Singapore," *Economist*, October 23, 2021, https://www.economist.com/middle-east-and-africa/2021/10/23/three-places-that -dream-of-becoming-africas-singapore.

6. See "Philips Blames Parliamentarians for Jamaica's Economic Stagnation," *Radio Jamaica News*, November 23, 2021. Samuel Braithwaite points out that politicians from different parties wield Singapore in their political rhetoric. Many thanks to Braithwaite for the references.

7. Jeevan Vasagar, "Singapore-on-Thames? This Is No Vision for Post-Brexit Britain," Opinion, *The Guardian*, November 24, 2017, https://www.theguardian.com/commentis free/2017/nov/24/singapore-on-thames-post-brexit-britain-wealthy-city-state.

8. See Tersita Cruz-del Rosario and Victor Kattan, "Opinion: Jared Kushner's Plan for Palestine Is Even Crazier Than You Thought," *Haaretz*, July 4, 2019, https://www.haaretz .com/middle-east-news/.premium-jared-kushner-s-plan-for-palestine-is-even-crazier -than-you-thought-1.7435303. The World Bank has also made a similar suggestion. See David

Rosenberg, "David's Harp/Can't Turn Palestine into Singapore," *Haaretz*, August 1, 2012, https://www.haaretz.com/david-s-harp-can-t-turn-palestine-into-singapore-1.5274971.

9. Lamb, "Singapore Swing," n.p.

10. William Gibson, "Disneyland with the Death Penalty," *Wired* 1.04, April 1, 1993, https://www.wired.com/1993/04/gibson-2/.

11. For discussion of Asian Miracle nations, see World Bank, *The East Asian Miracle: Economic Growth and Public Policy* (Oxford: Oxford University Press, 1993).

12. In 1994, as punishment for vandalizing cars and stealing road signs, Michael Fay was the first US citizen to be caned in Singapore.

13. Such robotic imagery is, of course, deeply racialized. See Michelle N. Huang and CA Davis's film essay, "Inhuman Figures: Robots, Clones, Aliens" Smithsonian Asian Pacific American Center, 2021, https://smithsonianapa.org/inhuman-figures/.

14. Lamb, "Singapore Swing," n.p.

15. In 2019, The World Bank ranked Singapore the second-best place in the world in its "Ease of Doing Business" rankings. In 2020, the Heritage Foundation ranked the city-state as number one for "economic freedom." See *Doing Business 2019: Training for Reform*, World Bank, 2019; and "2020 Index of Economic Freedom: Global Economic Freedom Hits All-Time High," Heritage Foundation, May 17, 2020, https://www.heritage.org/press/2020-index-economic-freedom-global-economic-freedom-hits-all-time-high.

16. *Bloomberg* has also reported that increasingly, China's billionaires are moving into Singapore as well. See Margaret Sutherlin, "China's Billionaires Jump Ship for Singapore," November 15, 2022, https://www.bloomberg.com/news/newsletters/2022-11-15/big-take-china-s-wealthy-elite-take-their-billions-to-singapore.

17. As Lily Cho and Susan J. Henders put it in their editorial introduction, Global Asia "underscores 'Asia' as a global site." See Lily Cho and Susan J. Henders. "Human Rights and the Arts in Global Asia: Conceptualizing Contexts," in *Human Rights and the Arts: Perspectives on Global Asia*, ed. Susan J. Henders and Lily Cho (Lanham, MD: Lexington Books, 2014), 6. Global Asia joins a number of cognate field formations with similar aims of changing the conditions of knowledge production about Asia. For Kuan-Hsing Chen and Chua Beng Huat, the Inter-Asia Cultural Studies project sought to recognize "very significant regional and sub-regional differences throughout 'Asia', including the effects of globalization on regionalization[,] . . . and move beyond nation-state boundaries to intersect the regional and sub-regional." See Kuan-Hsing Chen and Chua Beng Huat, "The *Inter-Asia Cultural Studies: Movements* Project," in *The Inter-Asia Cultural Studies Reader*, ed. Kuan-Hsing Chen and Chua Beng Huat (New York: Routledge, 2007), 2.

In a critique of inter-Asia discourses and their potential to produce an exclusionary Asia-centricity, Gladys Pak Lei Chong, Yiu Fai Chow, and Jeroen De Kloet write, "Trans-Asia as method recognizes the importance of 'Asia' as an affective and imagined framework, but it resists in drawing fixed boundaries that blocks exchanges, and therefore limits epistemological potentials." Gladys Pak Lei Chong, Yiu Fai Chow, and Jeroen De Kloet, "Towards Trans-Asia: Projects, Possibilities, Paradoxes," in *Trans-Asia as Method: Theory and Practices*, ed. Jeroen De Kloet, Yiu Fai Chow, and Gladys Pak Lei Chong (Lanham, MD: Rowman and Littlefield, 2020), 6.

In *Other Asias* (London: Blackwell, 2003), Gayatri Chakravorty Spivak calls for a pluralistic study of Asia, one that is guided by the "empowerment of an informed imagination" rather than "the directions of US foreign policy" (2).

Through the concept of "Global Asias," Tina Chen and Eric Hayot call for interdisciplinary approaches that bring together the fields of Asian, Asian American, and Asian diaspora studies, fields that have historically not had much exchange. See Tina Chen and Eric Hayot, "Introducing *Verge*: What Does It Mean to Study Global Asias?," *Verge: Studies in Global Asias* 1.1 (Spring 2015): vi–xv.

18. See Economic Strategies Committee Subcommittee, "Attracting and Rooting MNCs, Asian Enterprises and Global Mid-Sized Companies," National Archives Singapore, February 3, 2010; and Leo Yip, "The Road Ahead," in *Heart Work 2* (Singapore: Straits Times Press, 2011), 248–63.

19. Based on the flurry of socioeconomic policy reports and recommendations calling for cultural and economic restructurings, one would not have guessed that Singapore remained relatively insulated from the damage of the 1997 Asian financial crisis compared to neighboring Southeast Asian and East Asian countries. Indeed, during this period, the reports from almost every single sector foreground re-visioning their twenty-first-century future: *Singapore 21: Together, We Make the Difference* (1999), *Manpower 21: Vision of a Talent Capital* (1999), *Construction 21* (1999), *ProAct 21: Creating the Future* (1999), *Tourism 21: Vision of a Tourism Capital* (1996), and *Media 21: Transforming Singapore into a Global Media City* (2002), to name but a few. If not marked by "21," such reports often took on a title declaring some kind of extraordinary change: *Learning to Think: Thinking to Learn* (1998), *Changing Mindsets, Deepening Relationships* (2003), *New Challenges, Fresh Goals: Towards a Dynamic Global City* (2003), and *Renaissance City Report: Culture and the Arts in Renaissance Singapore* (1999), to name a few more.

20. Goh Chok Tong, "Singapore 21: Vision for a New Era," excerpt from a speech in Parliament, June 5, 1997, Annual Report FY 1997, National Library Board. To be clear, despite the language of transition in Goh's speech, policy papers were recommending a diversification of the economy rather than a total transition out of manufacturing.

21. Michael Hardt, "Affective Labor," *boundary 2* 26.2 (Summer 1999): 89–100, 90.

22. *Renaissance City Report*, 4.

23. Richard Florida, *The Rise of the Creative Class: And How It's Transforming Work, Leisure, and Everyday Life*, 2nd ed. (New York: Basic Books, 2012).

24. *Renaissance City Report*, 47. Prime Minister Goh's contrasting style of softer leadership seemed to validate the *Renaissance City's* recommendation that the state scale back its overt authority, particularly when compared to his predecessor, Lee Kuan Yew. Regarded as "extremely gentle and [with a] self-effacing personality," Goh was a sharp contrast to the unrelentingly results-focused Lee, even going as far as to allow "a new extremely relaxed and free atmosphere in the Cabinet and the caucus, encouraging open, virtually uninhibited debate and discussion." Ray Vasil, "Singapore 1991: Continuity and Change," *Southeast Asian Affairs* (1993): 297–312, 298–99.

25. See Joseph S. Nye Jr., *Soft Power: The Means to Success in World Politics* (New York: Public Affairs, 2004). Like Nye, I am thinking about soft power in terms of foreign policy, but I am also thinking through "softer" forms of governance.

26. My thinking about anglophonic legibility is informed by W. E. B. Du Bois's notion of "double consciousness" and Frantz Fanon's concept of the white gaze. These important thinkers were describing and analyzing the lived experience of anti-Black racism in the contexts of the early twentieth-century United States and the mid-twentieth-century French Empire, respectively. For Du Bois, double consciousness is the "sense of always looking at

one's self through the eyes of others, of measuring one's soul by the tape of a world that looks on in amused contempt and pity" (38). W. E. B. Du Bois, *The Souls of Black Folk*, ed. David W. Blight and Robert Gooding-Williams (New York: Bedford Books, 1997). This was Du Bois's sociological observation for understanding the psychic violence of continued oppression in the postslavery United States. Fanon also observes that "Blacks have had to deal with two systems of reference," further noting how the "white gaze" fixes Blackness (90). Frantz Fanon, *Black Skin, White Masks*, trans. Richard Philcox (New York: Grove Press, 2008).

Resonating with these concepts, the Singaporean texts under study in this book variously highlight an undue awareness by the state of how Singapore or Singaporeans look to the world at large. In the years of early independence, the "contempt and pity" Singapore faced as a Third World country were certainly wielded by politicians as structural conditions to overcome. Such dynamics of inferiority have changed with Singapore's ascendent economic status, yet the white/colonial/Western gaze continues to rationalize the construction of Singapore as a desirable capitalist haven. While Du Bois's and Fanon's works provide these terms to name the object of critique for the decolonial struggle of liberation and to describe the experience of racial violence, their optical metaphors help explain why legibility is so crucial in the context of postcolonial capitalism.

27. Also see Christopher B. Patterson's *Transitive Cultures: Anglophone Literature of the Transpacific* (New Brunswick, NJ: Rutgers University Press), 21–26. For Patterson, anglophone literatures "uncover responses to pluralist governmentality" in Southeast Asia (21) and offer a mode of comparison between Asian American and postcolonial literatures.

28. Why does "a particular combination of characteristics," to draw on Peter Hitchcock, "surface and subside at different moments of history"? See Hitchcock, "The Genre of Postcoloniality," *New Literary History* 34.2 (Spring 2003): 299–330, 312. Or to put it in S. Charusheela's language, these emergent genres offer keen insights into "a shift in the *ways*—and not just contents but also forms—in which national, political, and cultural subjective understandings of class and politics are constituted, because of the emergence of a new spatial locus for accumulation." Charusheela, "Where Is the 'Economy'? Cultural Studies and Narratives of Capitalism," in *The Renewal of Cultural Studies*, ed. Paul Smith (Philadelphia: Temple University Press, 2011), 177–87, 182; original emphasis. In this excellent essay, Charusheela is posing the part I quote as a question, but for my purposes here, it works as a statement.

29. Eng-Beng Lim, "Asian Megastructure and Queer Futurity," *Cultural Dynamics* 28.3 (2016): 309–19, at 311.

30. Naoki Sakai, "'You Asians': On the Historical Role of the West and Asia Binary," *South Atlantic Quarterly* 99.4 (Fall 2000): 789–817. Indeed, I have observed a number of North American academics talk about Singapore as if it is simply mimicking the United States. Beng Huat Chua has noted that "neoliberal" has been used to describe Singapore, despite "the Singapore state's presence in the domestic and global economy through its state-owned enterprises and sovereign wealth funds" (22). See *Liberalism Disavowed: Communitarianism and State Capitalism in Singapore* (Ithaca, NY: Cornell University Press, 2017).

31. Aihwa Ong, *Neoliberalism as Exception: Mutations in Citizenship and Sovereignty* (Durham, NC: Duke University Press, 2006).

32. Aihwa Ong, *Flexible Citizenship: The Cultural Logics of Transnationality* (Durham, NC: Duke University Press, 1999), 35.

33. Ong, *Flexible Citizenship*, 35.

34. Ong, *Flexible Citizenship*, 35.

35. Neil Lazarus, "Introducing Postcolonial Studies," in *The Cambridge Companion to Postcolonial Literary Studies*, ed. Neil Lazarus (Cambridge: Cambridge University Press, 2004), 1–18.

36. See Daniel Wei Boon Chua, *US-Singapore Relations, 1965–1975: Strategic Non-Alignment in the Cold War* (Singapore: National University of Singapore Press, 2017). For more on the critical relevance of China for American studies, see the special issue "The Chinese Factor: Reorienting Global Imaginaries in American Studies," *American Quarterly* 69.3 (2017).

37. Jini Kim Watson, *Cold War Reckonings: Authoritarianism and the Genres of Decolonization* (New York: Fordham University Press, 2021), 2.

38. Wen-Qing Ngoei asks, "Would our understanding of the U.S. encounter with Southeast Asia change if we pivoted from Vietnam to U.S. relations with Britain, Malaya, and Singapore (one, a declining empire; the other two, dominoes that historians have left at the margins of U.S. foreign relations?)" (5). See *Arc of Containment: Britain, the United States, and Anticommunism in Southeast Asia* (Ithaca, NY: Cornell University Press, 2019).

39. Viet Thanh Nguyen and Janet Alison Hoskins, "Introduction: Transpacific Studies: Critical Perspectives on an Emerging Field," in *Transpacific Studies: Framing an Emerging Field* (Honolulu: University of Hawai'i Press, 2014), 1–38, 4.

40. "Postcolonial" is of course a notoriously slippery term. It can variously describe the aftermath of formal colonialism, a geopolitical position, a politics of liberation, and an academic field that studies the literatures and cultures of formerly colonized world to interrogate the violent histories and epistemologies of European imperial power. Neil Lazarus notes that prior to Homi Bhabha's *Location of Culture*, "postcolonial" was a mere descriptor of a historical period rather than an ideological concept, project, or politics. See Lazarus, Introduction to *The Postcolonial Unconscious* (Cambridge: Cambridge University Press, 2011, 1–20), esp. 10–18; and Lazarus, "Introducing Postcolonial Studies," 3–5.

41. Ong, *Flexible Citizenship*, 35.

42. In the multiplicity school of thought, for example, Sandro Mezzadra, who specifically takes up the term "postcolonial capitalism," argues for the recognition of "diverse scales, places and histories" (166) of labor, which in turn challenges cohesive theories of abstract or free labor—the basis of many Marxian conceptions of capitalism. In Kalyan Sanyal's work, the heterogeneous character of capitalism is key for arresting developmental narratives of capitalism's spread and simplified accounts of capitalism's hegemony that undergird the assumptions of developmental economics. For Sanyal, comprehending postcolonial capitalism means "produc[ing] a vision of capitalism that is malleable and protean, see[ing] economic difference as an integral part of that capitalism and explor[ing] how capital successfully lives in that world of difference" (7). At stake in all these works is freeing the production of knowledge from the colonial tendencies that reify Western dominance and consequently miss the intricacies of capitalism.

In the second school of thought, theorists of racial capitalism and colonial capitalism center Europe in their accounts of what Couze Venn describes as the "process of pauperization across the world" (67). They also tend to take issue with the idea that class can be understood without race. As Cedric J. Robinson puts it, "ordering ideas" such as racialism "have little or no *theoretical* justification in Marxism for their existence" (2). Robinson thus turns his readers to the long history of Western Europe, tracking the ways that racialism is exported and implemented as an ordering principle of capitalism. Centering the role of race in racial capitalism, Gargi Bhattacharyya explains, "is a way of understanding the role of racism in enabling key moments of capitalist development—it is not a way of understanding capitalism as a racist conspiracy or racism as a capitalist conspiracy." At stake is the formation of class solidarity that is attentive to the politics of race. While distinct from discussions of racial capitalism in terms of subfield and aim, colonial capitalism shares with racial capitalism deep conceptual overlaps in their *longue durée* view of enslavement and British colonialism as key events in the production of global inequality. Like Robinson's characterization of capitalism as a "nonobjective" force, critics studying colonial capitalism also take issue with depictions of capitalism as driven by natural, market forces, hence David Harvey's notion of "accumulation by dispossession." For all of these critics, capitalism is an ordering force of power, not an impartial metric.

Although the "postcolonial" in these works tends to go untheorized and my own focus is on the role that postcoloniality plays in the makings of capitalism, they serve as an important reminder of how the continuing legacies of colonialism construct the unequal foundation of global capitalism. See Sandro Mezzadra, "How Many Histories of Labour? Toward a Theory of Postcolonial Capitalism," *Postcolonial Studies* 14.2 (2011): 151–70; Kalyan Sanyal, *Rethinking Capitalist Development: Primitive Accumulation, Governmentality and Post-Colonial Capitalism* (London: Routledge, 2013); Couze Venn, *After Capital* (Thousand Oaks, CA: Sage, 2018); Cedric J. Robinson, *Black Marxism: The Making of the Black Radical Tradition*, 3rd ed. (Chapel Hill: University of North Carolina Press, 2020); Gargi Bhattacharyya, *Rethinking Racial Capitalism: Questions of Reproduction and Survival* (Lanham, MD: Rowman and Littlefield, 2018); David Harvey, *The New Imperialism* (Oxford: Oxford University Press, 2003).

43. Ralph Cohen, "Genre Theory, Literary History, and Historical Change," in *Genre Theory and Historical Change: Theoretical Essays of Ralph Cohen*, ed. John L. Rowlett (Charlottesville: University of Virginia Press, 2017), 145–69, 145.

44. Aimé Césaire, *Discourse on Colonialism*, trans. Joan Pinkham (New York: Monthly Review Press, 2001), 44. Arif Dirlik, in "The Postcolonial Aura: Third World Criticism in the Age of Global Capitalism," *Critical Inquiry* 20.2 (1994): 328–56, writes that "postcolonial critics have been silent on the relationship of the idea of postcolonialism to its context in contemporary capitalism, indeed they have suppressed the necessity of considering such a possible relationship by repudiating a foundational role to capitalism in history" (331). Similar critiques emerged from Stuart Hall (1996) and Gayatri Spivak (1985). Of course, much has changed in postcolonial studies since the 1994 publication of Dirlik's essay, and there have since been a number of important works offering postcolonial literary perspectives on the world system of contemporary capitalism. These include Warwick Research Collective, *Combined and Uneven Development: Toward a New Theory of World-Literature* (Liverpool: Liverpool University Press, 2015); Ravinder Kaur, *Brand New Nation: Capitalist Dreams and Nationalist Designs in the Twenty-First-Century India* (Stanford, CA: Stanford University Press, 2020); Quinn Slobodian, *Globalists: The End of Empire and the Birth of Neoliberalism* (Cambridge, MA: Harvard University Press, 2018); Adom Getachew, *Worldmaking after Empire: The Rise and Fall of Self-Determination* (Princeton, NJ: Princeton University Press, 2019); and Watson, *Cold War Reckonings*.

45. BRICS, or Brazil, Russia, India, China, and South Africa, is a geopolitical bloc considered the main rival of the G7. The BRICS leaders have been described as "presenting their group . . . in the warm and fuzzy framework of benevolent South-South cooperation, an essential counterweight to the 'old' West and a better partner for the poor masses of the developing world." See Pascal Fletcher, "BRICS Chafe under Charge of 'New Imperialists' in Africa," Reuters, March 26, 2013, https://www.reuters.com/article/us-brics-africa/brics -chafe-under-charge-of-new-imperialists-in-africa-idUSBRE92P0FU20130326.

46. In a sense, postcolonial capitalism is the field of postcolonial studies' "bad object." See Naomi Schor, *Bad Objects: Essays Popular and Unpopular*, (Durham, NC: Duke University Press, 1995).

47. Ong, *Flexible Citizenship*, 34.

48. Gayatri Chakravorty Spivak, *A Critique of Postcolonial Reason: Toward a History of the Vanishing Present* (Cambridge, MA: Harvard University Press, 1999), 1.

49. "Remaking Singapore—Changing Mindsets," National Day Rally Address by Prime Minister Goh Chok Tong at the University Cultural Centre, NUS, Sunday, August 18, 2002, National Archives of Singapore.

50. Alfian Sa'at, Faris Joraimi, and Sai Siew Min, Introduction to *Raffles Renounced: Towards a Merdeka History*, ed. Alfian Sa'at, Faris Joraimi, and Sai Siew Min (Singapore: Ethos Books, 2021), 11–16, 14.

51. C. J. W.-L. Wee, "Contending with Primordialism: The 'Modern' Construction of Postcolonial Singapore," *positions: asia critique* 1.3 (1993): 719–20; original emphasis.

52. Such a stabilization of postcoloniality is a familiar ploy to critics who study colonialism. Much in the way that Fanon argues that the white gaze fixes blackness, the colonial gaze fixes postcoloniality, and Singapore's postcolonial capitalism exploits that essentialized stability. A significant body of scholarship reads for the ways that this colonial gaze and postcolonial fixity have been translated and systematized by institutions, such as the World Bank or transnational corporations. See, e.g., Amitava Kumar, *World Bank Literature* (Minneapolis: University of Minnesota Press, 2002); Bret Benjamin, *Invested Interests: Capital, Culture, and the World Bank* (Minneapolis: University of Minnesota Press, 2007); Purnima Bose and Laura E. Lyons, eds., *Cultural Critique and the Global Corporation* (Bloomington: Indiana University Press, 2010). A number of other works form their ideas from a critique of postcolonialism to think through the ways that contemporary capitalism affects literary productions and aesthetics in postcolonial contexts. For example, the Warwick Research Collective (WReC) proposes that world literature be understood as "the literature of the world-system—of the modern capitalist world-system, that is" (8). Sarah Brouillette investigates the ideological impact of UNESCO on twentieth-century understandings of the literary. See Warwick Research Collective, *Combined and Uneven Development*; Sarah Brouillette, *UNESCO and the Fate of the Literary* (Stanford, CA: Stanford University Press, 2019). Graham Huggan and other scholars such as Sarah Brouilette, Arif Dirlik, Stuart Hall, Timothy Brennan, and Rey Chow recognize the agency of, in this case, subjects who use postcoloniality in order to gain financial or social advantage. See Graham Huggan, *The Postcolonial Exotic: Marketing the Margins* (London: Routledge, 2001); Sarah Brouillette, *Postcolonial Writers in the Global Literary Market* (London: Palgrave Macmillan, 2007); Rey Chow, *Writing Diaspora: Tactics of Intervention in Contemporary Cultural Studies* (Bloomington: Indiana University Press, 1993); Arif Dirlik, *The Postcolonial Aura: Third World Criticism in the Age of Global Capitalism* (London: Routledge, 1997); Timothy Brennan,

At Home in the World: Cosmopolitanism Now (Cambridge, MA: Harvard University Press, 1997).

53. Nguyen and Hoskins, "Introduction," 20.

54. There is a local rumor in Singapore that Lee Kuan Yew's children were also fluent in Russian in case the former USSR emerged as victor in the Cold War. Rumors are just rumors, but the nature of this one is telling for it validates the point that Singaporean governance strategizes according to global order rather than a political or cultural attachment to a particular power.

55. In her conceptualization of Asian American studies as a subjectless discourse, Kandice Chuh calls attention to the ways that "Asian Americanist discourse can contribute to ways of thinking and producing knowledge formations that might interrupt the concepts that justify the sustenance of grossly unjust political and economic practices" (39–40). Kandice Chuh, *Imagine Otherwise: On Asian Americanist Critique* (Durham, NC: Duke University Press, 2003), 39–40. Part of my Asian Americanist training is the result of Tina Chen's leadership of the Global Asias Initiative (GSI), which she describes "as a conceptual infrastructure enabling diverse scholars, methods, and practices to meet without declaring new fealties or renouncing cherished loyalties." It has facilitated important exchange among scholars of Asia-related fields without the pressures of consensus. I was fortunate enough to participate in a Global Asias Summer Institute with a number of excellent junior scholars working in Asian American studies. See Tina Chen, "Global Asias: Method, Architecture, Praxis," *Journal of Asian Studies* 80.4 (November 2021): 997–1009, 1001.

56. The White House, "Peace to Prosperity: A Vision to Improve the Lives of the Palestinian and Israeli People," January 2020, https://trumpwhitehouse.archives.gov/wp-content/uploads/2020/01/Peace-to-Prosperity-0120.pdf.

57. Lamb, "Singapore Swing," n.p.

58. Lee Kuan Yew, *The Singapore Story: Memoirs of Lee Kuan Yew* (Upper Saddle River, NJ: Prentice Hall, 1998), 72.

59. Lee, *The Singapore Story*, 74.

60. Lee, *The Singapore Story*, 76.

61. Lee, *The Singapore Story*, 66.

62. Hong Lysa and Huang Jianli, *The Scripting of a National History: Singapore and Its Pasts* (Hong Kong: Hong Kong University Press, 2008), 6.

63. Lee, *The Singapore Story*, 51.

64. Lee, *The Singapore Story*, 66.

65. Kevin Kwan, *Rich People Problems* (New York: Doubleday, 2017), 376.

66. Kwan, *Rich People Problems*, 377.

67. Kwan, *Rich People Problems*, 381.

68. See Mamoru Shinozaki, *Syonan, My Story: The Japanese Occupation of Singapore* (Singapore: Times Books International, 1982).

69. Geraldine Heng and Janadas Devan, "State Fatherhood: The Politics of Nationalism, Sexuality, and Race in Singapore," in *The Gender/Sexuality Reader: Culture, History, Political Economy*, ed. Roger N. Lancaster and Micaela di Leonardo (London: Routledge, 1997), 107–21, 343.

70. *Becoming Global Asia* builds on the Marxist literary tradition encapsulated by works like Fredric Jameson's *The Political Unconscious* (1981) that thinks through the relationship between capitalism and literary form but with an eye to very different economic and

postcolonial contexts. Numerous literary and cultural studies demonstrate the importance of understanding the culture, logics, and ideologies of capitalism. As Paul Crosthwaite, Peter Knight, and Nicky Marsh argue in "Introduction: The Interwovenness of Literature and Economics," the turn to literary study to understand economic process has become more urgent following the 2008 global financial crisis (2). See *The Cambridge Companion to Literature and Economics* (Cambridge University Press, 2022), 1–16. Even economists such as Robert J. Shiller are drawing on literary methodologies to study the impact of storytelling on major economic events. Perhaps unsurprisingly, however, Shiller's *Narrative Economics: How Stories Go Viral and Drive Major Economic Events* (Princeton, NJ: Princeton University Press, 2019) hardly looks at the work that has already been done in literary and cultural studies.

71. Goh Chok Tong, "Remaking Singapore—Changing Mindsets," National Day Rally Address, August 18, 2002. National Archives of Singapore. Although the "stayer/quitter" binary tends to be attributed to Goh's divisive speech in the context of globalization's negative effects, it was first introduced by Prime Minister Lee Kuan Yew in a lesser-known 1969 speech when he declared that Singapore's future would be determined by "the quality of its top one to two per cent . . . [and] whether this one to two per cent consists of 'stayers' or 'quitters.'" The sheer repetition of the labels "stayer" and "quitter" in the context of Singapore's independence and in the aftermath of an economic crisis suggests that these two historical events—one signifying Global Asia and one signifying state developmentalism—must be read together. See Yeo Toon Joo, "Brain Drain Will Be Decisive: Lee," *Straits Times*, September 7, 1969, 1.

72. "About OS Portal," Overseas Singaporean Unit webpage, accessed December 2, 2013. In 2019, the OSU merged with a new agency, the Singapore Global Network, and is now known as such. See "A new home for Singaporeans, friends and fans: Singapore Global Network," February 19, 2020, accessed January 25, 2023, https://singaporeglobalnetwork.gov .sg/stories/culture/a-new-home-for-singaporeans-friends-and-fans-singapore-global -network/.

73. Singapore Economic Review Committee, *New Challenges, Fresh Goals*, 10.

74. "Speech by Mr Wong Kan Seng, Deputy Prime Minister and Minister for Home Affairs, at the Launch of the Overseas Singaporean Portal," August 16, 2006, Singapore Government Media Release, National Archives of Singapore.

75. Singapore 21 Committee, *Singapore 21: Together, We Make the Difference*, 45; Ministry of Information, Communications and the Arts, *Renaissance City Report*, 38.

76. *Renaissance City Report*, 5.

77. Ong, *Neoliberalism as Exception*, 53. In other words, there is a tendency to use "diaspora" as a mode of producing an exclusive group identity rather than to describe an organic sociological formation emerging from a particular historic violence. Wong's wielding of the term is certainly problematic from a critical diaspora studies perspective that, as Evelyn Hu-Dehart puts it, seeks to "regain some control over its meaning and parameters before it is totally reduced to a simple and simplistic essentialism denoting any kind of human mobility and scattering, or any kind of sentimental yearning by upper-class exiles." See "Diaspora," in *Keywords for Asian American Studies*, ed. Cathy J. Schlund-Vials, Linda Trinh Võ, and K. Scott Wong (New York: New York University Press, 2015), accessed July 17, 2021, https:// keywords.nyupress.org/asian-american-studies/essay/diaspora/.

78. Ong, *Neoliberalism as Exception*, 60.

79. *Renaissance City Report*, 5. With great thanks to Wen-Qing Ngoei for helping me understand the nebulous genre of the "report."

80. Exceptions include the translated versions of *Singapore 21* in Malay and Tamil, which are far less accessible. Publicly accessible copies are only available at the National Library in Singapore.

81. In *Cold War Reckonings*, Watson thinks through the ways authoritarian power presents a problem of representation, pointedly asking, "If earlier genres often privileged the *colonial state* as an unambiguous object of critique, what representation logic is demanded by authoritarian postcolonial regimes?" (21).

1. THE CULTURAL HISTORY OF SINGAPORE LITERARY ANTHOLOGIES

1. In the 1970s, there were only 16 anthologies and in the 1980s, about 28. It is the 1990s when the anthology began to take off: there were 86 anthologies in the 1990s; 82 in the 2000s; over 120 in the 2010s. These tabulations run up to 2018. I am grateful to Shawn Hoo, my research assistant, for his help compiling this information.

2. Joy Fang, "The Rise of the Anthology," *Today Online*, November 23, 2016, https://www.todayonline.com/entertainment/arts/rise-anthology.

3. In 2018, the Singapore Literature Festival by Singapore Unbound featured a panel, "The Anthologist's Dream," and in 2020, the National Institute of Education in Singapore held "The Anthology in Singapore: A Symposium."

4. Weihsin Gui, "Contemporary Literature from Singapore," in *Oxford Research Encyclopedia of Literature* (2017), https://oxfordre.com/literature/view/10.1093/acrefore/9780190201098.001.0001/acrefore-9780190201098-e-189?print=pdf.

5. Nair is described as a figure whose "contribution (in a Singapore where the support he envisaged is now the norm) has been largely forgotten." "Chandran Nair: Biography," *poetry.sg*, accessed April 20, 2022.

6. Nair, personal correspondence, February 4, 2021.

7. Nair, personal correspondence, February 4, 2021.

8. Following Michel Foucault, we should understand the anthologies of these periods as the prior, historical pieces of Global Asia rather than the pieces that caused Global Asia to occur. See Foucault, "Nietzsche, Genealogy, History," in *The Foucault Reader*, ed. Paul Rabinow (New York: Pantheon Books, 1984), 76–100.

9. Jeffrey R. Di Leo, "Analyzing Anthologies," in *On Anthologies: Politics and Pedagogy*, ed. Jeffrey R. Di Leo (Lincoln: University of Nebraska Press, 2004), 1–27, 3; original emphasis.

10. Di Leo, "Analyzing Anthologies," 3–4. Laura Mandell and Rita Raley's website on eighteenth-century anthologies and miscellanies states that the distinction between anthologies and miscellanies is the difference between selecting poems of "excellence" versus "interest" (accessed March 15, 2022). See http://oldsite.english.ucsb.edu/faculty/rraley/research/anthologies/.

11. Because of the anthology's authority and function as reference, Di Leo likens it to the atlas, which is notably a genre with colonial undertones in its role in making legible territories for conquest and resource extraction. Di Leo's geographic metaphor reminds us that the anthology accrues its authority in terms of both time and space. That is, the anthology at once asserts command over what constitutes literary history and, through its ability

to include many pieces, performs authority through coverage. These spatial implications become more literal when further considering how anthologies are often large, heavy, and thick tomes that take up space.

12. Recognizing how the anthology's roots in the literary canon create an issue of authority over history, Larissa Lai advances the notion of a "counter-anthology" with an orientation to "open-ended time—contingent moment upon contingent moment" (91). Lai sees such an orientation as a subversion of canonizing anthologies that act with a "kind of closure" because they are "fully invested in its place in history and [have] a vested role in canon formation" (91). Writing of African American and Black diasporic anthologies of the 1920s, Brent Hayes Edwards notes that the anthology operated "not in confirming the canon, not in a backward-looking survey of the highpoints in a trajectory, but instead in founding and enabling the very tradition it documents, 'at the beginning rather than the end of literary history making'" (44). With a similar temporal focus, Alice Te Punga Somerville also argues that "a multiple-author literary collection brings together a range of perspectives from many voices and thereby conveys . . . what Witi Ihimaera described [in an introduction to a Māori anthology] as 'an opportunity to say to the present, "This is how we are,"—to say to the future, "This is how we were"'" (255). See Larissa Lai, *Slanting I, Imagining We: Asian Canadian Literary Production in the 1980s and 1990s* (Waterloo, ON: Wilfrid Laurier University Press, 2014); Brent Hayes Edwards, *The Practice of Diaspora: Literature, Translation, and the Rise of Black Internationalism* (Cambridge, MA: Harvard University Press, 2003); Alice Te Punga Somerville, "Not Emailing Albert: A Legacy of Collection, Connection, Community," *Contemporary Pacific* 22.2 (2010): 253–70.

13. Te Punga Somerville, "Not Emailing Albert," 261. See also Cynthia Franklin's *Writing Women's Communities: the Politics and Poetics of Contemporary Multi-Genre Anthologies* (Madison: University of Wisconsin Press, 1997), for her discussion of 1980s women's anthologies from the United States and how they were a "privileged site for marginalized groups of women intent on theorizing and putting into practice communities founded upon a powerful but inherently unstable politics of identity" (5).

14. Barbara Benedict, *Making the Modern Reader: Cultural Mediation in Restoration and Eighteenth-Century Literary Anthologies* (Princeton, NJ: Princeton University Press, 1996), 242.

15. Colleen Lye sees the plural form of the anthology as reinforcing "additive" approaches to Asian American racial identity (95) and Gayatri Chakravorty Spivak problematizes how the anthology's erasure of incommensurability sanctions "populist" approaches to learning about cultural difference in the context of world literature. See Colleen Lye, "Racial Form," *Representations* 104.1 (2008): 92–101; David Damrosch and Gayatri Chakravorty Spivak, "Comparative Literature/World Literature: A Discussion with Gayatri Chakravorty Spivak," *Comparative Literature Studies* 48.4 (2011): 455–85.

16. Smaro Kamboureli, for example, argues that ethnic Canadian anthologies can reproduce official state multiculturalism. See chapter 3 of *Scandalous Bodies: Diasporic Literature in English Canada* (Waterloo, ON: Wilfrid Laurier University Press, 2009).

17. Timothy Brennan, "The National Longing for Form," in *Nation and Narration*, ed. Homi K. Bhabha (New York: Routledge, 1990), 44–90, 50.

18. He writes, "The city-state had no history of anti-colonial struggle in the name of the nation as it is now constituted to forge a national consciousness[,] . . . nor has Singapore a

ready-made high cultural precolonial past to summon in order to imagine a new nation." Philip Holden, "Postcolonial Desire: Placing Singapore," *Postcolonial Studies* 11.3 (2008): 345.

19. Brennan ("The National Longing for Form") too has highlighted the limitations of holding the novel as an esteemed form: "For under conditions of illiteracy and shortages, and given simply the leisure-time necessary for reading one, the novel has been an elitist and minority form in developing countries when compared to poem, song, television, and film. Almost inevitably it has been the form through which a thin, foreign-educated stratum (however sensitive or committed to domestic political interests) has communicated to metropolitan reading publics, often in translation. It has been, in short, a naturally cosmopolitan form that empire has allowed to play a national role, as it were, only in an international arena" (56). Brennan's remarks capture the limitations of the novel as well as the bias toward narrative for comprehending nation form.

20. Te Punga Somerville ("Not Emailing Albert") observes that "treatments of Wendt's work tend to focus on his individually authored fiction, poetry, drama, and scholarship," whereas his editorial work is excluded (254). She further speculates that part of the issue is that "his work as an editor of anthology is [treated as] a form of service to the field: behind-the scenes work that is more about making things possible than it is about standing in the limelight" (254). Those who take on strong service roles in the academy are acutely aware of the unequal value given to faculty who perform the behind-the-scenes labor that Te Punga Somerville describes: organizing a conference rather than giving a keynote address, writing reference materials for emerging subfields rather than single-authored articles, teaching "service" courses for general education credit rather than specialist courses, and the list goes on.

21. See Su Friedrich's website Edited By at http://womenfilmeditors.princeton.edu/, accessed March 16, 2022.

22. Kristine Kotecki, "After the Archive: Framing Cultural Memory in Ex-Yugoslav Collections" (PhD diss., University of Texas at Austin, 2013), 96–97.

23. Dipesh Chakrabarty, "The Legacies of Bandung: Decolonization and the Politics of Culture," in *Making a World after Empire: The Bandung Moment and Its Political Afterlives*, ed. Christopher J. Lee (Athens: Ohio University Press, 2010), 45–68, 53.

24. See Aihwa Ong's discussion of technocrats and technocratic governance in *Neoliberalism as Exception: Mutations in Citizenship and Sovereignty* (Durham, NC: Duke University Press, 2006), 20. In the emphasis on outcome, Ong is also thinking with Foucault through different modalities of power that emerge under neoliberalism, namely the move away from disciplinary power.

25. Writing of bricolage, Lévi-Strauss explains, "Rites and myths, on the other hand, like 'bricolage' (which these same societies only tolerate as a hobby or pastime), take to pieces and reconstruct sets of events (on a psychical, socio-historical or technical plane) and use them as so many indestructible pieces for structural patterns in which they serve alternative as ends of means" (32–33). Lévi-Strauss saw the engineer as the bricoleur's contrasting figure, a move that was critiqued as a constructed foil by Jacques Derrida. See Claude Lévi-Strauss, *The Savage Mind* (London: Trafalgar Square, 1966); Jacques Derrida, "Structure, Sign, and Play in the Discourse of the Human Sciences," in *Writing and Difference*, trans. Alan Bass (Chicago: University of Chicago Press, 1978), 278–94.

26. "Chandran Nair: Biography," *poetry.sg*, accessed May 6, 2022.

27. See Jini Kim Watson, *The New Asian City: Three-Dimensional Fictions of Space and Urban Form* (Minneapolis: University of Minnesota Press, 2011).

28. Chandran Nair, personal correspondence, February 4, 2021.

29. Interview with Chandran Nair by Ismail Kassim, "The High Cost of Publishing a Book," *New Nation*, December 16, 1974, 9.

30. Philip Holden, "The Social Life of Genres: Short Stories as a Singapore Form," in *Singapore Literature and Culture: Current Directions in Local and Global Contexts*, ed. Angelia Mui Cheng Poon and Angus Whitehead (London: Routledge, 2017), 99–113, 102.

31. Holden, "The Social Life of Genres," 102.

32. Another rich historical direction to pursue, as suggested to me by Nadine Chan, is the role of broadcast, with fifteen-minute to hour-long slots, in shaping the short form in Singapore. During this period of book development, UNESCO was also pumping resources into broadcast communications in the developing world after World War II.

33. Brouillette, *UNESCO and the Fate of the Literary*, 11.

34. Chandra Nair and Nalla Tan, eds., *The Proceedings of the Seminar on Developing Creative Writing in Singapore, Aug. 6th–7th, 1976* (Singapore: Woodrose Publications, 1977).

35. "Why Foreign Books Only?," *New Nation*, July 5, 1975, 3.

36. Holden, "The Social Life of Genres," 103. About some of the local publications at the time, Nair remarked, "We need a far greater critical consciousness than we have forged to date. In my opinion, there is too little assessment and critical writing. . . . Some of the poems so called, published in book form and in popular media, do serious poets in Singapore a disservice. It would seem that the immediate future will see the appearance of a good many anthologies and individual collections—some good, some bad. . . . We must however be aware that harsh judgements are the only way of separating the worthwhile from the not worthwhile." See "Back Efforts of Local Writers Call," *New Nation*, June 8, 1976, 4.

37. "Speech by Mr Ch'ng Jit Koon, Minister of State for Community Development, at the 1986 National Short Story Competition Prize-Giving Ceremony at The Drama Centre on 1 December 1987 at 6.00pm," Ministry of Communications and Information (1985–1990), Singapore National Archives.

38. Nair and Tan, *The Proceedings of the Seminar on Developing Creative Writing in Singapore*, 8. Here we might also be reminded of Audre Lorde's remark, "Of all art forms, poetry is the most economical" (116). See Lorde, "Age, Race, Class and Sex: Women Redefining Difference," in *Sister Outsider: Essays and Speeches*, 2nd ed. (Berkeley: Crossing Press, 2007).

39. Tan, "The Current State of Creative Writing in Singapore," 8, in Nair and Tan.

40. Brouillette, *UNESCO and the Fate of the Literary*, 78.

41. "Speech by Mr Ho Kah Leong, Parliamentary Secretary (Education) at the Opening Ceremony of the Workshop for Writers at the Lecture Hall Bukit Merah Branch Library on Monday, 12 September 1983 at 9.30am," Ministry of Culture, Singapore National Archives.

42. For a brief history of oil and petroleum corporations and their relation to Singapore literature, see Joanne Leow, "My Elusive Petrofictions," *Brick: A Literary Journal* (Summer 2021): 54–61.

43. "NUS" stands for the National University of Singapore.

44. Titles in this series include *Tranquerah* (1985) by Ee Tiang Hong, *5* (1985) by Simon Tay, *No Man's Grove* (1985) by Shirley Lim, *Remembering Grandma and Other Rumours* (1989) by Phui Nam Wong, and *Collected Poems* (1986) by Angeline Yap.

45. "ASEAN Literary Anthology Project Proposal," in *Report of the Conference of ASEAN Writers, Manila, 24–26 June 1981* (Jakarta: KITLV, 1987), 2.

46. Rebecca Chua, "Our Showcase," *The Straits Times*, March 1, 1986, 2.

47. The second volume, *The Fiction of Singapore*, would garner much more local press and even be commercially available as a paperback, suggesting the potential for a different kind of reader relationship with the text.

48. Benedict Anderson, *Imagined Communities: Reflections on the Origin and Spread of Nationalism*, 2nd ed. (New York: Verso, 2006), 5.

49. Edwin Thumboo, "The English Anthology in Singapore and Southeast Asia," The Anthology in Singapore: A Symposium, Writers@NIE Series, National Institute of Education, Singapore, August 12, 2020.

50. Étienne Balibar, "The Nation Form: History and Ideology," in *Race, Nation, Class: Ambiguous Identities*, trans. Chris Turner (London: Verso, 1991), 86–106, 86; David Lloyd, "Nationalisms against the State," in *The Politics of Culture in the Shadow of Capital*, ed. Lisa Lowe and David Lloyd (Durham, NC: Duke University Press, 1997), 173–97, 173.

51. Chua Beng Huat, "Multiculturalism in Singapore: An Instrument of Social Control," *Race & Class* 44.3 (2003): 58–77.

52. Slavoj Žižek, "Multiculturalism, Or, the Cultural Logic of Multinational Capitalism," *New Left Review*, September 1, 1997, 28–51, 44.

53. Jodi Melamed, *Represent and Destroy: Rationalizing Violence in the New Racial Capitalism* (Minneapolis: University of Minnesota Press, 2011).

54. Kunio Yoshihara, quoted in Lee Soo Ann, *Singapore Goes Transnational: A Study of the Economic Impact of Investment by Multinational Corporations in Singapore* (Singapore: Eastern Universities Press, 1977), 1.

55. K. P. Wong, "The Cultural Impact of Multinational Corporations in Singapore," UNESCO, 1980, 52.

56. Edwin Thumboo, *The Poetry of Singapore* (Singapore: ASEAN Committee of Culture and Information, 1985), 1.

57. Rey Chow's chapter, "Not Like a Native Speaker: The Postcolonial Scene of Languaging and the Proximity of the Xenophone," offers a way out of the impasse generated by the debates between Ngũgĩ wa Thiong'o and Chinua Achebe about the colonial status of the English language. See Rey Chow, *Not Like a Native Speaker: On Languaging as a Postcolonial Experience* (New York: Columbia University Press, 2014), 35–60.

58. John Miksic, "Temasik to Singapura: Singapore in the 14th and 15th Centuries," in *Singapore from Temasek to the 21st Century: Reinventing the Global City*, ed. Karl Hack and Jean-Louis Margolin with Karine Delaye (Singapore: National University of Singapore Press, 2005), 103–32.

59. Minae Mizumura, *The Fall of Language in the Age of English*, trans. Mari Yoshihara and Juliet Winters Carpenter (New York: Columbia University Press, 2015).

60. Jahan Ramazani, *A Transnational Poetics* (Chicago: University of Chicago Press, 2009), 19.

61. Thumboo, *The Poetry of Singapore*, 147.

62. Gayatri Chakravorty Spivak, "The Politics of Translation," in *Outside in the Teaching Machine* (London: Routledge, 1993), 179–200, 180.

63. Spivak, "The Politics of Translation," 197.

64. Michael F. Suarez SJ, "The Production and Consumption of the Eighteenth-Century Poetic Miscellany," in *Books and Their Readers in Eighteenth-Century England: New Essays*, ed. Isabel Rivers (Leicester: Leicester University Press, 2001), 217–51, 218–19.

65. My categorization of major anthologies in this period includes not only the texts put out by state-sponsored and international publishers but also ones put out by academics from National University of Singapore, which I take as an authoritative institution in defining Singaporean literature (and literariness). I have categorized anthologies published by secondary schools, such as *Vic Vox: Prize Winning Short Stories and Poems* (1990) by Victoria School and *Creative Expressions: Chinese High School Anthology of Stories* (1989) as popular anthologies because they are put out by institutions or publishers that have a less authoritative claim to Singaporean literature. Indeed, many of these anthologies issued by secondary schools are often memorializing a school writing competition.

66. "Book Bang," *Straits Times*, October 16, 1989, 1.

67. "Book Bang," 1.

68. Lai, *Slanting I, Imagining We*, 118.

69. Chua Beng Huat, "Communitarian Politics in Asia," in *Communitarian Politics in Asia*, ed. Chua Beng Huat (London: Routledge Curzon, 2004), 1–24, 10.

70. Chua, "Communitarian Politics in Asia," 11.

71. Chua, "Communitarian Politics in Asia," 3.

72. Chua, "Communitarian Politics in Asia," 11.

73. Chua, *Communitarian Ideology and Democracy in Singapore*, 89–91.

74. "Our National Ethic: Speech by Mr Goh Chok Tong, First Deputy Prime Minister and Minister for Defence, at the PAP Youth Wing Charity Night, At Neptune Theatre Restaurant on Friday, 28 October 1988, at 8.00pm," Singapore National Archives, 2–3.

75. Stephan Ortmann, "Singapore: The Politics of Inventing National Identity," *Journal of Current Southeast Asian Affairs* 28.4 (2009), pp. 23–46, p. 27.

76. "White Paper on 'Shared Values,'" in *In Search of Singapore's National Values*, ed. Jon S. T. Quah, Institute of Policy Studies (Singapore: Times Academic Press, 1990), 106–16, 115–16.

77. "White Paper on 'Shared Values,'" 116.

78. Some of these television appearances include "Publishing, Creative Writing and Singapore: Question and Answer Session with Poet and Publisher Chandran Nair," Television Corporation of Singapore, July 4, 1975; and "Opinion on National Identity: Is There a Singapore Identity," Singapore Broadcasting Corporation, July 25, 1980. See National Archive of Singapore.

79. Ng Yi-Sheng, "A History of Singapore Horror," *BiblioAsia*, July–September 2017, March 23, 2022, https://biblioasia.nlb.gov.sg/vol-13/issue-2/jul-sep-2017/historyofsghorror, accessed March 23, 2022.

80. Weihsin Gui, "Noir Fiction in Malaysia and Singapore as a Critical Aesthetic of Global Asia," *Global Asia*, ed. Nadine Chan and Cheryl Narumi Naruse, *Social Text Online*, accessed March 23, 2022.

81. Weihsin Gui, "Renaissance City and Revenant Story: The Gothic Tale as Literary Technique in Fiona Cheong's Fictions of Singapore," *Interventions: International Journal of Postcolonial Studies* 18.4 (2016): 559–72, 570. For more on postcolonial, Asian gothic literature, also see Andrew Hock Soon Ng, *Asian Gothic: Essays on Literature, Film and Anime* (Jefferson, NC: McFarland & Co., 2008).

82. Alfian Sa'at, "Some thoughts . . . ," Facebook, January 19, 2017, accessed March 23, 2022.

83. Alfian Sa'at, "Some thoughts . . . "

84. Chakrabarty, "The Legacies of Bandung," 54.

85. Chang Yau Hoon, "Revisiting the Asian Values Argument Used by Asian Political Leaders and Its Validity," *Indonesian Quarterly* 32.2 (2004): 154–74, 156.

86. Pugalenthi Ramakrishnan, "Good Point to Ponder," Facebook, January 19, 2017, accessed March 23, 2022.

87. Kirpal Singh, "Singapore Fiction in English: Some Reflections . . . ," *Singapore Book World* 23 (1993–94), pp. 21–23, p. 21.

88. Singh, "Singapore Fiction in English," 21.

89. Singh, "Singapore Fiction in English," 22–23.

90. Singh, "Singapore Fiction in English," 23. Singh writes, "It is a telling comment to note that a small country like Papua New Guinea (regarded by many Singaporeans as being 'primitive,' 'backward,' etc., and one where the tertiary education only started around the late sixties) has produced writers whose works are talked about and read internationally (names like Vincent Kri, Russel Soaba) whereas we have yet to get there."

91. "From Us to You," in *Motherland 1*, ed. Pugalenthi Sr (Singapore: VJ Times, 1993), n.p. Also notable is a Fitzgerald quote cited by Matthew J. Bruccoli, an F. Scott Fitzgerald scholar: "Literature is what lasts. Literary history demonstrates that critical reception is an inaccurate forecast of permanent merit. The writings that turn out to be literature are frequently ignored or savaged at the time of their initial publication." This quote comes from the preface to Fitzgerald's short stories, in which Bruccoli notes how Fitzgerald is rarely celebrated as a short story writer since those writings often were published in magazines–that is, those stories were likely economically motivated. By aligning himself with Fitzgerald, Pugalenthi suggests that his critics are also mistaken about VJ Times.

92. "Local Publisher Not Allowed to Stand at Book Fair," *Straits Times*, September 4, 1994, 23.

93. The end of *The Chrysanthemum Haiku*, for example, includes a mock quiz to assess writerly capability. Questions include "Are you a good story-teller?" and "Have people ever told you that you 'have a way with words' . . . that you 'really ought to write?'" Readers who answer yes to all the questions are invited to fill out a form with their personal details and then send in their works for publications.

94. Neil Duncan, "Ten-Year Cultural Development Plan," UNESCO, Serial No. FMR/CC/CD/80/158, 1980, 4.

95. Duncan, "Ten-Year Cultural Development Plan," 5.

96. Alvin Pang, personal correspondence, December 27, 2020. Thinking about the anthology as a generative form rather than solely a canon-confirming one builds on Eve Kosofsky Sedgwick's notion of a "reparative reading," though in this case, the onus is on the form rather than the critical reader as interpreter. See Alvin Pang's "Writing the Multiple: From Chapalang to Confluence" (PhD diss., Royal Melbourne Institute of Technology, 2020) for further discussion of the professional/amateur divide.

97. Pugalenthi Sr, *Motherland 1*, n.p.

98. Although the front matter in the *Motherland* volumes make mention of VJ Times's ambition to "globalise our writers and to make VJ Times a global publishing house," given the tone of the front matter as a whole, I take this as a defensive comment against critiques

of VJ Times as publishing vernacular or overly local literature rather than as a concession to the global literary marketplace.

99. See *Over There: Poems from Singapore and Australia* (2008), *Double Skin: New Poetic Voices From Italy and Singapore* (2009), *A Monsoon Feast: Short Stories to Celebrate the Cultures of Kerala and Singapore* (2012), *Get Lucky: An Anthology of Philippine and Singapore Writings* (2015). A good number of these were edited by Alvin Pang, who, we recall, was himself featured in a number of VJ Times anthologies.

2. OVERSEAS SINGAPOREANS AND THEIR USES: POPULATION AESTHETICS AND TERRITORIAL PRODUCTIONS OF SINGAPORE'S GLOBAL ASIA IMAGINARY

1. The demographic nature of such compilations is obscured by their categorization under the library subject headings "anecdotes" and "personal narratives." Such classifications reveal the genre's *testimonio* roots; what might be described as the earliest Singaporean demographic compilations of the twentieth century are POW accounts of Japanese occupation.

2. Some examples of recent titles are *Inspirations of a Nation: Tribute to 25 Singaporean South Asians* (2016), *PAP Pioneers: 50 Ordinary Stories* (2015), *50 Points of View: A Unique Celebration of Singapore by Students from Pathlight School* (2015), *Setia Dan Bakti: 50 Stories of Loyalty and Service* (2015), *Befriending Conversations: 20 Seniors, 20 Occupations, 20 Stories* (2020), *Conversations on Coming Home: 20 Singaporeans Share Their Stories* (2013) (which I discuss in chapter 3), *The Naysayer's Book Club: 26 Singaporeans You Need to Know* (2018).

3. Partha Chatterjee, *The Politics of the Governed* (New York: Columbia University Press, 2004), 34.

4. As Benedict Anderson writes, the census (as well as the map and the museum) "profoundly shaped the way in which the colonial state imagined its dominion" because constructions of ethnic-racial classifications and their systematic quantification were key for organizing colonial bureaucracies. Such instruments continue to be relevant under postcolonial governance in Singapore. See *Imagined Communities*, 164, 168–69.

5. Sunil Amrith, "Eugenics in Postcolonial Southeast Asia," in *The Oxford Handbook of the History of Eugenics*, ed. Alison Bashford and Philippa Levine (Oxford: Oxford University Press, 2010), 3.

6. Ong, *Neoliberalism as Exception*, 180.

7. For one, the national heroes in Anderson's readings of Jose Rizal's *Noli Me Tangere*, Francisco Balagtas's *Pinagdaanang Buhay ni Florante at ni Laura sa Cahariang Albania*, Jose Joaquin Fernandez De Lizardi's *El Periquillo Sarniento*, and Mas Marco Kartodikromo's *Semarang Hitam* are anticolonial revolutionaries. So too is the case with Lee Kuan Yew in *The Singapore Story*, who is understood as the founding leader of postcolonial Singapore. The nationalist role for such figures is clearcut: they are fighting to establish the sovereignty of the nation-state.

8. Philip Holden, *Autobiography and Decolonization: Modernity, Masculinity, and the Nation-State* (Madison: University of Wisconsin Press, 2008), 173.

9. Emily Steinlight, *Populating the Novel: Literary Form and the Politics of Surplus Life* (Ithaca, NY: Cornell University Press, 2018), 40. In her work, Steinlight argues that the

"concrete formal strategies" of literature establishes and responds to the new significance of population as introduced by Thomas Malthus.

10. Benedict Anderson, *The Spectre of Comparisons: Nationalism, Southeast Asia, and the World* (London: Verso, 1998), 40.

11. Anderson, *The Spectre of Comparisons*, 40.

12. Chatterjee, *The Politics of the Governed*, 5–6.

13. Chatterjee, *The Politics of the Governed*, 5–6.

14. Michel Foucault, *"Society Must Be Defended": Lectures at the College de France, 1975–1976*, trans. David Macey (London: Picador, 2003), 241.

15. See Colleen Lye's discussion of how crowds are central to the Yellow Peril imaginary. Lye, *America's Asia: Racial Form and American Literature, 1893–1945* (Princeton, NJ: Princeton University Press, 2004).

16. Robert Mitchell, "Biopolitics and Population Aesthetics," *South Atlantic Quarterly* 115.2 (2016): 367–98, 369.

17. Weihsin Gui, *National Consciousness and Literary Cosmopolitics: Postcolonial Literature in a Global Moment* (Columbus: Ohio State University Press, 2013), 11.

18. Justin Tyler Clark, "From Global City to 'City of Villages': Tracing the State Discourse of Cosmopolitanism in Modern Singaporean History," *Journal of Intercultural Studies* 40:4 (2019): 399–416, 402.

19. Brenda S. A. Yeoh, "Cosmopolitanism and Its Exclusions in Singapore," *Urban Studies* 41.12 (November 2004): 2431–45, 2434; original emphasis. One might also see the celebratory rhetoric around Singapore's cosmopolitan populace as an implicit jab at their former British colonizers, who struggled to govern its multilingual populace. See Rachel Leow's *Taming Babel: Language in the Making of Malaysia* (Cambridge: Cambridge University Press, 2016) for an excellent historical account of these governance struggles.

20. Yeoh, "Cosmopolitanism and Its Exclusions in Singapore," 2434. Put a little differently, my discussion of cosmopolitanism via the Overseas Singaporean operates in what Bruce Robbins calls a "descriptive register" rather than a "normative" one. That is, rather than investigating, say, vernacular definitions of cosmopolitanism in Singapore and how they compare to normative ones as derived from the European Enlightenment, my concern here is how cosmopolitanism serves as what Young describes as a "new form and practice of mediation, between the sovereignty of the state and the claims of the universal, between nation and individual, between the sovereign state and the ethics of human hospitality." See Bruce Robbins, Introduction to *Cosmopolitanisms*, ed. Bruce Robbins and Paulo Lemos Horta (New York: New York University Press, 2017), 1–20, 3; Robert J. C. Young, "The Cosmopolitan Idea and National Sovereignty," in Robbins and Horta, *Cosmopolitanisms*, 135–40, 136.

21. Michael Hill and Lian Kwen Fee, *The Politics of Nation Building and Citizenship in Singapore* (London: Routledge, 1995), 26.

22. Seng, quoted in Elgin Toh, "60 years of the Singapore Citizenship: From Hawkers to Millionaires, They All Queued Up," *Straits Times*, October 8, 2017, https://www.straitstimes.com/politics/60-years-of-the-singapore-citizenship-from-hawkers-to-millionaires-they-all-queued-up, accessed July 9, 2021.

23. Historically, the concerns state officials voiced about loyalty and belonging were mostly directed at the Chinese and Indian settler populations, which were seen as politically

suspect. Although the Malay people are regarded as Indigenous to the region, after independence, their Muslim faith was regarded as a threat to the possibility of national loyalty.

24. "Campaign to Make 250,000 Aliens Voters from Nov. 1," *Straits Times*, October 16, 1957, 4.

25. Paul Foo, "250,000 New Citizens," *Straits Times*, November 3, 1957, 10.

26. Or to put it in Kamal Sadiq's words, Singapore complicates historical accounts that propose "that citizens of newly independent postcolonial states were born into *a spirit* of constitutional equality through *jus soli* principles." While Kadiq here is discussing the various controversies around postcolonial citizenship (i.e., that of *jus soli* and *jus sanguinis* principles), the notion of the decolonizing spirit that he describes cannot be assumed in a location with as many transient workers as Singapore has. As Hill and Lian further point out, for example, the "Nanyang Chinese sentimental attachment to their homeland acted as a barrier to renouncing their Chinese nationality" (54). Kamal Sadiq, "Postcolonial Citizenship," in *The Oxford Handbook of Citizenship*, ed. Ayelet Shachar, Rainer Baubock, Irene Bloemraad, and Maarten Vink (Oxford: Oxford University Press, 2020), 178–99, 186.

27. From a 1969 newspaper article: "Hundreds take part in this annual student exodus—some lured by the traditions of famous universities; others in search of new science not yet available locally; and still others, because there are no places for them in local universities and colleges." See "Is This Annual Student Exodus Necessary?," *Straits Times*, September 21, 1969, 12.

28. The number of Singaporeans studying abroad peaked in 1999 and has remained steady since then, comprising about a tenth of the total tertiary enrollments in Singapore. See Christopher Ziguras and Cate Gribble, "Policy Responses to Address Student 'Brain Drain': An Assessment of Measures Intended to Reduce the Emigration of Singaporean International Students," *Journal of Studies in International Education* 19.4 (2015): 246–64, 249.

29. Phew Yew Kok, Joseph Tan Meng Kwan, Hashin Bin Idris, "Don't Waste Your Time on Parasites," *Straits Times*, January 14, 1971, 18.

30. "'Get Tough on Rich Parents': Unions' Call to Govt," *Straits Times*, October 13, 1970, 7.

31. "'Get Tough on Rich Parents.'"

32. Clark, "From Global City to 'City of Villages,'" 404.

33. "Question on Brain Drain for Parliament," *Straits Times*, December 9, 1987, 19.

34. See "Premier Lee Warns of 'Brain Drain,'" *Straits Times*, July 2, 1966, 6; and "Futility of Aid While U.S. Drains Afro-Asia of Their Brains," *Straits Times*, February 28, 1967, 3.

35. Warren Fernandez, "Give Them Second Chance, but Not Special Treatment," *Straits Times*, March 7, 1991, 19.

36. Lee commented, "The mass of people everywhere has to stay and face whatever is coming. But in a new society, the determinants are those who can leave, but do not, and help make things better for the majority." See Yeo Toon Joo, "Brain Drain Will Be Decisive: Lee," *Straits Times*, September 7, 1969, 1.

37. The main way in which we continue to see the state treat Overseas Singaporeans as a problematic population is in limitations on voting. See Jee Leong Koh, "The Right to Vote: The Stories of Overseas Singaporeans," Singapore Unbound, July 7, 2020, https://singapore unbound.org/blog/2020/7/6/the-right-to-vote-the-stories-of-overseas-singaporeans.

38. "Population in Brief 2020" (Singapore Department of Statistics, 2020), 15. The report notes that in 2020, during the COVID-19 pandemic, a significant number of Singaporeans returned home.

39. See No. 14 of "Date of Census and Particulars," under Census Act, Chapter 35, Section 3.

40. See Singapore's *Population in Brief* series, as put out by the Prime Minister's Office.

41. See the Enlistment Act of 1972 (Chapter 93, Section 33{2}) and the Constitution of the Republic of Singapore (No. 128 of Part X).

42. With thanks to Philip Holden for sharing this with me.

43. As Seng notes, official figures do not reveal "the virtual citizenry that identifies Singapore as home." See Eunice M. F. Seng, "Transnational Utopia: Diaspora as Creative Praxis," in *Singapore Dreaming: Managing Utopia*, ed. H. Koon Wee and Jeremy Chia (Singapore: Asian Urban Lab, 2016), 146–67, 148; Cherian George, "Sintercom: Harnessing of Virtual Community," in *Contentious Journalism and the Internet: Towards Democratic Discourse in Malaysia and Singapore* (Singapore: National University of Singapore Press, 2006), 99–119.

44. *Changing Mindsets, Deepening Relationships*, Ministry of Community Development and Sports, 2003, 30.

45. The Overseas Singaporean Unit would be transformed into the Singapore Global Network in 2019, merging with Contact Singapore.

46. Clark, "From Global City to 'City of Villages,'" 400.

47. In "The Cosmopolitan Idea and National Sovereignty," Robert J. C. Young writes: "Whereas the coalescence of nation and state meant the consolidation of citizenship with forms of ethnic or cultural belonging, the identification for individuals and groups of the one with the other, cosmopolitanism raises the question of how new forms of belonging in a world marked by migration, diaspora, and transnational labor might be understood in relation to those older forms of singular cultural identification" (137).

48. Camilo Arturo Leslie, "Territoriality, Map-mindedness, and the Politics of Place," *Theory and Society* 45.2 (2016): 169–201, 171.

49. Christina Klein writes that sentimental texts "uphold human connection as the highest ideal and emphasize the forging of bonds and the creation of solidarities among friends, family, and community." See Klein, *Cold War Orientalism: Asia in the Middlebrow Imagination, 1945–1961* (Oakland: University of California Press, 2003), 14.

50. Deepika Shetty, "A City of Contrasts," *Straits Time: The Sunday Times*, November 9, 2008, 10.

51. Deepika Shetty, "Marrakech's Magical Mix," *Straits Times: The Sunday Times*, December 28, 2008, 10.

52. In *Autobiography and Decolonization*, Holden discusses how the Singapore citizen-consumer has been a cornerstone of Singapore governmentality since the 1960s, as illustrated by the public housing policy and the "mushrooming of semiautonomous organs of the state that encourage citizenship as consumption" (184).

53. Sunny Xiang's discussion of Asian inscrutability was especially useful for this formulation. "Inscrutability," she writes, "conveys a faithless relationship between surface phenomena and inner truths." See *Tonal Intelligence: The Aesthetics of Asian Inscrutability during the Long Cold War* (New York: Columbia University Press, 2020), 38.

54. The most obvious example of this is Edward Said's notion of Orientalism. Another classic is Gayatri Chakravorty Spivak's "Three Women's Texts and a Critique of Imperialism,"

where she writes about the depiction of "the Third World as distant cultures, exploited but with rich intact literary heritages waiting to be recovered, interpreted, and curricularized in English translation" (243). See *Critical Inquiry* 12 (Autumn 1985): 243–261.

55. Mary Louise Pratt, *Imperial Eyes: Travel Writing and Transculturation*, 2nd ed. (New York: Routledge, 2003), 30.

56. Anderson, *Imagined Communities*, 177.

57. Foucault, *Security, Territory, Population*, 20–21.

58. Mitchell, "Biopolitics and Population Aesthetics," 373.

59. Foucault, *Security, Territory, Population*, 22.

60. Mitchell, "Biopolitics and Population Aesthetics," 373.

61. be movement, May 23, 2016, via Internet Archive Wayback Machine, accessed April 3, 2022; be movement, "About" and "Store."

62. Like Troy Chin, who I discuss in chapter 3, Lim's story is something of a post-coming-of-career narrative. After the experience of being trapped in a stairwell in Tokyo during the 2011 Tohoku earthquake and reflecting on the "meaninglessness" of her life and career (youtube), Lim decided to start be movement.

63. Gui, *National Consciousness and Literary Cosmopolitics*, 11.

64. "50 Red Dots Around the World," *be movement*, vol. 6 (2015), 35.

65. "50 Red Dots Around the World," 32.

66. In "50 Red Dots," Diana Saw comments that the state's economic agenda has been at the expense of affective ties: "Singapore's unrelenting focus on commerce means that foster community and identity are often sacrificed, such as the old buildings we grew up with and love, even Singlish, because it apparently interferes with how well we attract international trade and foreign investment." (185).

67. Joseph Slaughter, *Human Rights, Inc.: The World Novel, Narrative Form, and International Law* (New York: Fordham University Press, 2007), 274, 42.

68. Frantz Fanon, *The Wretched of the Earth* (New York: Grove Press, 2004), 160.

69. "50 Red Dots Around the World," 13.

70. "50 Red Dots Around the World," 30.

71. "50 Red Dots Around the World," 77.

72. "Profile," JCCI Singapore, accessed April 3, 2022, https://www.jcci.org.sg/profile/?lang=en.

73. "About JCCI Singapore Foundation," JCCI Singapore, accessed April 3, 2022, https://www.jcci.org.sg/about-singapore/?lang=en.

74. "50 Red Dots Around the World," 45.

75. Jeremy Tiang, *It Never Rains on National Day* (Singapore: Epigram Books, 2015), 1.

76. Singapore 21 Committee, *Singapore 21: Together, We Make the Difference*," 1999, 45.

77. Laurence Leong Wai Teng, "Sexual Governance and the Politics of Sex in Singapore," *Management of Success: Singapore Revisited*, ed. Terence Chong (Singapore: ISEAS Publishing, 2010), 582. Such unapologetic eugenic thinking is also evident in marriage laws for immigrants; while there are no restrictions on marriages between Singaporeans and those under "foreign talent" work visas, there are marriage restrictions between Singaporeans and migrants categorized as "unskilled labor." Foreign work permit holders "shall not go through any form of marriage under any law, religion, custom or usage with a Singapore Citizen or Permanent Resident in or outside Singapore without the prior approval of the Controller, while he/she holds a Work Permit, and also after his/her Work Permit has expired or has been

cancelled or revoked." See Employment of Foreign Manpower (Work Passes) Regulations 2012, S 569/12, November 8, 2012, issued under the Employment of Foreign Workers Act (Cap. 91A), online: http://www.mom.gov.sg/Documents/services-forms/passes/WPSPass Conditions.pdf, 1 March 2014. Consequences for the migrant worker include deportation.

78. *Changing Mindsets*, 65. In order to attract Overseas Singaporean women back to Singapore, the report advocated for automatic citizenship for their offspring, a privilege afforded at the time to Singaporean men but not to women.

79. Tiang, *It Never Rains on National Day*, 1

80. Tiang, *It Never Rains on National Day*, 1.

81. Tiang, *It Never Rains on National Day*, 2.

82. Tiang, *It Never Rains on National Day*, 2.

83. Tiang, *It Never Rains on National Day*, 2.

84. Tiang, *It Never Rains on National Day*, 3; emphasis added.

85. Tiang, *It Never Rains on National Day*, 5.

86. Tiang, *It Never Rains on National Day*, 6.

87. Tiang, *It Never Rains on National Day*, 7.

88. Tiang, *It Never Rains on National Day*, 9.

89. Tiang, *It Never Rains on National Day*, 11.

90. Tiang, *It Never Rains on National Day*, 10.

91. Young, "The Cosmopolitan Idea and National Sovereignty," 138–39.

92. Tiang, *It Never Rains on National Day*, 167.

93. Tiang, *It Never Rains on National Day*, 168.

94. Tiang, *It Never Rains on National Day*, 167.

95. Tiang, *It Never Rains on National Day*, 169, 176.

96. Tiang, *It Never Rains on National Day*, 177.

97. Tiang, *It Never Rains on National Day*, 177, 180.

98. Tiang, *It Never Rains on National Day*, 174.

3. COMING-OF-CAREER NARRATIVES, THE POSTCOLONIAL WORK ETHIC, AND THE PROMISE OF A NEW NATION

1. Isa Kamari, *The Tower*, trans. Alfian Sa'at (Singapore: Epigram Books, 2013), 16

2. Isa Kamari, *The Tower*, 74.

3. See also Cheryl Narumi Naruse, "Hwee Hwee Tan's *Mammon Inc.* as Bildungsroman, or the Coming-of-Career Narrative," *Genre: Forms of Discourse and Culture* 49.1 (April 2016): 95–115; Cheryl Narumi Naruse, "Diasporic Singaporeans, Coming-of-Career Narratives, and the Corporate Nation," *biography: an Interdisciplinary quarterly* 37.1 (Winter 2014): 143–67.

4. Early examples include Brontë's *Jane Eyre* (1847), which ties the protagonist's character development to her work as a governess. Twentieth-century examples are what Juliette Rogers describes as the female *berufsroman*, or novel of women's professional development, which emerged in post–World War I France. Also notable are career novels, serialized novels primarily published from the 1930s to the 1960s. As a precursor to the chick lit phenomenon, a typical career novel follows the professional and romantic adventures of a young woman about to embark on her first job, often concluding with a marriage proposal and

a job promotion. In the *berufsroman* and the career novel, the protagonist's formation as a total personality is the story of what it means to be a gendered body in the workforce. In the United States, career novel series include Avalon's Career Novels and Dodd Mead's Career Books. In the United Kingdom, there are the Bodley Head Career Books for Girls series and Chatto and Windus's Career Novels. Some examples of titles are Elizabeth Churchill's *Juliet in Publishing* (1956); Joan Owens's *Margaret Becomes a Doctor* (1957); Alberta Eiseman and Ingrid Sladkus's *Monica: The Story of a Young Magazine Apprentice* (1957); and Blanche L. Gibbs and Georgiana Adams's *Shirley Clayton, Secretary* (1941). See Juliette M. Rogers, *Career Stories: Belle Epoque Novels of Professional Development* (University Park: Pennsylvania State University Press, 2007). For a discussion of *Mammon Inc.* as chick-lit, see chapter 5 of Christopher B. Patterson's *Transitive Cultures: Anglophone Literature of the Transpacific* (New Brunswick, NJ: Rutgers University Press, 2018).

5. These include Singaporean classics *If We Dream Too Long* by Goh Poh Seng (Singapore: National University Press, 2020) and *Ricky Star* by Lim Thean Soo (Singapore: Epigram Books, 2012), as well as trade fiction such as *Beck and Call* (Singapore: Monsoon Books, 2012) by Eric Alagan (described as "a business thriller set in Singapore") and *Eat Company: Sleep Bunk Berth* by Wee Kiat (Singapore: Landmark Books, 1997).

6. Joseph R. Slaughter writes, "Humboldtian *Bildung* describes a civic course of acculturation by which the individual's impulses for self-expression and fulfillment are rationalized, modernized, conventionalized, and normalized within the social parameters, cultural patterns, and public institution of the modern nation-state." See *Human Rights, Inc.*, 113.

7. Marianne Hirsch, "The Novel of Formation as Genre: Between Great Expectations and Lost Illusions," *Genre* 12 (Fall 1979): 293–311, 300. See also Patricia M. Chu's *Assimilating Asians: Gendered Strategies of Authorship in Asian America* (Durham, NC: Duke University Press, 2000) and Jed Esty's *Unseasonable Youth: Modernism, Colonialism, and the Fiction of Development* (Oxford: Oxford University Press, 2011) for more works on how the bildungsroman has been repurposed as a mode of critique, despite its ideological roots.

8. *Mammon Inc.* handles this through the use of multiple settings. Other examples such as Dave Eggers's *The Circle* (New York: Knopf, 2013) portray the global economy through the world of the corporation. For Aravind Adiga's *The White Tiger*, (London: Atlantic Books, 2008), the transnationally connected world is made apparent in its epistolary address.

9. Kalyan Nadiminti, "Work, Neoliberal Development, and Global Anglophone Literatures," *Oxford Research Encyclopedia of Literature*, 2020, 2.

10. Isa Kamari, "Mind your (Inter)Culture: *The Tower*," Grassroots Book Room, Singapore, April 23, 2016.

11. Given Singapore's ability so quickly to metabolize the capitalist imperatives that accompanied developmentalism as the three-world order came into being, it seems unsurprising that Hwee Hwee Tan's *Mammon Inc.* (London: Penguin Books, 2001) would also be one of the first works of Asian finance fiction. Like other well-known examples of Asian finance fiction such as Adiga's *The White Tiger* (2008), Tash Aw's *Five Star Billionaire* (New York: Random House, 2014), Mohsin Hamid's *How to Get Filthy Rich in Rising Asia* (New York: Riverhead Books, 2014), and Zia Haider Rahman's *In Light of What We Know* (London: Picador, 2015), Tan's novel uses realist techniques to explore the confluences of the global economy and the nation in the context of Asia's increasing capitalist power.

12. Lee Kuan Yew, "31 August 1957: Message to Federation of Malaya on Attainment of Merdeka," National Archives of Singapore.

13. Fanon, *The Wretched of the Earth*, 57.

14. See Harvey, "The 'New' Imperialism."

15. See chapter 3 in Venn's *After Capital* for a useful historical summary of capitalism's relationship to colonialism.

16. Rey Chow, *The Protestant Ethnic and the Spirit of Capitalism* (New York: Columbia University Press, 2002), 40–41.

17. Chow, *The Protestant Ethnic and the Spirit of Capitalism*, 42, 45.

18. Fanon, *The Wretched of the Earth*, 44.

19. Though Lee envisioned a society based on meritocracy, the very notion of merit based on work was in essence the same logic of British colonial governance that classified different racial groups in colonial era Singapore according to their perceived quality of work.

20. Balibar, "The Nation Form," 86.

21. Lee's assertion that work performed liberation from colonialism, an ideological cornerstone of (economic) developmentalism, was not unique to his thinking; he was echoing many of the sentiments expressed throughout the Bandung Conference of 1955. In *Theory Is History* (Dordrecht: Springer, 2013), the Marxist economist Samir Amin writes, "The Bandung era, with the triumph of the ideology of development, was based on a range of seeming truths, specific to each region of the world but all deeply rooted in prevailing beliefs: Keynesianism; the myth of catching up through third world interdependence. These prevailing myths have been subject to critical examination, but to a limited and little-understood degree" (63).

22. Fanon, *The Wretched of the Earth*, 56.

23. Fanon, *The Wretched of the Earth*, 52; emphasis added.

24. As Mezzadra succinctly writes in "How Many Histories of Labour?," "To make a long (and complex) history short (and easy), the dyad citizen-worker assumed dominance worldwide after World War II, whether in the Stakhanov moment of the USSR, the heyday of US industrial towns such as Flint Michigan, or the disciplined working subject of the Nehru Plans" (155).

25. Sanyal, *Rethinking Capitalist Development*, 33.

26. Mezzadra, "How Many Histories of Labour?," 155.

27. Michel Foucault, *The Birth of Biopolitics: Lectures at the Collège de France 1978–1979*, trans. Graham Burchell (London: Palgrave Macmillan, 2008), 217.

28. Foucault, *The Birth of Biopolitics*, 220–21.

29. Foucault, *The Birth of Biopolitics*, 220–23.

30. Foucault, *The Birth of Biopolitics*, 226.

31. Foucault, *The Birth of Biopolitics*, 228.

32. Jamaica Kincaid, *A Small Place* (New York: Farrar, Straus and Giroux, 2000), 36–37; original emphasis.

33. Foucault, *The Birth of Biopolitics*, 230.

34. See the Guide from Cathy Park Hong's *Dance Dance Revolution* (2006), Balram of Adiga's *The White Tiger*, Phoebe from Aw's *Five Star Billionaire*, Helen of Derek Walcott's *Omeros* (New York: Farrar, Straus and Giroux, 1990), Ifemelu of Chimamanda Ngozi

Adichie's *Americanah* (New York: Vintage Books, 2014), Rajkumar of Amitav Ghosh's *The Glass Palace* (New York: Random House, 2002), the unnamed protagonist of Hamid's *How to Get Filthy Rich in Rising Asia*, to name a few. Moments of a postcolonial entrepreneurial spirit are also evident in works, both fictional and critical, now considered classic. Consider, for example, the market scene in which Tambudzai of Tsitsi Dangarembga's *Nervous Conditions* (London, Ayebia Clarke: 2004) sells mealies in order to pay for her school tuition or Epeli Hau'ofa's reference to his Tongan friend in "Our Sea of Islands," *The Contemporary Pacific* 6.1 (Spring 1994), an enterprising, resourceful man described as having "never heard of dependency" (160).

35. Tan, *Mammon Inc.*, 2.

36. Robbie B. H. Goh, "Writing 'the Global' in Singapore Anglophone Fiction," in *China Fictions, English Language: Literary Essays in Diaspora, Memory, Story*, ed. A. Robert Lee (Amsterdam: Rodopi, 2008), 239–58, 240.

37. Eddie Tay, *Colony, Nation, and Globalisation: Not at Home in Singaporean and Malaysian Literature* (Hong Kong: Hong Kong University Press, 2011), 127.

38. Paul Nadal, "A Literary Remittance: Juan C. Laya's *His Native Soil* and the Rise of Realism in the Filipino Novel in English," *American Literature* 89.3 (2017): 591–626, 596.

39. Tay, *Colony, Nation, and Globalisation*, 131.

40. Tan, *Mammon Inc.*, 64.

41. The concerns of economic decline following the 1997 Asian financial crisis spurred Prime Minister Goh Chok Tong to call for a reassessment of Singapore. He assembled the Singapore 21 Committee, a group of eighty-three individuals from the private and public business sectors and citizens, and tasked it with brainstorming solutions to what was regarded as the pressures of an increasingly globalized knowledge economy. In addition to the committee's recommendations to the government and its public readership, which include the need to strengthen family bonds and nationalist sentiment, the report details how to create a more transnational, geographically mobile, and worldly citizenry in Singapore. Though it seemed that the report was also an "attempt to give Singaporeans a cause to fight for other than the blind pursuit of wealth accumulation," its language and the rationale for many of the committee's recommendations ultimately made the state's economic imperative clear. See Yolanda Chin, "Community Confidence and Security," in *Management of Success: Singapore Revisited*, ed. Terence Chong (Singapore: ISEAS Publishing, 2010), 443–61, 449.

42. Singapore 21 Committee, *Singapore 21*, 45; emphasis added.

43. Hardt, "Affective Labor," 90.

44. Hardt, "Affective Labor," 94.

45. Hardt cautions that immaterial labor should not be understood within a developmentalist framework (i.e., service or knowledge economies are not signs of capitalist advancement), and part of resisting such a framework, I contend, requires that an analysis of how immaterial labor is at once the capitalist action of a knowledge economy and a reaction, in this instance, to previous economic paradigms.

46. C. J. W.-L. Wee, "The Indigenized West in Asian Multicultures: Literary-Cultural Production in Malaysia and Singapore," *Interventions: International Journal of Postcolonial Studies* 10.2 (2008): 188–206, 201.

47. Chiah Deng's knowledge and curiosity about other cultures and literature is hyperbolized: "I became friends with Tock Seng [her ex-boyfriend] because he was the only one

in my school who had read Dante and Derrida. For our class project, we used Chinese opera conventions to perform scenes from the Greek tragedy *Oedipus Rex*. . . . We would greet each other with—" You! *Hypocrite lecteur!—mon semblable—mon frère!*," knowing that we might possibly be the only couple in Singapore who knew this was an allusion to Baudelaire's *Les Fleurs du Mal* via T. S. Eliot's *The Waste Land*" (42). This is just one example of several in the novel.

48. Shashi R. Thandra, "Annihilation and Accumulation: Postcolonial Literatures on Genocide and Capital" (PhD diss., Wayne State University, 2014), 13.

49. Tan, *Mammon Inc.*, 3.

50. "Singapore 21 (Motion)," Singapore Parliamentary Debates, Parliament 9, Sess. 1, Vol. 70, Sitting 14, May 5, 1999, Col. 1626; emphasis added.

51. As evidenced by government bureaucracy—the National Productivity Centre, which was established in 1972, had an earlier iteration in the "National Productivity Centre and the Productivity Unit"—national emphasis on productivity was not necessarily new.

52. Publications by the National Productivity Board include *People-Centered Management: Programmes* (1985), *Our Story: 15 Years of NPB* (1981), *Report of the Committee on Productivity* (1981), *Handbook on Productivity Management* (1988), *Productivity Concepts and Their Application* (1992), and countless others.

53. Singapore National Productivity Board, *Tomorrow Shall Be Better Than Today: a Productivity Action Plan*, 1983, i.

54. Teh Cheang Wan, "We Must Be Productive in All Fields of Human Endeavour," in *The Way to Productivity: Thematic Speeches* (Singapore: Ministry of Culture, 1983), 19–20, 19.

55. As Chakrabarty writes, "In this vitalist understanding [of labor as articulated by Marx], life, in all its biological/conscious capacity for willful activity . . . is the excess that capital, for all its disciplinary procedures, always needs but can never quite control or domesticate" (60). See *Provincializing Europe: Postcolonial Thought and Historical Difference* (Princeton, NJ: Princeton University Press, 2008), 60.

56. Watson, *The New Asian City*, 116.

57. See, e.g., "Producing Better Towkays," *New Nation*, April 27, 1978, 8; "Coming Up with Solutions for Problems of Job Satisfaction," *Straits Times*, August 3, 1979, 16.

58. A 1979 National Day celebration speech by Chai Chong Yii offers some further insight into this notion that work is most significant to one's external environment. According to Chai, there were three "types" of workers: the first, clearly the most desirable, were the "hundreds of elderly people who work seven days a week, 365 days a year. They do not rest unless they fall sick. Even then, they may still give instruction on their sick beds to attend their business." Second, a middling group, were "people who believe in keeping a strict dividing line between work and play. They are diligent and conscientious in attending to their work. When business hours are over, they refuse to have anything to do with their office work. They maintain strictly a private life for themselves." The third, clearly the least desirable, were "people who put personal enjoyment above everything. They do not like to work for long hours if they can shorten them. They hate to dirty their hands if they can keep them clean. They do not enjoy working. Neither do they have pride in their work. They work because they need their pay."

Chai's classifications suggest first that there is the notion that work occupies the sphere of public life—and that the most hardworking are the ones who do not let their private life encroach into public/national life. Second, the "less productive" types are ones whose actions are driven by pleasure—as the emotive verb choices "do not like," "hate," or "do not enjoy" indicate—compared to the hard workers, who do not feel but just do. Taken as a whole, Chai's speech encapsulates the notion that the pleasure in work is external to one's inner life and that one's life is only ever part of the larger national whole. Moreover, the derisive phrase "They do not enjoy working" also suggests that he wants workers to enjoy work.

59. S. M. Muthu, "Wrong Ideas on Meritocracy: Chok Tong," *Straits Times*, May 1, 1981, 10.

60. "Speech by Dr Ahmad Mattar, Acting Minister for Social Affairs, and Member of Parliament for Brickworks at the Brickworks Constituency National Day Dinner," Singapore Government Press Release, Publicity Division, August 19, 1978.

61. In April 1996, the National Productivity Board Act was repealed and the NPB merged with the Singapore Institute of Standards and Industrial Research and was renamed the Singapore Productivity and Standards Board.

62. Goh Chok Tong, "Speech by Prime Minister Goh Chok Tong at the Opening of the 7th International Conference on Thinking on Monday, 2 June 1997, at 9.00am at the Suntec City Convention Centre Ballroom," *Shaping Our Future: Thinking Schools, Learning Nation*, National Archives of Singapore, 8.

63. Goh Chok Tong, "Speech," 8.

64. Colleen Lye, "Unmarked Character and the 'Rise of Asia': Ed Park's *Personal Days*," *Verge: Studies in Global Asias* 1.1 (2015): 230–54, 234.

65. Tan, *Mammon Inc.*, 131.

66. Hardt, "Affective Labor," 94.

67. Tan, *Mammon Inc.*, 131.

68. Tina Chen, "Agency/Asiancy," in *The Routledge Companion to Asian American and Pacific Islander Literature*, ed. Rachel Lee (London: Taylor and Francis, 2014), 56–67, 58.

69. Tan, *Mammon Inc.*, 3.

70. Tan, *Mammon Inc.*, 76.

71. Teo Youyenn, *Neoliberal Morality in Singapore: How Family Policies Make State and Society* (London: Routledge, 2011), 3; original emphasis.

72. At its core, for example, Dipesh Chakrabarty's image of a "waiting room of history" from *Provincializing Europe* comments on the violence of colonial emplotment: historicism is an act of restricting the colonial subject within a discrete event, or reading the colonial subject as forever stuck in an early plot point in the rising action of History. The (postcolonial) nation, however, operates with its own teleology as it "appears as the fulfillment of a 'project' stretching over centuries, in which there are different stages and moments of coming to self-awareness," as Balibar points out ("The Nation Form," 86). National subjects, or what Benedict Anderson describes as the galvanizing force of the nation as an "imagined community," are emplotted together, moving together though the unfolding of homogeneous, simultaneous time of the nation. In each of these instances, the national subject is imbued with a sense of broader structural power, whether that of colonialism or of the postcolonial nation.

73. Jed Esty writes in *Unseasonable Youth*, "To become an adult [is] to complete the passage from innocence—understood as a kind of ungroundedness—into citizenship, or full integration into the national community" (ix).

74. Tan, *Mammon Inc.*, 7.

75. Tan, *Mammon Inc.*, 7.

76. The Singapore Day I attended in 2012 in Brooklyn, New York, had an estimated crowd of 5,000 and a budget of S$4 million (roughly US$3.2 million). The event was a curious amalgamation of trade show—with various installations showcasing the latest infrastructural developments in Singapore—heritage festival and career fair. I was given the booklet as

I was surveying the scene at the career fair component of the event, which included booths that were offering lucrative positions at transnational corporations. Besides observing that these booklets were placed on nearly every table and that the booklet was made freely available on Contact Singapore's website, there is no other circulation information.

77. Leslie Sklair, *The Transnational Capitalist Class* (London: Wiley-Blackwell, 2000).

78. *Conversations on Coming Home* was available in PDF form on the website of Contact Singapore along with three other booklets that all promote Singapore as a place to develop careers but to different audiences: *Welcome to a New City of Opportunities* (2014) is aimed at a general audience; *Dreams Taking Shape* (n.d.) is geared to Southeast Asian expatriates; and *Connecting in the Heart of Asia* (2012) is specifically for South Asian professionals. The latter two booklets follow a similar structure as *Conversations* in its biographical focus on people moving to Singapore to work. *Dreams* reflects a similar sinocentric politics insofar as the people featured in it are Chinese passing while the racial politics of *Connecting* reveals a colorism. In other words, these booklets aimed at recruiting labor operate with a strong visual politics of racial capitalism.

79. Contact Singapore closed in 2017. Many of the services associated with Contact Singapore are now under the auspices of the Singapore Global Network, where the Overseas Singapore Unit now is.

80. *Conversations on Coming Home: 20 Singaporeans Share Their Stories*, Contact Singapore, 2012, 7.

81. *Conversations on Coming Home*, 29, 35.

82. *Conversations on Coming Home*, 19.

83. *Conversations on Coming Home*, 17.

84. *Conversations on Coming Home*, 25.

85. *Conversations on Coming Home*, 17.

86. The way that a common cosmopolitan taste consolidates returned Singaporeans with national outsiders is reminiscent of Fanon's discussion of the colonized intellectual's place in the production of national culture in *The Wretched of the Earth*: "The colonized intellectual who returns to his people through works of art behaves in fact like a foreigner. Sometimes he will not hesitate to use the local dialects to demonstrate his desire to be as close to the people as possible but the ideas he expresses, the preoccupations that haunt him are in no way related to the daily lot of the men and women of his country" (160). Fanon critiques the way that the colonized intellectual produces national culture according to colonial perceptions of exotic difference, and analogously we can critique the returned Singaporeans who make national culture legible according to state-produced tourist markers, which also operate according to the pleasure principles of cultural difference.

87. See "Latest Results," Migrant Poetry Competition, https://www.singaporeworker poetry.com/2014-results. With many thanks to Nasia Anam and Madhumita Lahiri for their help with my questions about the poem's English translation from the Bengali.

88. Tan, *Mammon Inc.*, 255.

89. See Brenda S. A. Yeoh, "Singapore: Hungry for Foreign Workers at All Skill Levels," *Migration Information Sources: The Online Journal of the Migration Policy Institute*, January 1, 2007.

90. Joanne Leow, "Strangers, Surrogates, Lovers: Foreign Domestic Workers in Contemporary Singapore Texts," in *Singapore Literature and Culture: Current Directions in Local and Global Contexts*, ed. Angelia Poon and Angus Whitehead (London: Routledge, 2017), 198–216, 200.

91. Alden Sajor Marte-Wood, "Philippine Reproductive Fiction and Crises of Social Reproduction," *Post45*, no. 1 (2019), https://post45.org/2019/01/philippine-reproductive -fiction-and-crises-of-social-reproduction/.

92. League of Cities of the Philippines Secretariat, "Iloilo City," online, accessed June, 23, 2021.

93. For example, Sherwin Mendoza notes the critical limits imposed by both the Singaporean state and the US Embassy in Singapore (a sponsor of the competition) and by the humanizing interpretive frame placed on the 2015 Migrant Worker Poetry Competition. Despite this, Mendoza observes that works by Monir Ahmod (Shromik Monir) and Rolinda O. Espanola offer important critical voices that call for international solidarity among migrant workers. See "Singapore's Migrant Worker Poetry, Worker Resistance, and International Solidarity," *Asia-Pacific Journal* 17.14 (2019), 1–18.

94. HDB, or Housing Development Board, buildings are government-subsidized apartment buildings that a majority of Singaporeans own and live in and are emblematic of Singapore's achievement of industrial modernity.

95. Many thanks to Alden Sajor Marte-Wood for his help with the Tagalog to English language translation.

96. Leow, "Strangers, Surrogates, Lovers," 198.

97. Troy Chin, *The Resident Tourist (Part 1)* (Singapore: Math Paper Press, 2007), n.p.

98. Chin, *The Resident Tourist (Part 1)*.

99. Rebecca Bustamante with Veronica Pulumbarit, *Maid to Made*, ed. Richard Mills (Manila: Chaire Consultancy Services, 2014), 27.

100. Bustamante, *Maid to Made*, 10.

101. Bustamante, *Maid to Made*, 10.

102. Spivak, *Other Asias*, 169.

103. "Overview of Asia CEO Forum," Asia CEO Forum, accessed June 24, 2021, https:// www.asia-ceo.org/Overview-of-Asia-CEO-Forum.

104. Bustamante, *Maid to Made*, foreword.

105. Moreover, the broad assumption is that domestic workers are governed by their employers. As Ong puts it in *Neoliberalism as Exception*, "The employer controls every aspect of the foreign maid's life" (202).

106. Singapore Ministry of Foreign Affairs, *Singapore National Report 2021*, 6.

107. "Who We Are," Aidha: Sustainable Futures through Financial Education, accessed June 23, 2021, https://www.aidha.org/about-us/who-we-are/.

108. "Course Overview," Aidha: Sustainable Futures through Financial Education, accessed June 23, 2021, https://www.aidha.org/courses/courses-overview/.

4. THE PRINCESS FANTASY OF SINGAPORE: SHORTER HISTORIES AND US DECLINE IN *CRAZY RICH ASIANS*

1. Rebecca Tan, "Flower Power: Singapore's Orchid Diplomacy," *BiblioAsia* 18.1 (April– June 2022), 8–15.

2. Annabeth Leow, "PM Lee Unveils Orchid Named after President Obama and His Wife at White House State Dinner," *Straits Times*, August 3, 2016.

3. Leow, "PM Lee Unveils Orchid."

4. Haunani-Kay Trask, *From a Native Daughter: Colonialism and Sovereignty in Hawai'i*, 2nd ed. (Honolulu: Latitude 20 Books, 1999), 136.

5. "Toast Speech by Prime Minister Lee Hsien Loong at the White House State Dinner," Prime Minister's Office Singapore, August 2, 2016, https://www.pmo.gov.sg/Newsroom /toast-speech-prime-minister-lee-hsien-loong-white-house-state-dinner.

6. Fareed Zakaria and Lee Kuan Yew, "Culture Is Destiny: A Conversation with Lee Kuan Yew," *Foreign Affairs* 73.2 (March–April 1994): 109–26, 112–13.

7. Pooja Nansi, "I'm tired of having to say this . . . ," Facebook, April 25, 2018, www .facebook.com/pnansi/posts/10155065574991442.

8. See Cristina Bacchilega, "An Introduction to the 'Innocent Persecuted Heroine' Fairy Tale," *Western Folklore* 52.1 (1993): 1–12.

9. Anne McClintock, *Imperial Leather: Race, Gender, and Sexuality in the Colonial Contest* (New York: Routledge, 1995), 6–7.

10. Edward Said, *Orientalism* (New York: Vintage Books, 1978), 6.

11. Steven Swann Jones, "The Innocent Persecuted Heroine Genre: An Analysis of its Structure and Themes," *Western Folklore* 52.1 (1993): 20–21.

12. JoAnn Conrad, "Docile Bodies of (Im)Material Girls: The Fairy Tale Construction of JonBenet Ramsey and Princess Diana," *Marvels & Tales* 13.2 (1999): 125–69, 133.

13. Conrad, "Docile Bodies of (Im)Material Girls," 133.

14. Kevin Kwan, *Crazy Rich Asians* (New York: Knopf, 2013), 36.

15. Kwan, *Crazy Rich Asians*, 110. Rachel's use of "Nanyang," or South Seas, invokes what Brian Bernards describes in *Writing the South Seas* (2018) as a "postcolonial literary trope of Chinese travel, migration, settlement, and creolization in Southeast Asia" (3). In this way, Rachel situates herself within (settler) colonial discourse. Brian C. Bernards, *Writing the South Seas: Imagining the Nanyang in Chinese and Southeast Asian Postcolonial Literature* (Seattle: University of Washington Press, 2018).

16. Kwan, *Crazy Rich Asians*, 110.

17. Drawing on the example of Christopher Columbus, who claimed the earth was shaped like a woman's breast, McClintock exposes "an uneasy sense of male anxiety, infantilization and longing for the female body" (*Imperial Leather*, 22).

18. McClintock, *Imperial Leather*, 22.

19. "ravish, v.," *OED Online*, Oxford University Press, June 2019.

20. McClintock, *Imperial Leather*, 22.

21. Kwan, *Crazy Rich Asians*, 114.

22. Kwan, *Crazy Rich Asians*, 116.

23. Kwan, *Crazy Rich Asians*, 87 (ellipsis in original).

24. Kwan, *Crazy Rich Asians*, 91.

25. Kwan, *Crazy Rich Asians*, 91–92.

26. Kwan, *Crazy Rich Asians*, 91.

27. Kwan, *Crazy Rich Asians*, 88.

28. Homi K. Bhabha, *The Location of Culture*, 2nd ed. (New York: Routledge, 2012), 128.

29. Kwan, *Crazy Rich Asians*, 91.

30. Kwan, *Crazy Rich Asians*, 214.

31. Kwan, *Crazy Rich Asians*, 92.

32. Elizabeth Currid-Halkett, *The Sum of Small Things: A Theory of the Aspirational Class* (Princeton, NJ: Princeton University Press, 2017), 20.

33. Jed Esty, *The Future of Decline: Anglo-American Culture at Its Limits* (Stanford: Stanford University Press, 2022), xi.

34. Economic decline in the west, Kimberly Kay Hoang points out, is also a loss of masculinity. See *Dealing in Desire: Asian Ascendancy, Western Decline, and the Hidden Currency of Global Sex Work* (Oakland: University of California Press, 2015), 6.

35. Kwan, *Crazy Rich Asians*, 137–38.

36. Some of the belittlement can be read as an indirect way of upholding British colonial culture—"If you did well enough, you entered the National University of Singapore (NUS) and if you did not, you were sent abroad to England (American colleges were deemed substandard)" (Kwan, *Crazy Rich Asians*, 72)—which suggests how postcoloniality can be read as navigating the power effects of both British and US empires.

37. Esty, *The Future of Decline*, ix.

38. Kwan, *Crazy Rich Asians*, 349.

39. Friedman further hypothesizes that "the discipline that the cold war imposed on America, by contrast [to Singapore], seems to have faded." See Thomas Friedman, "Singapore and Katrina," *New York Times*, Opinion, September 14, 2005, https://www.nytimes.com/2005/09/14/opinion/singapore-and-katrina.html.

40. See Peggy Orenstein, *Cinderella Ate My Daughter: Dispatches from the Front Lines of the New Girlie-Girl Culture* (New York: HarperCollins, 2011). Orenstein writes, "Recall that the current princess craze took off right around the terrorist attacks of September 11, 2001, and continued its rise through the recession: maybe, as another cultural historian suggested to me, the desire to encourage our girls' imperial fantasies is, at least in part, a reaction to a new unstable world. We *need* their innocence not only for consumerist but for *spiritual* redemption" (25; original emphasis).

41. Tina Jordan, "The 'It Books' of Summers Past," *New York Times*, June 5, 2019, https://www.nytimes.com/2019/06/05/books/beach-reads-summer.html.

42. Kwan, *Crazy Rich Asians*, 132–33.

43. Famously, Eduardo Saverin, cofounder of Facebook, renounced his US citizenship and moved to Singapore.

44. Kimberly Kay Hoang, "Risky Investments: How Local and Foreign Investors Finesse Corruption-Rife Emerging Markets," *American Sociological Review* 83.4 (2018): 657–85, 657. See the expansion of this work in Hoang's *Spiderweb Capitalism: How Global Elites Exploit Frontier Markets* (Princeton, NJ: Princeton University Press, 2022).

45. Hoang, "Risky Investments," 672.

46. When leveraging its colonial history for postcolonial capitalism, Singaporean state logic implicitly suggests that there is a relationship between the experience of British imperialism and the perception of Singapore as less risky, at least when compared to other Asian nations.

47. Toby Young, "Is Singapore the Template for New York? Uh-oh!," *Los Angeles Times*, March 15, 1998, https://www.latimes.com/archives/la-xpm-1998-mar-15-op-29087-story.html.

48. William Gibson, "Disneyland with the Death Penalty," *Wired*, April 1, 1993.

49. Jon Clifton, "Singapore Ranks as Least Emotional Country in the World," Gallup, November 21, 2012; Daniel Teo, "Singapore the 'Least Positive' Country in the World: Survey," *Yahoo! News*, December 20, 2012. While these surveys were conducted much later than 1997, I take them as a lagging indicator and one that continues to index the long shadow that the previous eras of postcolonial capitalism continue to cast into the moment of Global Asia. Interestingly, right around the time of this book's publication, Singapore ranked as the happiest Asian country in the world. See Izzah Imran, "#trending: Singapore Ranked

Happiest Country in Asia in UN's 2023 Happiness Report, but Some Raise Doubts Over Results," *Today*, March 27, 2023, https://www.todayonline.com/singapore/singapore-25th -happiest-country-2023-2135066.

50. "What SIA, Finance Sector Must Do to Stay Ahead—A Need to Become Globally Competitive," *Straits Times*, August 16, 1997, 39.

51. "What SIA, Finance Sector Must Do to Stay Ahead," 39.

52. Fanon, *The Wretched of the Earth*, 101.

53. See Singapore Tourist Promotion Board, *Tourism 21: Vision of a Tourism Capital*, Pagesetters Services, 1996.

54. See "Speech by S Dhanabalan, Minister for National Development, at the Opening of the Park Network System, Kallang River Phase I on Friday 14 Aug 91 at 5.00pm at Kallang River Park Connector (Bishan Road)," Singapore National Archives.

55. The emergence of Singapore as a city of pleasure is, of course, class based, so it seems unsurprising that coterminous with its now more fun global image Singapore has come to be seen as a haven of millionaires. From the 1990s on, seemingly to reassure the populace of the nation's economic success, Singaporean newspapers regularly reported the local growth of the millionaire population and its growth within Asia more generally. Singapore's global reputation as a place for the rich seems to have emerged around 2007, when the *New York Times* reported the appeal of Singapore's private banking system for the wealthy, reflecting the changes in tax and immigration laws that allowed foreigners to avoid taxes on their income and to apply for residency if they held more than S$5 million. Singapore has since been consistently listed as having the highest number of wealthy individuals in the world.

56. There are too many Asian television sitcoms to name, but a relevant one here is *Masters of the Sea* (1994), a Singaporean TV series that also featured the rich elite and their dramas.

57. Kok Xing Hui and Annabeth Leow, "Singapore's New International Brand by STB and EDB: Passion Made Possible," *Straits Times*, August 14, 2017, https://www.straitstimes.com /singapore/singapores-new-international-brand-by-stb-and-edb-passion-made-possible.

58. Postcolonial studies with regard to questions of the subaltern (e.g., Gayatri Chakravorty Spivak, Ranajit Guha), resistance literature (e.g., Barbara Harlow), and the English canon (e.g., Edward Said) have been especially instructive in offering methodologies that challenge the effects of master narratives on knowledge production by accounting for the postcolonial subject's agency.

59. Lauren Christensen, "*Crazy Rich Asians* Author Kevin Kwan on the Lavish Culture of Asia's Upper Crust: 'The Reality Is Simply Unbelievable,'" *Vanity Fair*, June 14, 2019, https://www.vanityfair.com/culture/2013/06/crazy-rich-asians-kevin-kwan-asia-upper -crust?verso=true.

60. Elaine Lies, "Book Talk: 'Crazy Rich Asians' Tackles Stereotypes via Satire," Reuters, June 14, 2019, https://www.reuters.com/article/us-books-authors-kwan-book-talk-crazy -rich-asians-tackles-stereotypes-via-satire-idUSBRE98401H20130905.

61. Lies, "Book Talk."

62. Even as Kwan demonstrates this investment in the contemporary, he has been criticized locally for his belated understandings of Singapore, particularly since he has not returned to Singapore in years because he is avoiding military conscription.

63. Wee, *The Asian Modern*, 2; "contemporary, adj. and n.," *OED Online*, June 2019.

64. Pratt, *Imperial Eyes*, 7.

65. C. M. Turnbull, *A History of Singapore 1819–1988* (Oxford: Oxford University Press, 1989), 5.

66. My use of "soft" at once draws from Joseph Nye's "soft power" and Nigel Thrift's "soft capitalism" to describe the mode in which Singapore brings in capital. For Nye, soft power describes "the ability to get what you want through attraction rather than coercion or payments. It arises from the attractiveness of a country's culture, political ideals, and policies" (x). When thinking in the mode of immateriality, also useful is Dora Zhang's discussion of atmosphere, which she argues "alter[s] the kinds of things that can be said in a space, the kinds of actions that are thinkable, and the modes of sociality that are possible" (121). Of course, there is always the specter of repressive power, as evidenced in the ways that the Singaporean state will wield its authority to keep its own political body in check. Developing a nation's "attractiveness" aligns with what Thrift describes as the culturalist emphasis on personal development in managerial discourse (41). See Joseph S. Nye Jr., *Soft Power: The Means to Success in World Politics* (New York: Public Affairs, 2004); Nigel Thrift, *Knowing Capitalism* (Thousand Oaks, CA: Sage, 2005); Dora Zhang, "Notes on Atmosphere," *Qui Parle* 27.1 (June 2018): 121–55.

67. Fred Pawle, "Kevin Kwan Satirizes the Lives of Asia's Crazy Rich," *Weekend Australian*, Life, September 12, 2013, https://www.theaustralian.com.au/life/kevin-kwan-satirises-the-lives-of-asias-crazy-rich/news-story/0ca546d5b987b775333187dfac837ebd?sv=8c7a574341d09da2702981b144e057f0.

68. Kwan, *Crazy Rich Asians*, 79.

69. Julia Vitale, "*Crazy Rich Asians* Author Kevin Kwan on Finishing His Trilogy and the Movie Adaptation to Come," *Vanity Fair*, May 18, 2017, https://www.vanityfair.com/style/2017/05/rich-people-problems-crazy-rich-asians-movie-kevin-kwan.

70. Rey Chow, *Woman and Chinese Modernity: The Politics of Reading Between West and East* (Minneapolis: University of Minnesota Press, 2003), xiii.

71. Anne Anlin Cheng, "Anxious Pedigree: From Fresh-Off-the-Boat to 'Crazy Rich Asians,'" *LA Review of Books*, April 24, 2018, https://lareviewofbooks.org/article/anxious-pedigree-from-fresh-off-the-boat-to-crazy-rich-asians/.

72. Grace Kyungwon Hong, "Speculative Surplus: Asian American Racialization and the Neoliberal Shift," *Social Text* 36. 2 (2018): 107–22, 109.

73. Hong, "Speculative Surplus," 112.

74. Hong, "Speculative Surplus," 117–18.

75. Hong, "Speculative Surplus," 114.

76. Kwan, *Crazy Rich Asians*, 7.

77. Kwan, *Crazy Rich Asians*, 5.

78. Kwan, *Crazy Rich Asians*, 6.

79. Bhabha, *The Location of Culture*, 123.

80. Hong, "Speculative Surplus," 118.

81. Kwan, *Crazy Rich Asians*, 3.

82. Spivak, *A Critique of Postcolonial Reason*, 1.

83. Andrew Liu, "How Asia Got Crazy Rich: Toward a materialist history of *Crazy Rich Asians*," *n+1 Magazine*, film review, June 14, 2019, https://nplusonemag.com/online-only/online-only/how-asia-got-crazy-rich/. This difference between reading the prologue as an

allegory for postcolonial revenge and an allegory for the emergence of diasporic Singaporeans stages debates about Marxist versus Foucauldian approaches to power. What is interesting to me about these contrasting perspectives is how they also map onto the politics of postcolonial criticism. My sense is that at stake for critics like Aihwa Ong, Pheng Cheah, and Beng Huat Chua is an understanding that subjectivity under global capitalism should not simply be regarded as ideologically deluded.

84. Hong, "Speculative Surplus," 118.

85. Foucault writes, "We must cease once and for all to describe the effects of power in negative terms: it 'excludes,' it 'represses,' it 'censors,' it 'abstracts,' it 'masks,' it 'conceals.' In fact, power produces; it produces reality; it produces domains of objects and ritual of truth" (*Discipline and Punish*, 2nd ed., trans. Alan Sheridan [New York: Vintage, 1995], 194).

86. Kwan, *Crazy Rich Asians*, 132–133.

87. Goh Poh Seng's *If We Dream Too Long* also focalizes state discourse through characters, in this case Boon Teik.

88. See Goh Chok Tong's 2001 National Day Rally Speech.

89. Kwan, *Crazy Rich Asians*, 298.

90. Kwan, *Crazy Rich Asians*, 298.

91. As evidenced in speeches during Malaya's independence, for Lee, the notion of a meritocracy was held up as a decolonial, multicultural philosophy, against the racialism of the British: "Let us all resolve to work hard together to build a happy and prosperous Malaya, to remove ignorance and poverty by education and production and to establish a more just social order where every man is judged on his merits and his contribution to society." See "Message to Federation of Malaya on Attainment of Merdeka." For Goh, meritocracy emphasized proper, monetary reward, as evidenced by a 1993 parliamentary speech: "The Government's primary duty is to build the right conditions for Singaporeans to create wealth for themselves. These conditions include security, law and order, political stability, social discipline, a level playing field, the free market, meritocracy and reward in accordance with a person's ability, performance and contribution. Within this framework, how wealthy a person becomes depends on himself. If he has the ability and puts in the effort he will do well. If he has exceptional ability, entrepreneurial spirit and good business sense, he can become extremely wealthy. In short, the more successful Singaporeans will end up better off than the less successful Singaporeans."

92. Kwan, *Crazy Rich Asians*, 302; original emphasis.

93. At a 1997 education conference, Goh Chok Tong noted the need to produce "highly creative, entrepreneurial individuals" like Americans and launched an initiative called "Thinking Schools, Learning Nations" in an attempt to cultivate them. See *Shaping Our Future: Thinking Schools, Learning Nation*. Also see Petrus Liu and Colleen Lye, "Liberal Arts for Asians: A Commentary on Yale-NUS," for a discussion of one Singaporean higher education institution that was formed in the vision that Goh advocated.

94. Kwan, *Crazy Rich Asians*, 302.

95. Hong, "Speculative Surplus," 117; original emphasis.

96. Kwan, *Crazy Rich Asians*, 19.

97. Kwan, *Crazy Rich Asians*, 379; Janet Maslin, "'Crazy Rich Asians,' Guilty Pleasure, or Cult of Opulence," *New York Times*, Books, June 30, 2013, https://www.nytimes.com/2013/07/01/books/kevin-kwans-crazy-rich-asians-depicts-a-cult-of-opulence.html.

98. Tash Aw, "'Crazy Rich Asians': Lives of the .0001 Percent," NPR, Book Reviews, June 20, 2013, https://www.npr.org/2013/06/20/191389836/crazy-rich-asians-lives-of-the-0001-percent.

99. Kwan, *Crazy Rich Asians*, 173–74.

100. Chow, *Woman and Chinese Modernity*, 85.

101. Kwan, *Crazy Rich Asians*, 341.

102. Kwan, *Crazy Rich Asians*, 341–342.

103. Kwan, *Crazy Rich Asians*, 342.

104. Kwan, *Crazy Rich Asians*, 341.

105. Kwan's writing follows an aesthetic tendency to present racialization in non-characterological ways, as Sunny Xiang observes in post–Cold War Asian American writing. Xiang turns her readers to tone as a method for reading the instability of race and "to read imperial archives for something other than the empirical fact of race or the melancholic absence of race" (17). See Xiang, *Tonal Intelligence*.

106. "Minimalist" here might seem contrary to what I was describing about the overperformed and melodramatic, but by "minimalist," I mean underdeveloped.

107. Anne Anlin Cheng, "Ornamentalism: A Feminist Theory for the Yellow Woman," *Critical Inquiry* 44.3 (Spring 2018): 415–46, 425.

108. Achille Mbembe, "Aesthetics of Superfluity," in *Johannesburg: The Elusive Metropolis* (Johannesburg: Wits University Press, 2008), 37–67, 38.

109. "The Bachelor 'Goes to Singapore,'" *The Bachelor*, ABC, Season 23, Episode 4, 2019.

110. Kwan, *Crazy Rich Asians*, 79–80.

111. Kwan, *Crazy Rich Asians*, 80.

112. Kwan, *Crazy Rich Asians*, 134, 136.

113. Marina Fang, "10 'Crazy Rich Asians' Culturally Nuanced Moments That Speak Directly to Asian Viewers," HuffPost, Asian Voices, August 21, 2018, https://www.huffpost.com/entry/crazy-rich-asians-cultural-references_n_5b7b29ede4b0a5b1febe0336.

114. Lenika Cruz, Emily Jan, Ashley Fetters, and Rosa Inocencio Smith, "Which *Crazy Rich Asians* Scenes Were Most Memorable?," *The Atlantic*, Culture, August 21, 2018, https://www.theatlantic.com/entertainment/archive/2018/08/crazy-rich-asians-roundtable/567844/.

115. Sarah Whitten, "'Crazy Rich Asians' Director Jon M Chu on Asian Representations in Hollywood: 'I think the doors are opening now,' cnbc.com, March 31, 2021.

116. Amy Chin, "Worries Grow in Singapore over China's Calls to Help 'Motherland,'" *New York Times*, August 5, 2018, https://www.nytimes.com/2018/08/05/world/asia/singapore-china.html, accessed November 12, 2022.

CONCLUSION

1. Stuart Hall, "Cultural Studies and Its Theoretical Legacies," in *Essential Essays*, vol. 1: *Foundations of Cultural Studies* (Durham, NC: Duke University Press, 2019), 71–100, 84.

2. Petrus Liu and Colleen Lye, "Liberal Arts of Asians: A Commentary on Yale-NUS," *Interventions: International Journal of Postcolonial Studies* 18.4 (2016): 573–87, 573–74.

3. Pericles Lewis, "In Asia, for the World: The Creation of Yale-NUS College," *Pericles Lewis: Yale University*, https://campuspress.yale.edu/pericleslewis/in-asia-for-the-world-the-creation-of-yale-nus-college/, accessed December 14, 2022.

4. "PM Lee Hsien Loong at the Inauguration of the Yale-NUS College Campus," Prime Minister's Office Singapore, October 12, 2015, https://www.pmo.gov.sg/Newsroom/speech -prime-minister-lee-hsien-loong-inauguration-yale-nus-college-campus.

5. "PM Lee Hsien Loong at the Inauguration."

6. See "A Planned Catastrophe: Yale-NUS to Close in 2025," *The Octant*, August 28, 2021; Yojana Sharma, "Students, faculty angry over closure of Yale-NUS College," *University World News*, September 1, 2021.

7. See David Bloom, "The Yale-NUS Closure's Unanswered Questions," *Yale Globalist*, December 14, 2021; and Sandra Davie, Ang Qing, and Ng Wei Kai, "What's Behind the Decision to Close Yale-NUS College," *Straits Times*, September 5, 2021.

8. Yojana Sharma, "Parliament Scrutiny Provides Few Clues to Yale-NUS Shutdown," *University World News*, September 15, 2021.

9. Shawn Hoo, "The Neoliberal Arts," *The Octant*, April 29, 2021, https://theoctant.org /edition/issue/allposts/opinion/the-neoliberal-arts/.

10. See Jothie Rajah's *Authoritarian Rule of Law: Legislation, Discourse and Legitimacy in Singapore* (Cambridge: Cambridge University Press, 2012). Insofar as she examines what I have described throughout this project as harder forms of power (i.e., the power of the repressive state apparatus), if one assumes power as singular or totalizing, Rajah's project might appear diametrically opposed to mine. Notably, however, we have methodological similarities. Throughout this project, I have looked to Singapore to think through the contraction of "postcolonial capitalism" and in a similar logic, Rajah examines how the seemingly incompatible terms of "authoritarism" and "rule of law" operate in Singapore. Her important study demonstrates how these terms are not mutually exclusive. It is from this methodological parallel that we can build a systemic sense of power.

11. Watson, *The New Asian City*, 254.

12. See Nasia Anam, "Introduction: Forms of the Global Anglophone," *Post45*, February 22, 2019, https://post45.org/2019/02/introduction-forms-of-the-global-anglophone/.

13. Jini Kim Watson and Gary Wilder, "Thinking the Postcolonial Contemporary," in *The Postcolonial Contemporary: Political Imaginaries for the Global Present*, ed. Jini Kim Watson and Gary Wilder (New York: Fordham University Press, 2018), 1–30, 1.

BIBLIOGRAPHY

"About OS Portal." Overseas Singaporean Unit, webpage, accessed December 2, 2013.

Adichie, Chimamanda Ngozi. *Americanah.* New York: Anchor, 2014.

Adiga, Aravind. *The White Tiger.* London: Atlantic Books, 2008.

Ahmed, Sara. *The Promise of Happiness.* Durham, NC: Duke University Press, 2010.

"Aidha: Sustainable Futures through Financial Education." Accessed June 23, 2021. https://www.aidha.org/.

Alagan, Eric. *Beck and Call.* Singapore: Monsoon Books, 2012.

Alfian Sa'at, Faris Joraimi, and Sai Siew Min, eds. *Raffles Renounced: Towards a Merdeka History.* Singapore: Ethos Books, 2021.

Alfian Sa'at. "Some thoughts . . ." Facebook, January 19, 2017. Accessed March 23, 2022. https://www.facebook.com/alfiansaat/posts/10154164954387371.

Amin, Samir. *Theory Is History.* Dordrecht: Springer, 2013.

Amrith, Sunil. "Eugenics in Postcolonial Southeast Asia." In *The Oxford Handbook of the History of Eugenics,* edited by Alison Bashford and Philippa Levine, 3. Oxford: Oxford University Press, 2010.

Anderson, Benedict. *Imagined Communities: Reflections on the Origin and Spread of Nationalism.* 2nd ed. London: Verso, 2006.

———. *The Spectre of Comparisons: Nationalism, Southeast Asia, and the World.* London: Verso, 1998.

Ang, Ien. "Stuart Hall and the Tension between Academic and Intellectual Work." *International Journal of Cultural Studies* 19.1 (2016): 1–13.

"ASEAN Literary Anthology Project Proposal." In *Report of the Conference of ASEAN Writers, Manila, 24–26 June 1981,* 2. Jakarta: KITLV, 1987.

Aw, Tash. "'Crazy Rich Asians': Lives of the .0001 Percent." NPR, Book Reviews, June 20, 2013. https://www.npr.org/2013/06/20/191389836/crazy-rich-asians-lives-of-the-0001-percent.

———. *Five Star Billionaire.* New York: Random House, 2014.

Bacchilega, Cristina. "An Introduction to the 'Innocent Persecuted Heroine' Fairy Tale." *Western Folklore* 52.1 (1993): 1–12.

"The Bachelor 'Goes to Singapore.'" *The Bachelor*, ABC, Season 23, Episode 4, 2019.

"Back Efforts of Local Writers Call." *New Nation*, June 8, 1976, 4.

Balasupramaniam, Krishna, ed. *Creative Expressions: Chinese High School Anthology of Stories.* Singapore: Shing Lee Publishers, 1989.

Balibar, Étienne. "The Nation Form: History and Ideology." In *Race, Nation, Class: Ambiguous Identities*, translated by Chris Turner, 86–106. London: Verso, 1991.

Benedict, Barbara. *Making the Modern Reader: Cultural Mediation in Restoration and Eighteenth-Century Literary Anthologies.* Princeton, NJ: Princeton University Press, 1996.

Benjamin, Bret. *Invested Interests: Capital, Culture, and the World Bank.* Minneapolis: University of Minnesota Press, 2007.

Bernards, Brian C. *Writing the South Seas: Imagining the Nanyang in Chinese and Southeast Asian Postcolonial Literature.* Seattle: University of Washington Press, 2018.

Bhabha, Homi K. "Introduction: Narrating the Nation." In *Nation and Narration*, edited by Homi K. Bhabha, 1–7. New York: Routledge, 1990.

———. *The Location of Culture.* 2nd ed. New York: Routledge, 2012.

Bhathal, R. S., Dudley de Souza, and Kirpal Singh, eds. *Singapore Science Fiction.* Singapore: Rotary Club of Jurong Town, 1980.

Bhattacharyya, Gargi. *Rethinking Racial Capitalism: Questions of Reproduction and Survival.* Lanham, MD: Rowman & Littlefield, 2018.

"Book Bang." *Straits Times*, October 16, 1989, 1.

Bose, Purnima, and Laura E. Lyons, eds. *Cultural Critique and the Global Corporation.* Bloomington: Indiana University Press, 2010.

Braziel, Jana Evans, and Anita Mannur, "Nation, Migration, Globalization: Points of Contention in Diaspora Studies. In *Theorizing Diaspora: A Reader*, 1–22. London: Blackwell, 2003.

Brennan, Timothy. *At Home in the World: Cosmopolitanism Now.* Cambridge, MA: Harvard University Press, 1997.

———. "The National Longing for Form." In *Nation and Narration*, edited by Homi K. Bhabha, 44–90. New York: Routledge, 1990

Brouillette, Sarah. *Postcolonial Writers in the Global Literary Market.* London: Palgrave Macmillan, 2007.

———. *UNESCO and the Fate of the Literary.* Stanford, CA: Stanford University Press, 2019.

Bustamante, Rebecca, with Veronica Pulumbarit. *Maid to Made.* Edited by Richard Mills. Manila: Chaire Consultancy Services, 2014.

"Campaign to Make 250,000 Aliens Voters from Nov. 1." *Straits Times*, October 16, 1957, 4.

Caryl, Christian. "Africa's Singapore Dream." *Foreign Policy*, April 2, 2015. https://foreign policy.com/2015/04/02/africas-singapore-dream-rwanda-kagame-lee-kuan-yew/.

Césaire, Aimé. *Discourse on Colonialism.* 1950. Translated by Joan Pinkham. New York: Monthly Review Press, 2001.

Chakrabarty, Dipesh. "The Legacies of Bandung: Decolonization and the Politics of Culture." In *Making a World after Empire: The Bandung Moment and Its Political Afterlives*, edited by Christopher J. Lee, 45–68. Athens: Ohio University Press, 2010.

———. *Provincializing Europe: Postcolonial Thought and Historical Difference.* Princeton, NJ: Princeton University Press, 2008.

Chandler, David, Norman G. Owen, William R. Roff, David Joel Steinberg, Jean Gelman Taylor, Robert H. Taylor, Alexander Woodside, and David K. Wyatt. *The Emergence of Modern Southeast Asia: A New History.* Edited by Norman G. Owen. Honolulu: University of Hawaii Press, 2004.

"Chandran Nair: Biography." *poetry.sg*, accessed April 20, 2022. http://www.poetry.sg/chandran-nair-bio.

Chang Yau Hoon, "Revisiting the Asian Values Argument used by Asian Political Leaders and Its Validity." *Indonesian Quarterly* 32.2 (2004): 154–74.

Charusheela, S. "Where Is the 'Economy'? Cultural Studies and Narrative of Capitalism." In *The Renewal of Cultural Studies*, edited by Paul Smith, 177–87. Philadelphia: Temple University Press, 2011.

Chatterjee, Partha. *The Politics of the Governed.* New York: Columbia University Press, 2004.

Cheah, Pheng. *Inhuman Conditions: On Cosmopolitanism and Human Rights.* Cambridge, MA: Harvard University Press, 2007.

Chen, Anthony, dir. *Ilo Ilo.* Golden Village, 2013.

Chen, Kuan-Hsing, and Chua Beng Huat. "The *Inter-Asia Cultural Studies: Movements* Project." In *The Inter-Asia Cultural Studies Reader*, edited by Kuan-Hsing Chen and Chua Beng Huat, 1–6. New York: Routledge, 2007.

Chen, Tina. "Agency/Asiancy." In *The Routledge Companion to Asian American and Pacific Islander Literature*, edited by Rachel Lee, 56–67. London: Taylor and Francis, 2014.

———. "Global Asias: Method, Architecture, Praxis." *Journal of Asian Studies* 80.4 (November 2021): 997–1009.

Chen, Tina, and Eric Hayot. "Introducing *Verge*: What Does It Mean to Study Global Asias?" *Verge: Studies in Global Asia* 1.1 (Spring 2015): vi–xv.

Cheng, Anne Anlin. "Anxious Pedigree: From Fresh-Off-the-Boat to 'Crazy Rich Asians.'" *LA Review of Books*, April 24, 2018. https://lareviewofbooks.org/article/anxious-pedigree-from-fresh-off-the-boat-to-crazy-rich-asians/.

———. "Ornamentalism: A Feminist Theory for the Yellow Woman." *Critical Inquiry* 44.3 (Spring 2018): 415–46.

Chin, Troy. *The Resident Tourist (Part 1).* Singapore: Math Paper Press, 2007.

Chin, Yolanda. "Community Confidence and Security." In *Management of Success: Singapore Revisited*, edited by Terence Chong, 443–61. Singapore: ISEAS Publishing, 2010.

Cho, Lily, and Susan J. Henders. "Human Rights and the Arts in Global Asia: Conceptualizing Contexts." In *Human Rights and the Arts: Perspectives on Global Asia*, edited by Susan J. Henders and Lily Cho, 1–20. Lanham, MD: Lexington Books, 2014.

Chong, Gladys Pak Lei, Yiu Fai Chow, and Jeroen De Kloet. "Towards Trans-Asia: Projects, Possibilities, Paradoxes." In *Trans-Asia as Method: Theory and Practices*, edited by Jeroen De Kloet, Yiu Fai Chow, and Gladys Pak Lei Chong, 1–24. Lanham, MD: Rowman & Littlefield, 2020.

Chow, Rey. *Not Like a Native Speaker: On Languaging as a Postcolonial Experience.* New York: Columbia University Press, 2014.

———. *The Protestant Ethnic and the Spirit of Capitalism.* New York: Columbia University Press, 2002.

———. *Woman and Chinese Modernity: The Politics of Reading between West and East.* Minneapolis: University of Minnesota Press, 1991.

———. *Writing Diaspora: Tactics of Intervention in Contemporary Cultural Studies*. Bloomington: Indiana University Press, 1993.

Christensen, Lauren. "*Crazy Rich Asians* Author Kevin Kwan on the Lavish Culture of Asia's Upper Crust: 'The Reality Is Simply Unbelievable.'" *Vanity Fair*, June 14, 2019. https://www.vanityfair.com/culture/2013/06/crazy-rich-asians-kevin-kwan-asia-upper-crust?verso=true.

Chu, John M., dir. *Crazy Rich Asians*. Warner Brothers Pictures, 2018.

Chu, Patricia M. *Assimilating Asians: Gendered Strategies of Authorship in Asian America*. Durham, NC: Duke University Press, 2000.

Chua Beng Huat. *Communitarian Ideology and Democracy in Singapore*. London: Routledge, 1995.

———. "Communitarian Politics in Asia." In *Communitarian Politics in Asia*, edited by Chua Beng Huat, 1–24. London: Routledge Curzon, 2004.

———. *Liberalism Disavowed: Communitarianism and State Capitalism in Singapore*. Ithaca, NY: Cornell University Press, 2017.

———. "Multiculturalism in Singapore: An Instrument of Social Control." *Race & Class* 44.3 (2003): 58–77.

Chua, Daniel Wei Boon. *US-Singapore Relations, 1965–1975: Strategic Non-Alignment in the Cold War*. Singapore: National University of Singapore Press, 2017.

Chuh, Kandice. *Imagine Otherwise: On Asian Americanist Critique*. Durham, NC: Duke University Press, 2003.

Clark, Justin Tyler. "From Global City to 'City of Villages': Tracing the State Discourse of Cosmopolitanism in Modern Singaporean History." *Journal of Intercultural Studies* 40.4 (2019): 399–416.

Clifton, Jon. "Singapore Ranks as Least Emotional Country in the World." Gallup, November 21, 2012. https://news.gallup.com/poll/158882/singapore-ranks-least-emotional-country-world.aspx.

Cohen, Ralph. "Genre Theory, Literary History, and Historical Change." In *Genre Theory and Historical Change: Theoretical Essays of Ralph Cohen*, edited by John L. Rowlett, 145–69. Charlottesville: University of Virginia Press, 2017.

Cohen, Robin. *Global Diasporas: An Introduction*. 2nd ed. London: Routledge, 2008.

"Coming up with Solutions for Problems of Job Satisfaction." *Straits Times*, August 3, 1979, 16.

Connecting in the Heart of Asia. Singapore: Contact Singapore, 2012.

Conrad, JoAnn. "Docile Bodies of (Im)Material Girls: The Fairy Tale Construction of JonBenet Ramsey and Princess Diana." *Marvels & Tales* 13.2 (1999): 125–69.

Construction 21. Singapore: Ministry of Manpower and Ministry of National Development, 1999.

Contreras-Cabrera, Manuelita, Migs Bravo-Dutt, and Eric Tinsay Valles. *Get Lucky: An Anthology of Philippine and Singapore Writings*. Singapore: Ethos Books, 2015.

Conversations on Coming Home: 20 Singaporeans Share Their Stories. Singapore: Contact Singapore, 2012.

Crosthwaite, Paul, Peter Knight, and Nicky Marsh. "Introduction: The Interwovenness of Literature and Economics." In *The Cambridge Companion to Literature and Economics*, 1–16. Cambridge: Cambridge University Press, 2022.

Cruz, Lenika, Emily Jan, Ashley Fetters, and Rosa Inocencio Smith. "Which *Crazy Rich Asians* Scenes Were Most Memorable?" *The Atlantic*, Culture, August 21, 2018. https://

www.theatlantic.com/entertainment/archive/2018/08/crazy-rich-asians-roundtable
/567844/.

Cruz–del Rosario, Tersita, and Victor Kattan. "Opinion: Jared Kushner's Plan for Palestine Is Even Crazier Than You Thought." *Haaretz*, July 4, 2019. https://www.haaretz.com
/middle-east-news/.premium-jared-kushner-s-plan-for-palestine-is-even-crazier-than
-you-thought-1.7435303.

Currid-Halkett, Elizabeth. *The Sum of Small Things: A Theory of the Aspirational Class*.
Princeton, NJ: Princeton University Press, 2017.

Damrosch, David, and Gayatri Chakravorty Spivak. "Comparative Literature/World Literature: A Discussion with Gayatri Chakravorty Spivak." *Comparative Literature Studies*
48.4 (2011): 455–85.

Dangarembga, Tsitsi. *Nervous Conditions*. London: Ayebia Clarke Publishing, 1988.

Derrida, Jacques. "Structure, Sign, and Play in the Discourse of the Human Sciences." In
Writing and Difference, translated by Alan Bass, 278–94. Chicago: University of Chicago
Press, 1978.

Di Leo, Jeffrey R. "Analyzing Anthologies." In *On Anthologies: Politics and Pedagogy*, edited
by Jeffrey R. Di Leo, 1–27. Lincoln: University of Nebraska Press, 2004.

Dirlik, Arif. "The Postcolonial Aura: Third World Criticism in the Age of Global Capitalism." *Critical Inquiry* 20.2 (1994): 328–56.

———. *The Postcolonial Aura: Third World Criticism in the Age of Global Capitalism*.
London: Routledge, 1997.

Doing Business 2019: Training for Reform. Washington, DC: World Bank, 2019.

Dreams Taking Shape. Singapore: Contact Singapore, n.d.

Du Bois, W. E. B. *The Souls of Black Folk*. Edited by David W. Blight and Robert Gooding-
Williams. New York: Bedford Books, 1997.

Duncan, Neil. "Ten-Year Cultural Development Plan." UNESCO, Serial No. FMR/CC/
CD/80/158, 1980.

During, Simon. "Empire's Present." *New Literary History* 43.2 (2012): 331–40.

Economic Strategies Committee Subcommittee. "Attracting and Rooting MNCs, Asian
Enterprises and Global Mid-sized Companies." National Archives Singapore, February
3, 2010.

Edwards, Brent Hayes. *The Practice of Diaspora: Literature, Translation, and the Rise of Black
Internationalism*. Cambridge, MA: Harvard University Press, 2003.

Ee Tiang Hong. *Tranquerah*. Singapore: National University of Singapore Press, 1985.

Eggers, Dave. *The Circle*. New York: Knopf, 2013.

Esty, Jed. *The Future of Decline: Anglo-American Culture at Its Limits*. Stanford: Stanford
University Press, 2022.

———. *Unseasonable Youth: Modernism, Colonialism, and the Fiction of Development*.
Oxford: Oxford University Press, 2011.

Fang, Joy. "The Rise of the Anthology." *Today Online*, November 23, 2016, https://www
.todayonline.com/entertainment/arts/rise-anthology.

Fang, Marina. "10 'Crazy Rich Asians' Culturally Nuanced Moments That Speak Directly
to Asian Viewers." *HuffPost*, Asian Voices, August 21, 2018. https://www.huffpost.com
/entry/crazy-rich-asians-cultural-references_n_5b7b29ede4b0a5b1febe0336.

Fanon, Frantz. *Black Skin, White Masks*. Translated by Richard Philcox. New York: Grove
Press, 2008.

———. *The Wretched of the Earth*. New York: Grove Press, 2004.

Fernandez, Warren. "Give Them Second Chance, but Not Special Treatment." *Straits Times*, March 7, 1991, 19.

50 Points of View: A Unique Celebration of Singapore by Students from Pathlight School. Singapore: Pathlight School, 2015.

"50 Red Dots Around the World." *be movement*, vol. 6 (2015).

Florida, Richard. *The Rise of the Creative Class: And How It's Transforming Work, Leisure, and Everyday Life.* 2nd ed. New York: Basic Books, 2012.

Foo, Paul. "250,000 New Citizens." *Straits Times*, November 3, 1957, 10.

Foucault, Michel. *The Birth of Biopolitics: Lectures at the Collège de France 1978–1979.* Translated by Graham Burchell. London: Palgrave Macmillan, 2008.

———. *Discipline and Punish.* 2nd ed. Translated by Alan Sheridan. New York: Vintage, 1995.

———. "Nietzsche, Genealogy, History." In *The Foucault Reader*, edited by Paul Rabinow, 76–100. New York: Pantheon Books, 1984.

———. *Security, Territory, Population: Lectures at the Collège de France (1977–1978).* Translated by Graham Burchell. London: Picador, 2004.

———. *"Society Must Be Defended": Lectures at the Collège de France, 1975–1976.* Translated by David Macey. London: Picador, 2003.

Franklin, Cynthia. *Writing Women's Communities: the Politics and Poetics of Contemporary Multi-Genre Anthologies.* Madison: University of Wisconsin Press, 1997.

Fratus, Tiziano and Alvin Pang. *Double Skin: New Poetic Voices From Italy and Singapore.* Singapore: Ethos Books, 2009.

Friedman, Thomas. "Serious in Singapore." *New York Times*, January 29, 2011. https://www.nytimes.com/2011/01/30/opinion/30friedman.html.

———. Singapore and Katrina." *New York Times*, Opinion, September 14, 2005. https://www.nytimes.com/2005/09/14/opinion/singapore-and-katrina.html.

Friedrich, Su. "Edited By." Accessed March 16, 2022. http://womenfilmeditors.princeton.edu/.

"Futility of Aid While U.S. Drains Afro-Asia of Their Brains." *Straits Times*, February 28, 1967, 3.

George, Cherian. "Sintercom: Harnessing of Virtual Community." In *Contentious Journalism and the Internet: Towards Democratic Discourse in Malaysia and Singapore*, 99–119. Singapore: Singapore University Press, 2006.

"'Get Tough on Rich Parents': Unions' Call to Govt." *Straits Times*, October 13, 1970, 7.

Getachew, Adom. *Worldmaking after Empire: The Rise and Fall of Self-Determination.* Princeton, NJ: Princeton University Press, 2019.

Ghosh, Amitav. *The Glass Palace.* New York: Random House, 2001.

Gibson, William. "Disneyland with the Death Penalty." *Wired* 1.04, April 1, 1993. https://www.wired.com/1993/04/gibson-2/.

Goh Chok Tong. "Global City, Best Home." National Day Rally Speech, Singapore, 1997.

———. "Remaking Singapore—Changing Mindsets." National Day Rally Address by Prime Minister Goh Chok Tong at the University Cultural Centre, NUS, Sunday, August 18, 2002. National Archives of Singapore.

———. "Singapore 21: Vision for a New Era." Excerpt From a Speech Made in Parliament, June 5, 1997. Annual Report FY 1997, National Library Board.

———. "Speech by Prime Minister Goh Chok Tong at the Opening of the 7th International Conference on Thinking on Monday, 2 June 1997, at 9.00 a.m. at the Suntec City

Convention Centre Ballroom." Shaping Our Future: Thinking Schools, Learning Nation, Singapore National Archives.

Goh Poh Seng. *If We Dream Too Long*. Singapore: National University of Singapore Press, 2020.

Goh, Robbie B. H. "Writing 'the Global' in Singapore Anglophone Fiction." In *China Fictions, English Language: Literary Essays in Diaspora, Memory, Story*, edited by A. Robert Lee, 239–58. Amsterdam: Rodopi, 2008.

Gui, Weihsin. "Contemporary Literature from Singapore." In *Oxford Research Encyclopedia of Literature* (2017). https://oxfordre.com/literature/view/10.1093/acrefore/9780190201098.001.0001/acrefore-9780190201098-e-189?print=pdf.

———. *National Consciousness & Literary Cosmopolitics: Postcolonial Literature in a Global Moment*. Columbus: Ohio State University Press, 2013.

———. "Noir Fiction in Malaysia and Singapore as a Critical Aesthetic of Global Asia." In *Global Asia*, edited by Nadine Chan and Cheryl Narumi Naruse. *Social Text Online*, accessed March 23, 2022. https://socialtextjournal.org/periscope_article/noir-fiction-in-malaysia-and-singapore-as-a-critical-aesthetic-of-global-asia/.

———. "Renaissance City and Revenant Story: The Gothic Tale as Literary Technique in Fiona Cheong's Fictions of Singapore." *Interventions: International Journal of Postcolonial Studies* 18.4 (2016): 559–72.

Hall, Stuart. "Cultural Studies and Its Theoretical Legacies." In *Essential Essays*, vol. 1: *Foundations of Cultural Studies*, 71–100. Durham, NC: Duke University Press, 2019.

Hamid, Mohsin. *How to Get Filthy Rich in Rising Asia*. New York: Riverhead Books, 2014.

Handbook on Productivity Management. Singapore: National Productivity Board, 1988.

Hardt, Michael. "Affective Labor." *boundary 2* 26.2 (Summer 1999): 89–100.

Harvey, David. *A Brief History of Neoliberalism*. Oxford: Oxford University Press, 2005.

———. *The New Imperialism*. Oxford: Oxford University Press, 2003.

———. "The 'New' Imperialism: Accumulation by Dispossession." *Socialist Register* 40 (2004): 63–87.

Hau'ofa, Epeli. "Our Sea of Islands." *Contemporary Pacific* 6.1 (Spring 1994): 148–61.

Heng, Geraldine, ed. *The Sun in Her Eyes*. Singapore: Woodrose Publications, 1976.

Heng, Geraldine, and Janadas Devan. "State Fatherhood: The Politics of Nationalism, Sexuality, and Race in Singapore." In *The Gender/Sexuality Reader: Culture, History, Political Economy*, edited by Roger N. Lancaster and Micaela di Leonardo, 107–21. London: Routledge, 1997.

Hill, Michael, and Lian Kwen Fee. *The Politics of Nation Building and Citizenship in Singapore*. London: Routledge, 1995.

Hirsch, Marianne. "The Novel of Formation as Genre: Between Great Expectations and Lost Illusions." *Genre* 12 (Fall 1979): 293–311.

Hitchcock, Peter. "The Genre of Postcoloniality." *New Literary History* 34.2 (Spring 2003): 299–330.

Hoang, Kimberly Kay. *Dealing in Desire: Asian Ascendancy, Western Decline, and the Hidden Currency of Global Sex Work*. Oakland: University of California Press, 2015.

———. "Risky Investments: How Local and Foreign Investors Finesse Corruption-Rife Emerging Markets." *American Sociological Review* 83.4 (2018): 657–85.

———. *Spiderweb Capitalism: How Global Elites Exploit Frontier Markets*. Princeton, NJ: Princeton University Press, 2022.

Holden, Philip. *Autobiography and Decolonization: Modernity, Masculinity, and the Nation-State*. Madison: University of Wisconsin Press, 2008.

———. "Postcolonial Desire: Placing Singapore." *Postcolonial Studies* 11.3 (2008): 345–61.

———. "The Social Life of Genres: Short Stories as a Singapore Form." In *Singapore Literature and Culture: Current Directions in Local and Global Contexts*, edited by Angelia Mui Cheng Poon and Angus Whitehead, 99–113. London: Routledge, 2017.

Hong, Cathy Park. *Dance Dance Revolution*. New York: Norton, 2008.

Hong, Grace Kyungwon. "Speculative Surplus: Asian American Racialization and the Neoliberal Shift." *Social Text* 36.2 (2018): 107–22.

Hong Lysa and Huang Jianli. *The Scripting of a National History: Singapore and Its Pasts*. Hong Kong: Hong Kong University Press, 2008.

Hoo, Shawn. "The Neoliberal Arts." *The Octant*, April 29, 2021. https://theoctant.org/edition/issue/allposts/opinion/the-neoliberal-arts/.

Huang, Michelle N. and CA Davis. "Inhuman Figures: Robots, Clones, Aliens." Smithsonian Asian Pacific American Center, 2021. https://smithsonianapa.org/inhuman-figures/.

Hu-Dehart, Evelyn. "Diaspora." In *Keywords for Asian American Studies*, edited by Cathy J. Schlund-Vials, Linda Trinh Võ, and K. Scott Wong. New York: New York University Press, 2015. Accessed July 17, 2021. https://keywords.nyupress.org/asian-american-studies/essay/diaspora/.

Huggan, Graham. *The Postcolonial Exotic: Marketing the Margins*. London: Routledge, 2001.

Isa Kamari. "Mind your (Inter)Culture: *The Tower*." Grassroots Book Room, Singapore, April 23, 2016.

———. *The Tower*. Translated by Alfian Sa'at. Singapore: Epigram Books, 2013.

"Is This Annual Student Exodus Necessary?" *Straits Times*, September 21, 1969, 12.

Jones, Steven Swann. "The Innocent Persecuted Heroine Genre: An Analysis of Its Structure and Themes." *Western Folklore* 52.1 (1993): 20–21.

Jordan, Tina. "The 'It Books' of Summers Past." *New York Times*, June 5, 2019. https://www.nytimes.com/2019/06/05/books/beach-reads-summer.html.

Kamboureli, Smaro. *Scandalous Bodies: Diasporic Literature in English Canada*. Waterloo, ON: Wilfrid Laurier University Press, 2009.

Kassim, Ismail. "The High Cost of Publishing a Book." *New Nation*, December 16, 1974, 9.

Kaur, Ravinder. *Brand New Nation: Capitalist Dreams and Nationalist Designs in Twenty-First-Century India*. Stanford, CA: Stanford University Press, 2020.

Kincaid, Jamaica. *A Small Place*. New York: Farrar, Straus and Giroux, 2000.

Kinsella, John, and Alvin Pang. *Over There: Poems from Singapore and Australia*. Singapore: Ethos Books, 2008.

Klein, Christina. *Cold War Orientalism: Asia in the Middlebrow Imagination, 1945–1961*. Oakland: University of California Press, 2003.

Koh, Jee Leong. "The Right to Vote: The Stories of Overseas Singaporeans." *Singapore Unbound*, July 7, 2020. https://singaporeunbound.org/blog/2020/7/6/the-right-to-vote-the-stories-of-overseas-singaporeans.

Koh Tai, Ann. *Singapore Literature in English: An Annotated Bibliography*. Singapore: National Library Board Singapore and Centre for Liberal Arts and Social Sciences, 2008.

Kok Xing Hui and Annabeth Leow. "Singapore's New International Brand by STB and EDB: Passion Made Possible." *Straits Times*, August 14, 2017. https://www.straitstimes.com/singapore/singapores-new-international-brand-by-stb-and-edb-passion-made-possible.

Kotecki, Kristine. "After the Archive: Framing Cultural Memory in Ex-Yugoslav Collections." PhD dissertation, University of Texas at Austin, 2013.

Kumar, Amitava. *World Bank Literature*. Minneapolis: University of Minnesota Press, 2002.

Kwan, Kevin. *Crazy Rich Asians*. New York: Knopf, 2013.

———. *Rich People Problems*. New York: Doubleday, 2017.

Lai, Larissa. *Slanting I, Imagining We: Asian Canadian Literary Production in the 1980s and 1990s*. Waterloo, ON: Wilfrid Laurier University Press, 2014.

Lamb, David. "Singapore Swing: Peaceful and Prosperous, Southeast Asia's Famously Uptight Nation Has Let Its Hair Down." *Smithsonian Magazine*, September 2007.

Lazarus, Neil. "The Global Dispensation since 1945." In *The Cambridge Companion to Postcolonial Literary Studies*, edited by Neil Lazarus, 19–40. Cambridge: Cambridge University Press, 2004.

———. "Introducing Postcolonial Studies." In *The Cambridge Companion to Postcolonial Literary Studies*, edited by Neil Lazarus, 1–18. Cambridge: Cambridge University Press, 2004.

———. *The Postcolonial Unconscious*. Cambridge: Cambridge University Press, 2011.

League of Cities of the Philippines. Secretariat. "Iloilo City." League of Cities of the Philippines. Accessed June, 23, 2021. https://lcp.org.ph/98/iloilo-city.

Learning to Think: Thinking to Learn. Singapore: Ministry of Education, 1998.

Lee Kuan Yew. "Message to Federation of Malaya on Attainment of Merdeka." National Archives of Singapore.

———. *The Singapore Story: Memoirs of Lee Kuan Yew*. Upper Saddle River, NJ: Prentice Hall, 1998.

Lee Soo Ann. *Singapore Goes Transnational: A Study of the Economic Impact of Investment by Multinational Corporations in Singapore*. Eastern Universities Press, 1977.

Leong, Laurence Wai Teng. "Sexual Governance and the Politics of Sex in Singapore." In *Management of Success: Singapore Revisited*, edited by Terence Chong, 579–93. Singapore: ISEAS Publishing, 2010.

Leow, Annabeth. "PM Lee Unveils Orchid Named after President Obama and His Wife at White House State Dinner." *Straits Times*, August 3, 2016.

Leow, Joanne. "Strangers, Surrogates, Lovers: Foreign Domestic Workers in Contemporary Singapore Texts." In *Singapore Literature and Culture: Current Directions in Local and Global Contexts*, edited by Angelia Poon and Angus Whitehead, 198–216. New York: Routledge, 2017.

Leow, Rachel. *Taming Babel: Language in the Making of Malaysia*. Cambridge: Cambridge University Press, 2016.

Leslie, Camilo Arturo. "Territoriality, Map-mindedness, and the Politics of Place." *Theory and Society* 45.2 (2016): 169–201.

L'essai, 1953, Std. VIIIB. Singapore: Raffles Institution, 1953.

Lévi-Strauss, Claude. *The Savage Mind*. London: Trafalgar Square, 1966.

Lies, Elaine. "Book Talk: 'Crazy Rich Asians' Tackles Stereotypes via Satire." Reuters, June 14, 2019. https://www.reuters.com/article/us-books-authors-kwan/book-talk-crazy-rich-asians-tackles-stereotypes-via-satire-idUSBRE98401H20130905.

Lim, Eng-Beng. "Asian Megastructure and Queer Futurity." *Cultural Dynamics* 28.3 (2016): 309–19.

———. *Brown Boys and Rice Queens: Spellbinding Performance in the Asias*. New York: New York University Press, 2013.

Lim, Shirley. *No Man's Grove*. Singapore: National University of Singapore Press, 1985.

Lim, Thean Soo. *Ricky Star*. Singapore: Epigram Books, 2012.

Liu, Andrew. "How Asia Got Crazy Rich: Toward a Materialist History of *Crazy Rich Asians*." Film review. *n+1 Magazine*, June 14, 2019. https://nplusonemag.com/online-only/online-only/how-asia-got-crazy-rich/.

Liu, Petrus, and Colleen Lye. "Liberal Arts for Asians: A Commentary on Yale-NUS." *Interventions: International Journal of Postcolonial Studies* 18.4 (2016): 573–87.

Lloyd, David. "Nationalisms against the State." In *The Politics of Culture in the Shadow of Capital*, edited by Lisa Lowe and David Lloyd, 173–97. Durham, NC: Duke University Press, 1997.

"Local Publisher Not Allowed to Stand at Book Fair." *Straits Times*, September 4, 1994, 23.

Loh Kah Seng, Thum Ping Tjin, and Jack Meng-Tat Chia, eds. *Living with Myths in Singapore*. Singapore: Ethos Books, 2017.

Lorde, Audre. "Age, Race, Class and Sex: Women Redefining Difference." In *Sister Outsider: Essays and Speeches*. 2nd ed. Berkeley, CA: Crossing Press, 2007.

Lye, Colleen. *America's Asia: Racial Form and American Literature, 1893–1945*. Princeton, NJ: Princeton University Press, 2004.

———. "Racial Form." *Representations* 104.1 (2008): 92–101.

———. "Unmarked Character and the 'Rise of Asia': Ed Park's *Personal Days*." *Verge: Studies in Global Asias* 1.1 (2015): 230–54.

Lynch, Deidre Shauna. *The Economy of Character: Novels, Market Culture, and the Business of Inner Meaning*. Chicago: University of Chicago Press, 1998.

Mandell, Laura, and Rita Raley. "Anthologies and Miscellanies." November 4, 2002. Accessed March 15, 2022. http://oldsite.english.ucsb.edu/faculty/rraley/research/anthologies/.

Manpower 21: Vision of a Talent Capital. Singapore: Ministry of Manpower, 1999.

Marte-Wood, Alden Sajor. "Philippine Reproductive Fiction and Crises of Social Reproduction." *Post45*, no. 1 (2019). https://post45.org/2019/01/philippine-reproductive-fiction-and-crises-of-social-reproduction/.

Marx, John. "What Happened to the Postcolonial Novel: The Urban Longing for Form." *NOVEL: A Forum on Fiction* 50.3 (2017): 409–25.

Maslin, Janet. "'Crazy Rich Asians,' Guilty Pleasure, or Cult of Opulence." *New York Times*, Books, June 30, 2013. https://www.nytimes.com/2013/07/01/books/kevin-kwans-crazy-rich-asians-depicts-a-cult-of-opulence.html.

Mbembe, Achille. "Aesthetics of Superfluity." In *Johannesburg: The Elusive Metropolis*, 37–67. Johannesburg: Wits University Press, 2008.

McClintock, Anne. *Imperial Leather: Race, Gender, and Sexuality in the Colonial Contest*. New York: Routledge, 1995.

Media 21: Transforming Singapore into a Global Media City. Singapore: Media Development Authority, 2003.

Melamed, Jodi. *Represent and Destroy: Rationalizing Violence in the New Racial Capitalism*. Minneapolis: University of Minnesota Press, 2011.

Mendoza, Sherwin. "Singapore's Migrant Worker Poetry, Worker Resistance, and International Solidarity." *Asia-Pacific Journal* 17.14 (2019).

Mezzadra, Sandro. "How Many Histories of Labour? Toward a Theory of Postcolonial Capitalism." *Postcolonial Studies* 14.2 (2011): 151–70.

Miksic, John. "Temasik to Singapura: Singapore in the 14th and 15th Centuries." In *Singapore from Temasek to the 21st Century: Reinventing the Global City*, edited by Karl Hack and Jean-Louis Margolin with Karine Delaye, 103–32. Singapore: National University of Singapore Press, 2005.

Mitchell, Robert. "Biopolitics and Population Aesthetics." *South Atlantic Quarterly* 115.2 (2016): 367–98.

Mizumura, Minae. *The Fall of Language in the Age of English*. Translated by Mari Yoshihara and Juliet Winters Carpenter. New York: Columbia University Press, 2015.

Mulvey, Laura. "Visual Pleasure and Narrative Cinema." In *Media and Cultural Studies: KeyWorks*, 2nd ed., edited by Meenakshi Gigi Durham and Douglas M. Kellner, 267–74. New York: Blackwell, 1999.

Muthu, S. M. "Wrong Ideas on Meritocracy: Chok Tong." *Straits Times*, May 1, 1981, 10.

Nadal, Paul. "A Literary Remittance: Juan C. Laya's *His Native Soil* and the Rise of Realism in the Filipino Novel in English." *American Literature* 89.3 (2017): 591–626.

Nadiminti, Kalyan. "Work, Neoliberal Development, and Global Anglophone Literatures." In *Oxford Research Encyclopedia of Literature*, 2020, 2.

Nag, Abhijit. *Inspirations of a Nation: Tribute to 25 Singaporean South Asians*. Singapore: World Scientific Publishing, 2016.

Nair, Chandran, ed. *Singapore Writing*. Singapore: Woodrose Publications, 1977.

Nair, Chandran, and Nalla Tan, eds. *The Proceedings of the Seminar on Developing Creative Writing in Singapore, Aug. 6th–7th, 1976*. Singapore: Woodrose Publications, 1977.

Nansi, Pooja. "*Crazy Rich Asians* Is One of Our Saddest Moments." *Inkstone*, August 22, 2018. https://www.inkstonenews.com/opinion/pooja-nansi-crazy-rich-asians-hailed -representative-it-ignores-people-singapore/article/2160802.

———. "I'm tired of having to say this . . . " Facebook, April 25, 2018. www.facebook.com /pnansi/posts/10155065574991442.

Naruse, Cheryl Narumi. "Diasporic Singaporeans, Coming-of-Career Narratives, and the Corporate Nation." *biography: An Interdisciplinary Quarterly* 37.1 (Winter 2014): 143–67.

———. "Hwee Hwee Tan's *Mammon Inc.* as Bildungsroman, or the Coming-of-Career Narrative." *Genre: Forms of Discourse and Culture* 49.1 (April 2016): 95–115.

Ng, Andrew Hock Soon. *Asian Gothic: Essays on Literature, Film and Anime*. Jefferson, NC: McFarland & Co., 2008.

Ng Yi-Sheng. "A History of Singapore Horror." *BiblioAsia*, July–September 2017. Accessed March 23, 2022. https://biblioasia.nlb.gov.sg/vol-13/issue-2/jul-sep-2017/historyofsg horror.

Ngoei, Wen-Qing. *Arc of Containment: Britain, The United States, and Anticommunism in Southeast Asia*. Ithaca, NY: Cornell University Press, 2019.

Nguyen, Viet Thanh, and Janet Alison Hoskins. "Introduction: Transpacific Studies: Critical Perspectives on an Emerging Field." In *Transpacific Studies: Framing an Emerging Field*, 1–38. Honolulu: University of Hawai'i Press, 2014.

"No Laughing Matter: Singapore." *Economist: Asia*, May 24, 2001. https://www.economist .com/asia/2001/05/24/no-laughing-matter.

Nye, Joseph S., Jr. *Soft Power: The Means to Success in World Politics*. New York: Public Affairs, 2004.

Ong, Aihwa. *Flexible Citizenship: The Cultural Logics of Transnationality*. Durham, NC: Duke University Press, 1999.

———. *Neoliberalism as Exception: Mutations in Citizenship and Sovereignty*. Durham, NC: Duke University Press, 2006.

"Opinion on National Identity: Is There a Singapore Identity." Singapore Broadcasting Corporation, July 25, 1980.

Orenstein, Peggy. *Cinderella Ate My Daughter: Dispatches from the Front Lines of the New Girlie-Girl Culture*. New York: HarperCollins, 2011.

Ortmann, Stephan. "Singapore: The Politics of Inventing National Identity." *Journal of Current Southeast Asian Affairs* 28.4 (2009): 23–46.

"Our National Ethic: Speech by Mr Goh Chok Tong, First Deputy Prime Minister and Minister for Defence, at the PAP Youth Wing Charity Night, at Neptune Theatre Restaurant on Friday, 28 October 1988, at 8.00pm." Singapore National Archives.

Our Story: 15 Years of NPB. Singapore: National Productivity Board, 1981.

"Overview of Asia CEO Forum." Asia CEO Forum. Accessed June 24, 2021. https://www.asia-ceo.org/Overview-of-Asia-CEO-Forum.

Ow Yeong Wai Kit and Muzakkir Samat, eds. *From Walden to Woodlands: An Anthology of Nature Poems*. Singapore: Ethos Books, 2015.

PAP Pioneers: 50 Ordinary Stories. Singapore: People's Action Party, 2015.

Patterson, Christopher B. *Transitive Cultures: Anglophone Literature of the Transpacific*. New Brunswick, NJ: Rutgers University Press, 2018.

Pawle, Fred. "Kevin Kwan Satirises the Lives of Asia's Crazy Rich." *Weekend Australian*, Life, September 12, 2013. https://www.theaustralian.com.au/life/kevin-kwan-satirises-the-lives-of-asias-crazy-rich/news-story/0ca546d5b987b775333187dfac837ebd?sv=8c7a574341d09da702981b144e057f0.

People-Centered Management: Programmes. Singapore: National Productivity Board. 1985.

Phew Yew Kok, Joseph Tan Meng Kwan, and Hashin Bin Idris. "Don't Waste Your Time on Parasites." *Straits Times*, January 14, 1971, 18.

"Population." Department of Statistics Singapore. https://www.singstat.gov.sg/publications/reference/ebook/population/population.

"Population in Brief 2020." Singapore Department of Statistics, 2020. https://www.strategygroup.gov.sg/files/media-centre/publications/population-in-brief-2020.pdf.

Pratt, Mary Louise. *Imperial Eyes: Travel Writing and Transculturation*. 2nd ed. New York: Routledge, 2003.

"Premier Lee Warns of 'Brain Drain.'" *Straits Times*, July 2, 1966, 6.

ProAct 21: Creating the Future. Singapore: Productivity and Standards Board, 1999.

"Producing Better Towkays." *New Nation*, April 27, 1978, 8.

Productivity Concepts and Their Application. Singapore: National Productivity Board, 1992.

"Publishing, Creative Writing and Singapore: Question and Answer Session with Poet and Publisher Chandran Nair." Television Corporation of Singapore, July 4, 1975.

Pugalenthi Sr, ed. *Motherland, Vol. 2*. Singapore: VJ Times, 1993.

"Question on Brain Drain for Parliament." *Straits Times*, December 9, 1987, 19.

Rahman, Zia Haider. *In the Light of What We Know*. London: Picador, 2015.

Rajah, Jothie. *Authoritarian Rule of Law: Legislation, Discourse and Legitimacy in Singapore*. Cambridge: Cambridge University Press, 2012.

Ramakrishnan, Pugalenthii. "Good Point to Ponder." Facebook, January 19, 2017. Accessed March 23, 2017. https://www.facebook.com/permalink.php?story_fbid=10212450620847412&id=1438388260.

Ramazani, Jahan. *A Transnational Poetics*. Chicago: University of Chicago Press, 2009.

Remaking Singapore Committee. *Changing Mindsets, Deepening Relationships*. Singapore: Ministry of Community Development and Sports, 2003.

Renaissance City Report: Culture and the Arts in Renaissance Singapore. Singapore: Ministry of Information and the Arts, 1999.

"Report of the Committee on Productivity." Singapore: National Productivity Board, *1981*.

Robbins, Bruce. Introduction to *Cosmopolitanisms*, edited by Bruce Robbins and Paulo Lemos Horta, 1–20. New York: New York University Press, 2017.

Robinson, Cedric J. *Black Marxism: The Making of the Black Radical Tradition*. 3rd ed. Chapel Hill: University of North Carolina Press, 2020.

Rogers, Juliette M. *Career Stories: Belle Epoque Novels of Professional Development*. University Park: Pennsylvania State University Press, 2007.

Rosenberg, David. "David's Harp/Can't Turn Palestine into Singapore," *Haaretz*, August 1, 2012. https://www.haaretz.com/david-s-harp-can-t-turn-palestine-into-singapore-1.5274971.

Sadiq, Kamal. "Postcolonial Citizenship." In *The Oxford Handbook of Citizenship*, edited by Ayelet Shachar, Rainer Baubock, Irene Bloemraad, and Maarten Vink, 178–99. Oxford: Oxford University Press, 2020.

Said, Edward. *Orientalism*. New York: Vintage Books, 1978.

Sakai, Naoki. "'You Asians': On the Historical Role of the West and Asia Binary." *South Atlantic Quarterly* 99.4 (Fall 2000): 789–817.

Sanyal, Kalyan. *Rethinking Capitalist Development: Primitive Accumulation, Governmentality and Post-Colonial Capitalism*. New York: Routledge, 2013.

Schor, Naomi. *Bad Objects: Essays Popular and Unpopular*. Durham, NC: Duke University Press, 1995.

Sedgwick, Eve Kosofsky. "Paranoid Reading and Reparative Reading, or, You're So Paranoid, You Probably Think This Essay Is about You." In *Touching Feeling: Affect, Pedagogy, Performativity*, 123–52. Durham, NC: Duke University Press 2003.

Seng, Eunice M. F. "Transnational Utopia: Diaspora as Creative Praxis." In *Singapore Dreaming: Managing Utopia*, edited by H. Koon Wee and Jeremy Chia, 146–67. Singapore: Asian Urban Lab, 2016.

Shetty, Deepika. "A City of Contrasts." *Straits Times, The Sunday Times*, November 9, 2008, 10.

———. "Marrakech's Magical Mix." *Straits Times, The Sunday Times*, December 28, 2008, 10.

Shiller, Robert J. *Narrative Economics: How Stories Go Viral and Drive Major Economic Events*. Princeton, NJ: Princeton University Press, 2019.

Shinozaki, Mamoru. *Syonan, My Story: The Japanese Occupation of Singapore*. Singapore: Times Books International, 1982.

Sim, Susan, and Francis Chan. *Setia Dan Bakti: 50 Stories of Loyalty and Service*. Singapore: Singapore Police Force, 2015.

Singapore Department of Statistics. *Census of Population 2010: Demographic Characteristics, Education, Language and Religion*. Accessed May 13, 2022. https://www.singstat.gov.sg/publications/cop2010/census10_stat_release1.

Singapore Economic Review Committee. *New Challenges, Fresh Goals: Towards a Global Dynamic City*. Singapore: Ministry of Trade and Industry, 2003.

Singapore National Report 2021. Singapore: Ministry of Foreign Affairs, 2021.

Singapore Tourist Promotion Board. *Tourism 21: Vision of a Tourism Capital*. Singapore: Pagesetters Services, 1996.

Singapore 21. Motion, Singapore Parliamentary Debates, Parliament 9, Sess. 1, Vol. 70, Sitting 14, May 5, 1999.

Singapore 21: Together, We Make the Difference. Singapore: Singapore 21 Committee, 1999.

Singh, Kirpal. "Singapore Fiction in English: Some Reflections . . ." *Singapore Book World* 23 (1993–94): 21–23.

Sklair, Leslie. *The Transnational Capitalist Class.* London: Wiley-Blackwell, 2000.

Slaughter, Joseph. *Human Rights, Inc.: The World Novel, Narrative Form, and International Law.* New York: Fordham University Press, 2007.

Slobodian, Quinn. *Globalists: The End of Empire and the Birth of Neoliberalism.* Cambridge, MA: Harvard University Press, 2018.

"Speech by Dr Ahmad Mattar, Acting Minister for Social Affairs, and Member of Parliament for Brickworks at the Brickworks Constituency National Day Dinner." Singapore Government Press Release, Publicity Division, August 19, 1978, Singapore National Archives.

"Speech by Mr Chai Chong Yii, Senior Minister of State for Education and Member of Parliament for Bukit Batok, At the National Day Celebration Dinner at the HDB Bukit Batok Housing Estate Car Park on Saturday, 11 August, '79 at 8.00pm." Singapore Government Press Release, Singapore National Archives.

"Speech by Mr Ch'ng Jit Koon, Minister of State for Community Development, at the 1936 National Short Story Competition Prize-Giving Ceremony at The Drama Centre on 1 December 1987 at 6.00pm." Ministry of Communications and Information (1985–90), Singapore National Archives.

"Speech by Mr Ho Kah Leong, Parliamentary Secretary (Education) at the Opening Ceremony of the Workshop for Writers at the Lecture Hall Bukit Merah Branch Library on Monday, 12 September 1983 at 9.30am." Ministry of Culture, Singapore National Archives.

"Speech by Mr Wong Kan Seng, Deputy Prime Minister and Minister for Home Affairs, at the Launch of the Overseas Singaporean Portal." August 16, 2006. Singapore Government Media Release, National Archives of Singapore.

"Speech by Prime Minister Mr Goh Chok Tong in Parliament on Tuesday, 9 March 1993." National Archives of Singapore.

"Speech by S Dhanabalan, Minister for National Development, at the Opening of the Park Network System, Kallang River Phase I on Friday 14 Aug 91 at 5.00pm at Kallang River Park Connector (Bishan Road)." Singapore National Archives.

Spivak, Gayatri Chakravorty. *A Critique of Postcolonial Reason: Toward a History of the Vanishing Present.* Cambridge, MA: Harvard University Press, 1999.

———. *Other Asias.* London: Blackwell, 2003.

———. "The Politics of Translation." In *Outside in the Teaching Machine*, 179–200. London: Routledge, 1993.

———. "Three Women's Texts and a Critique of Imperialism." *Critical Inquiry* 12 (Autumn 1985): 243–61.

Steinlight, Emily. *Populating the Novel: Literary Form and the Politics of Surplus Life.* Ithaca, NY: Cornell University Press, 2018.

Stoler, Ann Laura. *Duress: Imperial Durabilities in Our Times.* Durham, NC: Duke University Press, 2016.

Suarez, Michael F., SJ. "The Production and Consumption of the Eighteenth-Century Poetic Miscellany." In *Books and Their Readers in Eighteenth-Century England: New Essays*, edited by Isabel Rivers, 217–51. Leicester: Leicester University Press, 2001.

Sutherlin, Margaret. "China's Billionaires Jump Ship for Singapore." *Bloomberg*, November 15, 2022, https://www.bloomberg.com/news/newsletters/2022–11–15/big-take-china-s-wealthy-elite-take-their-billions-to-singapore.

Tan, E. K. "In Search of New Forms: The Impact of Bilingual Policy and the 'Speak Mandarin' Campaign on Sinophone Singapore Poetry." *Interventions* 18.4 (2016): 526–42.

Tan, Han Hoe. *Prize Poems: Winning Entries of the First Ministry of Culture Poetry Writing Competition.* Singapore: Educational Publications Bureau, 1979.

Tan, Hwee Hwee. *Mammon Inc.* London: Penguin Books, 2001.

Tan, Rebecca. "Flower Power: Singapore's Orchid Diplomacy." *BiblioAsia* 18.1 (April–June 2022): 8–15.

Tay, Eddie. *Colony, Nation, and Globalisation: Not at Home in Singaporean and Malaysian Literature.* Hong Kong: Hong Kong University Press, 2011.

Tay, Simon. *5.* Singapore: National University of Singapore Press, 1985.

Tay, Verena. *A Monsoon Feast: Short Stories to Celebrate the Cultures of Kerala and Singapore.* Singapore: Monsoon Books, 2012.

Te Punga Somerville, Alice. "Not Emailing Albert: A Legacy of Collection, Connection, Community." *Contemporary Pacific* 22.2 (2010): 253–70.

Teh Cheang Wan. "We Must Be Productive in All Fields of Human Endeavour." In *The Way to Productivity: Thematic Speeches.* Singapore: Ministry of Culture, 1983.

Teo, Justina, and Lions Befrienders Service Association. *Befriending Conversations: 20 Seniors, 20 Occupations, 20 Stories.* Singapore: Candid Creation Publishing, 2019.

Teo Youyenn. *Neoliberal Morality in Singapore: How Family Policies Make State and Society.* London: Routledge, 2011.

Thandra, Shashi. "Annihilation and Accumulation: Postcolonial Literatures on Genocide and Capital." PhD dissertation, Wayne State University, 2014.

"Three Places That Dream of Becoming Africa's Singapore." *Economist*, October 23, 2021. https://www.economist.com/middle-east-and-africa/2021/10/23/three-places-that-dream-of-becoming-africas-singapore.

Thrift, Nigel. *Knowing Capitalism.* Thousand Oaks, CA: Sage, 2005.

Thumboo, Edwin. "The English Anthology in Singapore and Southeast Asia." The Anthology in Singapore: A Symposium, Writers@NIE Series. National Institute of Education, Singapore, August 12, 2020.

———, ed. *The Poetry of Singapore.* Singapore: ASEAN Committee on Culture and Information, 1985.

Tiang, Jeremy. *It Never Rains on National Day.* Singapore: Epigram Books, 2015.

"Toast Speech by Prime Minister Lee Hsien Loong at the White House State Dinner." Prime Minister's Office Singapore, August 2, 2016. https://www.pmo.gov.sg/Newsroom/toast-speech-prime-minister-lee-hsien-loong-white-house-state-dinner.

Toh, Elgin. "60 Years of the Singapore Citizenship: From Hawkers to Millionaires, They All Queued Up." *Straits Times*, October 8, 2017. https://www.straitstimes.com/politics/60-years-of-the-singapore-citizenship-from-hawkers-to-millionaires-they-all-queued-up.

Tomorrow Shall Be Better Than Today: a Productivity Action Plan. Singapore: National Productivity Board, 1983.

Trask, Haunani-Kay. *From a Native Daughter: Colonialism and Sovereignty in Hawai'i.* 2nd ed. Honolulu: Latitude Books, 1999.

Turnbull, C. M. *A History of Singapore 1819–1988.* Oxford: Oxford University Press, 1989.

"2020 Index of Economic Freedom: Global Economic Freedom Hits All-Time High." Heritage Foundation, May 17, 2020. https://www.heritage.org/press/2020-index-econo mic-freedom-global-economic-freedom-hits-all-time-high.

Vasagar, Jeevan. "Singapore-on-Thames? This Is No Vision for Post-Brexit Britain." *The Guardian*, Opinion, November 24, 2017. https://www.theguardian.com/commentisfree /2017/nov/24/singapore-on-thames-post-brexit-britain-wealthy-city-state.

Vasil, Ray. "Singapore 1991: Continuity and Change." *Southeast Asian Affairs* (1993): 297–312.

Venn, Couze. *After Capital*. Thousand Oaks, CA: Sage, 2018.

Vic Vox: Prize Winning Short Stories and Poems. Singapore: Victoria School, 1990.

Vincent, Simon. *The Naysayer's Book Club: 26 Singaporeans You Need to Know*. Singapore: Epigram Books, 2018.

Vitale, Julia. "*Crazy Rich Asians* Author Kevin Kwan on Finishing His Trilogy and the Movie Adaptation to Come." *Vanity Fair*, May 18, 2017. https://www.vanityfair.com/style /2017/05/rich-people-problems-crazy-rich-asians-movie-kevin-kwan.

Walcott, Derek. *Omeros*. New York: Farrar, Straus and Giroux, 1992.

Warwick Research Collective. *Combined and Uneven Development: Toward a New Theory of World-Literature*. Liverpool: Liverpool University Press, 2015.

Watson, Jini Kim. *Cold War Reckonings: Authoritarianism and the Genres of Decolonization*. New York: Fordham University Press, 2021.

———. *The New Asian City: Three-Dimensional Fictions of Space and Urban Form*. Minneapolis: University of Minnesota Press, 2011.

Watson, Jini Kim, and Gary Wilder. "Thinking the Postcolonial Contemporary." In *The Postcolonial Contemporary: Political Imaginaries for the Global Present*, edited by Jini Kim Watson and Gary Wilder, 1–30. New York: Fordham University Press, 2018.

Wee, C. J. W.-L. *The Asian Modern: Culture, Capitalist Development, Singapore*. Singapore: National University of Singapore Press, 2007.

———. "Contending with Primordialism: The 'Modern' Construction of Postcolonial Singapore." *positions: asia critique* 1.3 (1993): 719–20.

———. "The Indigenized West in Asian Multicultures: Literary-Cultural Production in Malaysia and Singapore." *Interventions: International Journal of Postcolonial Studies* 10.2 (2008): 188–206.

Wee Kiat. *Eat Company: Sleep Bunk Berth*. Singapore: Landmark Books, 1997.

Welcome to a New City of Opportunities. Singapore: Contact Singapore, 2014.

"What SIA, Finance Sector Must Do to Stay Ahead—a Need to Become Globally Competitive." *Straits Times*, August 16, 1997, 39.

White House. "Peace to Prosperity: A Vision to Improve the Lives of the Palestinian and Israeli People," January 2020. https://trumpwhitehouse.archives.gov/wp-content/uploads /2020/01/Peace-to-Prosperity-0120.pdf.

"White Paper on 'Shared Values.'" In *In Search of Singapore's National Values*, edited by Jon S. T. Quah, 106–16. Institute of Policy Studies. Singapore: Times Academic Press, 1990.

"Why Foreign Books Only?" *New Nation*, July 5, 1975, 3.

Wong, K. P. "The Cultural Impact of Multinational Corporations in Singapore." UNESCO, 1980.

Wong, Phui Nam. *Remembering Grandma and Other Rumours*. Singapore: National University of Singapore Press, 1989.

World Bank. *The East Asian Miracle: Economic Growth and Public Policy*. Oxford: Oxford University Press, 1993.

Xiang, Sunny. *Tonal Intelligence: The Aesthetics of Asian Inscrutability during the Long Cold War*. New York: Columbia University Press, 2020.

Yap, Angeline. *Collected Poems*. Singapore: National University of Singapore Press, 1986.

Yeo, Robert, ed. *Prize Winning Plays I*. Singapore: Federal Publications, 1980.

Yeo, Toon Joo. "Brain Drain Will Be Decisive: Lee." *Straits Times*, September 7, 1969, 1.

Yeoh, Brenda S. A. "Cosmopolitanism and Its Exclusions in Singapore." *Urban Studies* 41.12 (November 2004): 2431–45.

———. "Singapore: Hungry for Foreign Workers at All Skill Levels." *Migration Information Sources: The Online Journal of the Migration Policy Institute*, January 1, 2007.

Yip, Leo. "The Road Ahead." In *Heart Work* 2, 248–63. Singapore: Straits Times Press, 2011.

Young, Robert J. C. "The Cosmopolitan Idea and National Sovereignty." In *Cosmopolitanisms*, edited by Bruce Robbins and Paulo Lemos Horta, 135–40. New York: New York University Press, 2017.

———. "Postcolonial Remains." *New Literary History* 43 (2012): 19–42.

Young, Toby. "Is Singapore the Template for New York? Uh-oh!" *Los Angeles Times*, March 15, 1998. https://www.latimes.com/archives/la-xpm-1998-mar-15-op-29087-story.html.

Zakaria, Fareed, and Lee Kuan Yew. "Culture Is Destiny: A Conversation with Lee Kuan Yew." *Foreign Affairs* 73.2 (March–April 1994): 109–26.

Zhang, Dora. "Notes on Atmosphere." *Qui Parle* 27.1 (June 2018): 121–55.

Ziguras, Christopher, and Cate Gribble. "Policy Responses to Address Student 'Brain Drain': An Assessment of Measures Intended to Reduce the Emigration of Singaporean International Students." *Journal of Studies in International Education* 19.4 (2015): 246–64.

Žižek, Slavoj. "Multiculturalism, Or, the Cultural Logic of Multinational Capitalism." *New Left Review*, September 1, 1997, 28–51.

INDEX

Singapore 21 report, 18, 89–91, 158n80, 173n41
Singapore Writers Festival, 23
Singh, Kirpal, 45, 164n90
Sing Lit Station, 48
sinocentrism, 66, 99, 141, 176n78
Sklair, Leslie, 99
Slaughter, Joseph, 67, 171n6
Smithsonian Magazine, 1–2, 4–5
socialism, 41. *See also* communism
social media, 4, 58. *See also* media
soft power, 5–6, 16, 19, 22; Japanese, 66, 69–70
Southeast Asia, 1, 8, 21, 119; British colonies of, 86; economic might of, 127; impossibility of political solidarity in, 107; Japanese diplomacy strategy in, 69–70; modernization of, 70; national sovereignty and modernity in, 26; Singapore as distinct from the rest of, 100; United States empire in, 8, 13; United States encounter with, 153n38. *See also* Indonesia; Malaysia; Philippines; Singapore; Thailand; Vietnam
South Korea, 1, 29, 40, 62; decolonization struggles in, 8. *See also* Asian Miracle/Asian Tiger nations
Soviet Union, 41, 156n54
Spivak, Gayatri Chakravorty, 11, 26, 38, 112, 132, 150n17, 154n44, 159n15, 168n54, 180n58
Steinlight, Emily, 51–52, 165n9
Straits Times, 40, 53, 55. *See also* "Singaporean Abroad" (newspaper series)
Suarez, Michael F., 39
subjectivity: domestic worker, 107, 111; globalized and modern, 85, 182n83; and national identity, 88; personality and, 62; power and legible through its effects on, 64; production of neoliberal, 87; Singaporean, 82
Switzerland, 71–75, 123, 133

Taiwan, 29, 40. *See also* Asian Miracle/Asian Tiger nations
Tan, Amy, 127
Tan, Hwee Hwee: *Mammon, Inc.*, 19, 21, 81–82, 87–90, 93–98, 102, 105–6, 109–13, 121, 171n11
Tan, Nalla: "The Current State of Creative Writing in Singapore," 31
Tay, Eddie, 88
Tay, Simon, 32, 57, 91
Teh Cheang Wan, 92
television, 4, 43, 163n78. *See also* media
Teo, Youyenn, 96–97
Te Punga Somerville, Alice, 25–27, 38, 159n12, 160n20
Thailand, 33, 71; classical religious texts of, 34. *See also* Southeast Asia

Thandra, Shashi R., 90
Thrift, Nigel, 181n66
Thumboo, Edwin, 24, 32–37
Tiang, Jeremy: *It Never Rains on National Day*, 21, 53, 70–76; "Sophia's Honeymoon," 6–7, 71–78, 133; "Sophia's Party," 71, 76–78
Times International, 29
tourism, 6, 59, 61–64, 102, 117; food, 120; infrastructure of, 125; "Passion Made Possible" campaign of Singaporean, 117, 126, 137. *See also* Singapore
transnational corporations, 13, 81, 103, 112, 155n52; demands of, 35; and nation-states, 97; Singaporean accommodation of, 123–24; work ethic for the benefit of, 92–95. *See also* global economy; neoliberalism
transpacificism, 13; dynamics of, 146
Trans-Pacific Partnership, 114
Trask, Haunani-Kay, 114
travel writing, 100–101

UNESCO, 20, 24, 30–32, 38, 45, 47; broadcast communications supported by, 161n32; "The Cultural Impact of Multinational Corporations in Singapore," 35
United Kingdom, 1, 89; publishers of the, 29; writing in the, 47. *See also* British Empire
United States, 89; anti-Black racism in the, 151n26; audiences in the, 127; decline of the, 117, 122–23, 140; education in the, 71; empire of the, 8, 13; feminization of the, 114, 117–18; and Global Asia, 116–17; as global signifier, 75; as improper and undesirable, 115; publishers of the, 29; Singaporean immigrant population in the, 8, 13, 56; as the "West," 25; writing in the, 47

Venn, Couze, 9, 153n42; *After Capital*, 172n15
Vietnam, 8, 153n38; foreign investors in, 124. *See also* Southeast Asia
Vietnam War, 47
violence: capitalist, 96; colonial, 10, 70; psychic, 152n26; racial, 152n26
VJ Times, 40, 42–48; *The Chrysanthemum Haiku*, 46, 164n93; horror anthologies published by, 25, 43; *Motherland* series, 46–47, 164n98. *See also* anthologies: popular

Warwick Research Collective (WReC), 155n52
Watson, Jini Kim, 8, 29, 85, 102, 146–47; *Cold War Reckonings*, 158n81; *The New Asian City*, 128

Founded in 1893,
UNIVERSITY OF CALIFORNIA PRESS
publishes bold, progressive books and journals
on topics in the arts, humanities, social sciences,
and natural sciences—with a focus on social
justice issues—that inspire thought and action
among readers worldwide.

The UC PRESS FOUNDATION
raises funds to uphold the press's vital role
as an independent, nonprofit publisher, and
receives philanthropic support from a wide
range of individuals and institutions—and from
committed readers like you. To learn more, visit
ucpress.edu/supportus.